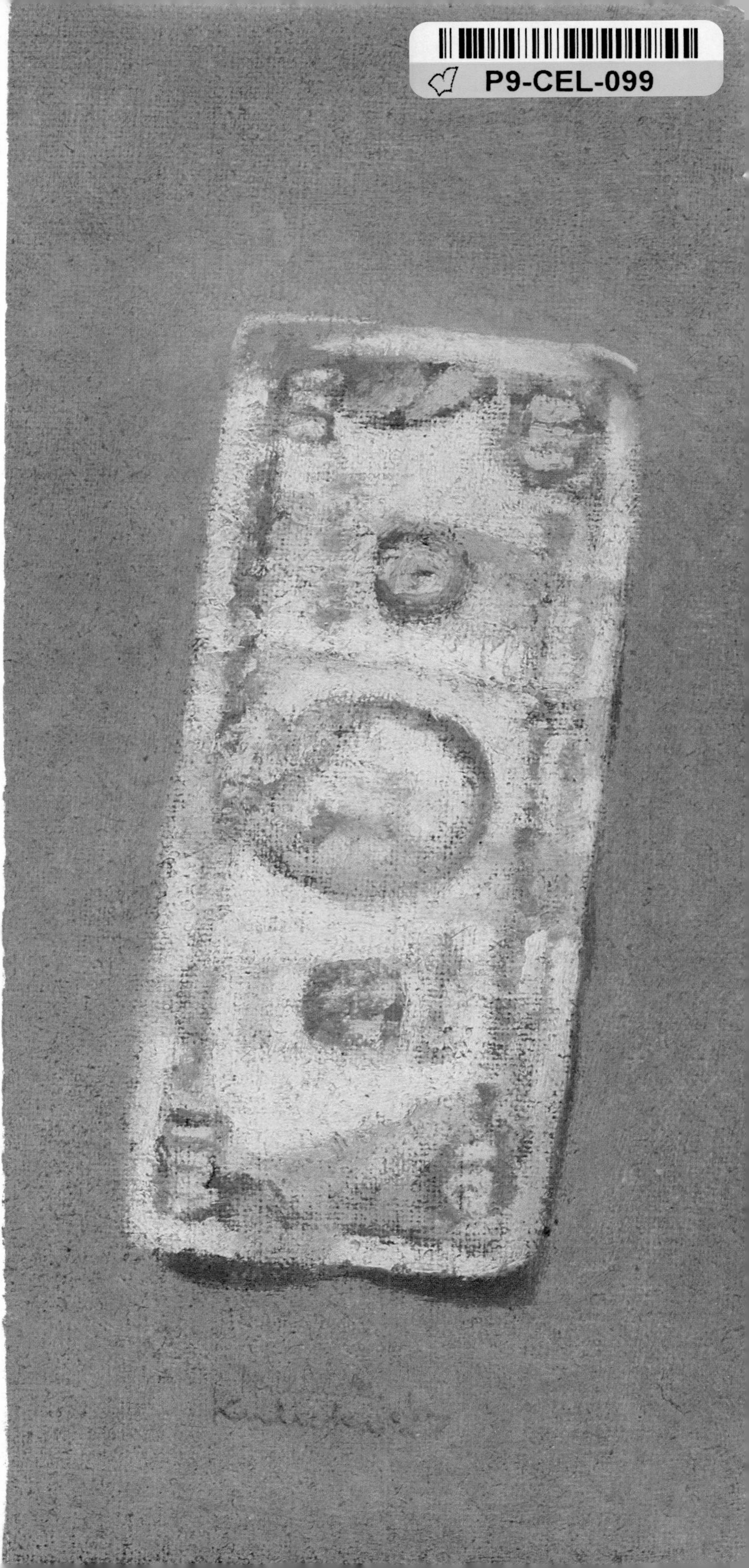

THE WALL STREET JOURNAL.

GUIDE to UNDERSTANDING MONEY & MARKETS

4

Investors exchange money for stock certificates which represent ***part-ownership in corporations***. While these investors may retain part-ownership for a while, they expect to eventually sell it to other investors – hopefully at a profit.

42

Investors ***lend money to corporations and governments in exchange for IOUs***, represented by bond certificates. The borrowers promise to repay the loan by a certain date and to pay interest regularly to the investors in the interim.

Published by **ACCESS**PRESS, a division of HarperCollins & Siegel & Gale, Inc. A Fireside Book, Published by Simon & Schus

62

There's power in numbers. With that in mind, people often ***band together to invest in groups*** called mutual funds. Mutual funds offer two major benefits: greater diversification of investments and experts to make specific investment decisions.

74

Futures contracts are ***deals made now to take place in the future***. They are the direct descendants of trading's earliest days when people bartered everything from cattle to seeds.

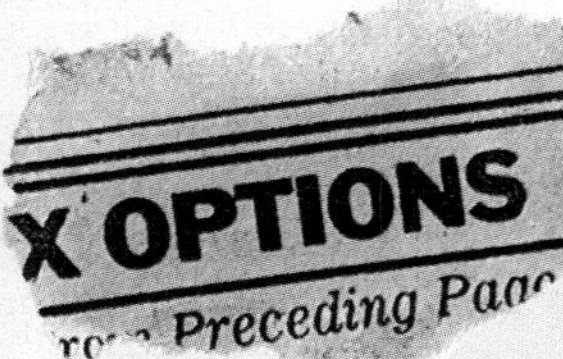

92

An option gives you the ***right to buy or sell something without the obligation*** to do so. In today's market, options also provide a way to control assets for a fraction of their full cost.

96

In early days of trade, when people bartered cows for sheep, corn for barley, ***commodities were money***. In today's world, where you can trade one currency for another currency anywhere in the world, any time of day, almost instantaneously, ***money has itself become a commodity***.

The Stock Certificate

A stock certificate is a very valuable document because it certifies exactly how much of a corporation you own.

The $1 ***par value*** on stock certificates is used only for bookkeeping purposes. It has no relationship to the stock's actual value.

Name of issuer

A human figure with plainly discernible features must appear with at least a 3/4 frontal view on all New York Stock Exchange certificates. Delicate flesh tones are almost always engraved right next to heavy shadows to make the artwork hard to reproduce.

SEC Registration Number assigned by the Securities and Exchange Commission.

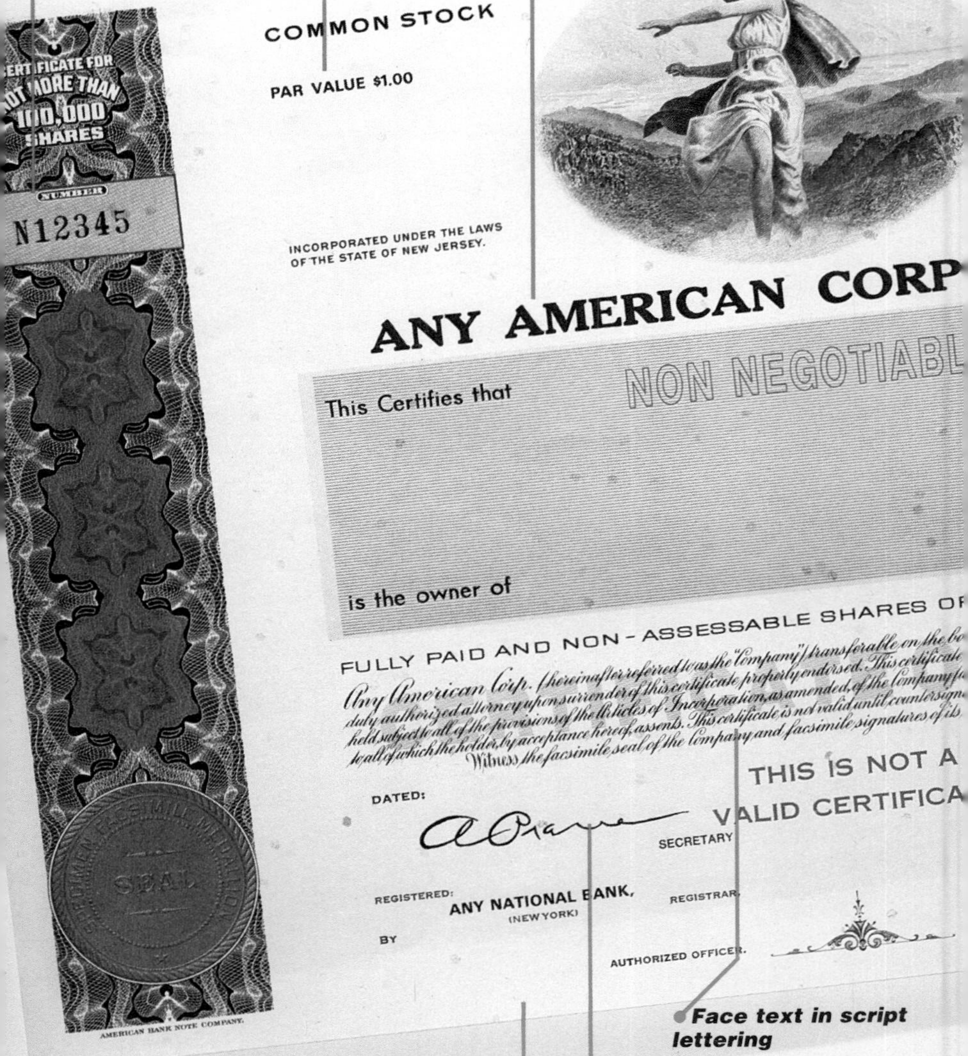

CERTIFICATE FOR NOT MORE THAN 100,000 SHARES

NUMBER

N12345

COMMON STOCK

PAR VALUE $1.00

INCORPORATED UNDER THE LAWS OF THE STATE OF NEW JERSEY.

ANY AMERICAN CORP

NON NEGOTIABL

This Certifies that

is the owner of

FULLY PAID AND NON-ASSESSABLE SHARES OF

Any American Corp. (hereinafter referred to as the "Company") transferable on the bo duly authorized attorney upon surrender of this certificate properly endorsed. This certificate held subject to all of the provisions of the Articles of Incorporation, as amended, of the Company to all of which the holder, by acceptance hereof, assents. This certificate is not valid until countersign Witness the facsimile seal of the Company and facsimile signatures of its

THIS IS NOT A VALID CERTIFICA

DATED:

SECRETARY

REGISTERED: ANY NATIONAL BANK, (NEW YORK) REGISTRAR

BY

AUTHORIZED OFFICER.

SPECIMEN FACSIMILE MEDALLION SEAL

AMERICAN BANK NOTE COMPANY.

Face text in script lettering

Facsimile signatures of corporate officers

Stocks are printed on specially-made ***paper*** incorporating little colored discs, called ***planchettes***, which are treated with secret chemicals. Security devices can automatically sense the planchettes.

Holograms are images with a 3-dimensional appearance like those found on some credit cards. They may be added to the anti-counterfeiting arsenal of stock certificate issuers in the near future.

Every time you buy stock, you receive a certificate. You cannot sell stock without surrendering the stock certificate. You can have the certificate made out in your own name and sent to you for safekeeping. Or, you can have it made out in ***street name*** (the brokerage firm's name) and have your broker store it for you. Most investors choose the latter. That way, it can't be lost or stolen, and time isn't wasted sending the certificate to the broker before selling.

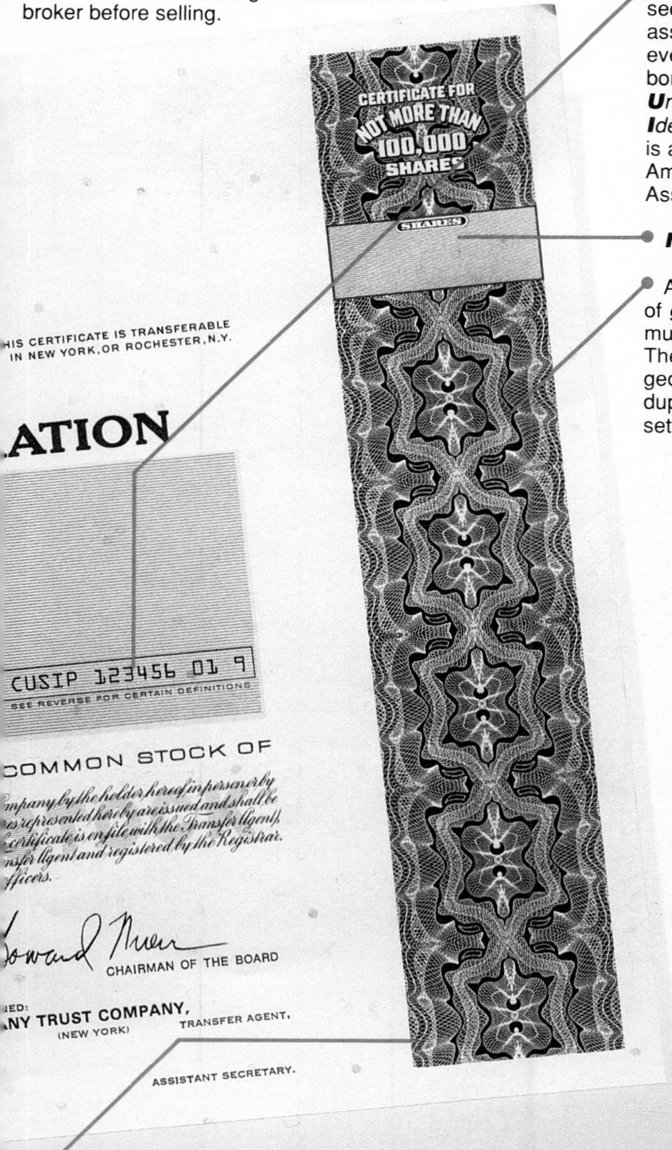

The CUSIP number is a security identification number assigned to every stock and to every corporate and municipal bond. The ***C****ommittee on* ***U****niform* ***S****ecurities* ***I****dentification* ***P****rocedures* is a committee set up by the American Banker's Association.

Number of shares

At least 20 square inches of ***geometric lathe work*** must appear on the certificate. The pattern created by a geometric lathe can't be duplicated unless the exact settings are known.

Certificates are printed using a minimum of two separate ***intaglio plates***. A distinguishing characteristic of intaglio printing is that the image feels raised to the touch. Normal photo/offset printing cannot duplicate this effect.

Difficult to match, off-shades of ink are also used during printing.

In a number of countries, such as Japan, certificates have been dispensed with altogether, and stock ownership is merely a matter of accounting records. This is also happening in the US, but at a slower pace.

Since 1933 there have been only about a dozen known attempts at stock certificate forgery. For some reason, statistics on successful forgeries are unavailable.

What Is a Stock?

A share of stock represents ownership in a corporation. A corporation is owned by its stockholders – often thousands of people and institutions – each owning a fraction of the corporation.

When you buy stock in a corporation you become a part-owner or ***stockholder*** (also known as shareholder). You immediately own a part, no matter how small, of every building, piece of office furniture, machinery – whatever that company owns.

As a shareholder, you stand to profit when the company profits. You are also legally entitled to a say in major policy decisions, such as whether to issue additional stock, sell the company to outside buyers, or change the board of directors. The rule is that each share has the same voting power, so the more shares you own, the greater your power.

You can vote in person by attending a corporation's annual meeting. Or you can vote by using an absentee ballot, called a ***proxy***, which is mailed before each meeting.

The proxy allows a Yes or No vote on a number of proposals. Alternatively, stockholders may authorize their votes to be cast consistently with the Board of Directors' recommendations.

ITT CORPORATION—COMMON AND/OR PREFE

PROXY SOLICITED BY THE BOARD OF DI

The undersigned hereby appoints Howard J. Aibel or Walter F. Diehl, Jr. or John substitute and hereby authorizes each of them at the Annual Meeting of Shareholders of I 1987 in the Chesapeake Ballroom of the Sheraton Inner Harbor Hotel, Baltimore, Maryla of ITT Common and Preferred Stock, including full shares held in the ITT Common Divid vote if personally present as designated below and upon any other matter properly broug **proxy will be voted as designated below, or if no designation is made, will be voted FO**

Directors recommend a vote **FOR** the following:

1. Election of Directors—Nominees are: B. B. Anderson, R. V. Araskog, N. D. Archibald, R. A. Burnett, E. M. Carpenter, M. David-Weill, L. S. Eagleburger, T. W. Keesee, Jr., E. C. Meyer, C. R. Powell, R. A. Schoellhorn, D. C. Thomas, M. E. White and M. C. Woodward, Jr.—pages 9-23 of proxy statement.

Mark One Box Only

☐ FOR ALL Nominees

☐ FOR ALL Nominees EXCEPT the following:

☐ WITHHOLD Authority To Vote For ALL Nominees

2. Reappointment of Auditors—page 24. FOR ☐ AGAINST ☐ ABSTAIN ☐

3. Amen lin di

4. Sha s

5. Sh

The ***proxy ballot*** allows you to vote for the board of directors who are charged with setting long-term goals for the company.

Stock prices are unpredictable...

A stock does not have a fixed, objective worth. At any moment, it's only as valuable as people think it is.

When you buy a stock, you're making a bet that a lot of other people are going to want to buy that stock, too – and that the price will go up as a result. Your bet is a gamble – but it's not like playing roulette, where the ball may land on 11 even if everyone in the room has bet on 23.

In the stock market, the betting itself influences the outcome. If many investors bet on XYZ stock, the price of XYZ stock will rise. It will become a more valuable stock...simply because a number of people thought it would.

When you're trading stock, then, you have to keep one eye on the other traders to see how they're betting.

...but not arbitrary.

The stock market is, however, more than a lot of investors watching what other investors do. They also watch the companies very carefully. Since the value of shares is directly related to how well the company is doing, investors naturally look for the companies with the best prospects for strong, sustained earnings.

How do you judge a company's prospects? By current or anticipated earnings, the desirability of its product or service, the competition, availability of new markets, management strengths and many other considerations. These are the factors that ***stock analysts*** track in trying to predict whether a stock's value will rise or fall.

How do investors make money?

As a rule, the better a company does and the higher its profits, the more money its stockholders make.

Investors buy stock to make money in one or both of two ways:

- Through dividend payments while they own the stock.
- By selling the stock for more than they paid.

Many companies parcel out portions of their annual profits to stockholders in the form of quarterly ***dividend*** payments. Dividend payments vary from stock to stock. Stocks with consistent histories of paying high dividends are known as ***income stocks*** because investors often buy these stocks for the current dividends rather than for the company's future prospects.

Some companies, however, reinvest most of their profits back into the business in order to expand and strengthen it. As a result, companies that pay little or no dividend are called ***growth stocks*** because investors expect the company to grow – and the stock price to grow with it.

Which corporation has the largest number of stockholders? As of December 31, 1987, AT&T had 2,701,876 holders of common stock on record. The total number of shares in the market totalled 1,073,795,524.

TOCK PROXY

as proxy, each with power to appoint his
ation to be held at 10:30 A.M. on May 12,
ny adjournments thereof to vote all shares
stment Plan, which the undersigned could
e meeting. **The shares represented by this**
2, and 3 and AGAINST Items 4 and 5.

recommend a vote **FOR** the following:
Certificate of Incorporation and By-laws re:
ors' liability and providing for indemnification of
cers, employees and agents—pages 25-33
FOR ☐ AGAINST ☐ ABSTAIN ☐

s recommend a vote **AGAINST** the following:
roposal for disclosure of prior governmental
ges 34-35. FOR ☐ AGAINST ☐ ABSTAIN ☐
oposal for cumulative voting of directors—pages
FOR ☐ AGAINST ☐ ABSTAIN ☐
and to be dated and signed on other side)

You may vote in accord with the directors' recommendations or against them on selected issues.

*The term **blue chips** was introduced in 1904 to mean the stocks of the largest, most consistently profitable corporations. The term comes from the blue chips used in poker – always the most valuable chips.*

A Portrait of the Stock Market

*Unofficially, there are four tiers of stocks in the market. Foremost are the **blue chips**, the older generation, the elite of American industry, the companies of unquestioned strength, like IBM and AT&T.*

***Secondary issues** are the solid, well-established businesses which receive a little less investor confidence than the blue chips.*

***Growth stocks** generally are relatively young companies with growth potential but no assurance of success.*

***Penny stocks** are the long-shots, companies with virtually no value other than their speculative potential.*

Issuing New Stock

Why does a company issue stock?

When stocks are traded in the market, the company that issued the stock doesn't make a cent on the deal. A company only makes money when new stock is issued – put up for sale. The first time a company's stock is issued, the company is said to be ***going public***. In other words, the owners of the company are selling part-ownership to the general public. The formal name for this process is an ***initial public offering (IPO)***.

Typically, a company goes public when it needs to raise cash, usually for expansion. In exchange for the cash, the company management gives up a measure of decision-making control to the shareholders.

When a company goes public, it also benefits from the fact that its stock is trading in the open market. This trading tends to give the company legitimacy: its performance, its financial vitality, becomes visible to all.

How do companies notify investors?

When a company goes public, the financial community is notified through ads in the financial press. These ads are commonly known as ***tombstones***, because of their traditional black border and heavy print.

You'll find a number of different companies' ads in any issue of ***The Wall Street Journal.*** They look alike, but each provides different specific information of interest to potential investors.

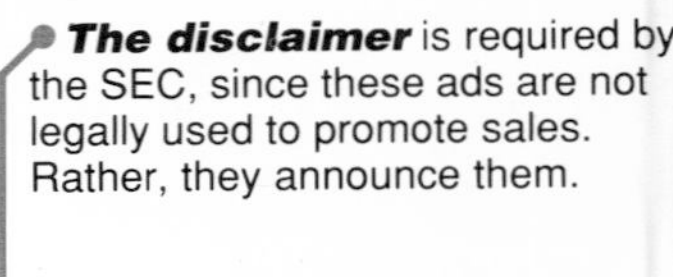

The disclaimer is required by the SEC, since these ads are not legally used to promote sales. Rather, they announce them.

Number of shares being offered for sale.

Name of the company issuing the stock.

Type of issue being offered.

This is the ***market value*** of the stock. The price of the shares upon their first offering to the public is called the ***initial offer***. Once the shares begin trading, even during that very first day, the price may rise or fall, depending on the stock's popularity with the public.

The ***prospectus*** must, by law, be available to anyone interested in investing. It provides detailed financial information not given in the advertisement.

The ***underwriters*** are the ***investment bankers*** who handle the offering. The investment banking division of a securities firm will ***underwrite*** (buy up) all the shares for sale from the company and then sell them on the market – to the public – at the best possible price. The lead firm has its name displayed most prominently. Other firms, with smaller roles in the offering, are then listed below.

This is not an offer to sell nor a solicitation of offers
This offer is made only by the P

1,100,000 Sh

MINDSCAPE I

Mindscap

Common S

Price $9 Per

Copies of the Prospectus may be obtain
Underwriter who may lawfully offer th

William Blair

Dillon, Read & Co

Alex. Brown & Sons
Incorporated

Hambrecht & Quist
Incorporated

Prudential-Bache Capital Funding

Advest, Inc.

Ladenburg, Thalmann &

The Robinson-Humphrey Company, Inc.

Sanford C. Bernstein & Co., Inc.

Furman Selz Mager Dietz & Birney
Incorporated

Johnson, Lane, Space, Smith & Co., Inc.

Ne

Gabelli & C

Common and Preferred Stock

Companies can issue two types of stock: common and preferred. Each type of stock has its own characteristics and trades independently of the other in the marketplace.

What is common stock?

A corporation issues common stock first. It represents the ***basic ownership*** of a corporation. Owners of common stock share directly in the success or failure of the business. If the company prospers, common stock owners can benefit through dividend increases and higher stock prices. In return for the ability to participate in higher profits, however, common stock owners take a back seat to preferred stockholders when it comes to distributing dividends.

What is preferred stock?

A corporation only issues preferred stock after common stock has been issued. Preferred stock is just what it sounds like: preferred stockholders receive ***preferential treatment.*** Dividends are distributed to them before being distributed to common stockholders. And, should the company be forced to go out of business and sell its assets – a process called ***liquidation*** – preferred stockholders are entitled to receive the money they've invested before common stockholders receive theirs. In exchange for these benefits, though, preferred stockholders must accept a fixed dividend payment, regardless of any increase in company profits.

28½	15¼	IntlAlum		.80	3.0	10	2	26¾	26¾	26¾	– ⅛
175⅞	100	IBM	IBM	4.40	3.5	15	19214	126½	125½	125¾	
58	37¼	IntlFlav	IFF	1.60	3.2	15	389	50	49⅝	49⅝	– ⅜
53	28	IntlMinrl	IGL	1.00	2.4	17	1371	41¼	40⅜	41⅛	+ ⅝
67	48½	IntlMinrl pfA		3.75	6.8	...	123	55	54½	55	+ ½
67¼	48⅛	IntlMinrl pfB		3.25	5.8	...	3	56	56	56	...
39¾	22½	IntlMultfds	IMC	1.18	3.7	14	58	32⅜	32	32	– ¼
56	27	IntlPaper	IP	1.30	2.8	9	4960	46⅜	45½	46	+ ¼
[illegible]	[illegible]	IntlRect	IRF		...	...	54	6¾	6¾	6¾	– ⅛
					...	...	267	3⅜	3¼	[illegible]	+ ⅛

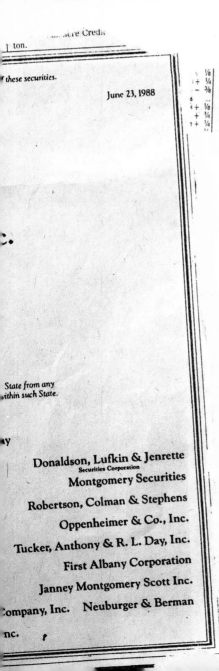

Companies may issue several ***classes*** of stock, often labelled A, B, C, and so on. The different classes have different market prices, different dividend payments and different restrictions on ownership. This clipping from the New York Stock Exchange Quotations in ***The Wall Street Journal*** shows that International Minerals and Chemicals Corporation has issued a common stock and two classes of preferred stock.

What's a stock split?

When a company finds that its high stock price is discouraging new investors, it may initiate a stock split to lower the price and increase trading.

In a stock split, the company gives you more shares but lowers the price of each share. If the stock splits two for one, the price of the stock is cut in half and stockholders are given twice as many shares. The initial effect for the stockholder, then, is no different than trading a dime for two nickels. The longer term effect is that now there are twice as many shares available to buy in the market at half the price.

Stocks can split 3 for 1, 3 for 2, 10 for 1, or any other combination. There can even be a reverse split, where you exchange, say, 10 shares for 5 shares, with each new share worth twice as much as an old one.

Who Buys Stocks?

According to a recent New York Stock Exchange survey, the typical American stock investor is not – contrary to popular opinion – a titan of industry.

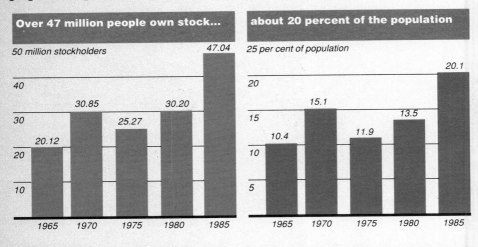

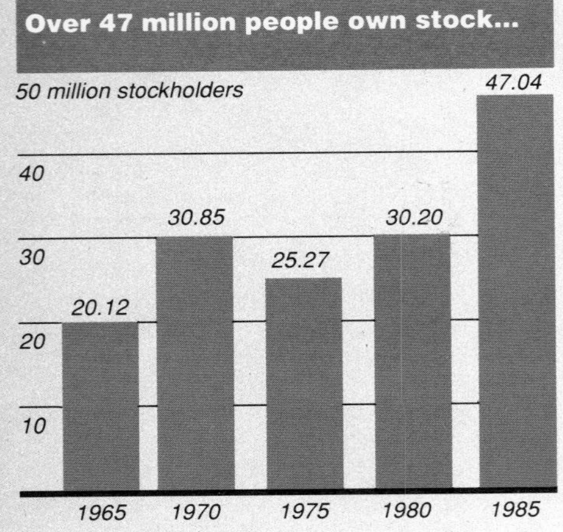

about 20 percent of the population

25 per cent of population

20
15
10
5
10.4
15.1
11.9
13.5
20.1
1965
1970
1975
1980
1985

How the average shareholder compares to the average US citizen

	Shareholders	*U.S. population*
Median Age (pop. over 21)	45 years	42 years
Median Income	$36,800	$22,400
Median Education Level	15.5 years	12.6 years
Male/Female ratio	50/50	48/52
Average stock portfolio (holdings)	$6,100	—

Can you buy stock in any company?

No, you may only buy stock in a ***publicly held corporation***. Some companies are ***privately held***, meaning they are completely owned by an individual or group of individuals, who retain control of the company. Some corporations are ***closely held***, meaning that a few people, often members of a family, hold all or most of the shares, thereby controlling the company.

Who are institutional investors?

A very different sort of investor is increasingly important in the stock market. This investor isn't an individual at all, but an institution, like a ***pension fund*** or a ***mutual fund***, with large sums to invest.

In recent years, institutions have acquired enormous clout in affecting prices. A company's employee pension fund investing hundreds of millions of dollars can influence stock prices considerably based on its buying and selling patterns.

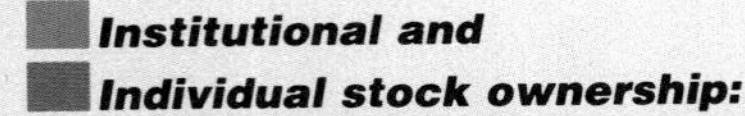

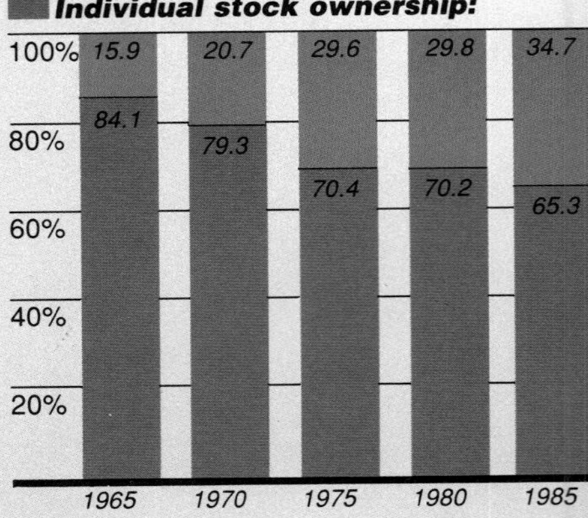

Buying Stocks: The Brokers

The business of a broker is to find customers the best trade price available and, when asked, to provide timely, sound investment advice.

Why do you need a broker?

Only a broker can execute an order to buy or sell stocks. And only a broker whose brokerage firm is a member of a stock exchange can trade stocks on that exchange.

Every firm employs two kinds of brokers. **Stockbrokers** work out of their offices. They spend a lot of time researching investments, helping clients develop goals, and giving advice. Investing has become so complex today that "stockbroker" is actually a misnomer. To devote the time required to provide good service, many brokers now specialize, restricting their work to one or two particular products. Stockbrokers are also called ***registered representatives***, meaning they have passed a ***series 7*** exam and are registered with the Securities and Exchange Commission, the SEC, to represent their brokerage firms.

Discount brokers act strictly as agents for your transactions and do not offer investment advice.

Stockbrokers pass their orders to the ***floorbrokers***. Floorbrokers are the ones who actually buy and sell – and though member firms are said to hold ***seats*** on the exchange, nobody ever sits while the deals are made.

How do brokers make money?

Each time you buy or sell stock you pay a ***commission***. A portion of that commission goes to your broker. The rest goes to the firm to cover costs and, hopefully, provide a profit.

Although brokers will quote you their commissions, all commissions are negotiable. Usually, though, only investors who trade frequently or in large blocks of stock are accorded commission discounts.

What is program trading?

Often institutions use ***computer-based buying or selling programs***. Since some of these programs are triggered automatically when prices reach a certain level, computer-based activity can often accentuate sudden swings in the price of stock, or cause dramatic shifts in the entire market, as the stock collapse of 1987 showed.

*The term **broker** was first used around 1622 to mean an agent in financial transactions. Originally, it referred to wine retailers – those who broach (break) wine casks.*

Top US Brokerage Firms Ranked by Total Capital *(figures in millions of dollars)*

Firm	*12/80*
Merrill Lynch, Pierce, Fenner & Smith Inc.	$969
Shearson Loeb Rhoades Inc.	470
EF Hutton	448
Salomon Holding Co.	330
Dean Witter	274
Bache Halsey Stewart Shields Inc.	252
PaineWebber	243
Goldman Sachs & Co.	219
Stephens Inc.	167

Firm	*1/1/88*
Shearson Lehman Brothers*	4,584
Salomon Brothers Inc.	3,133
Merrill Lynch, Pierce, Fenner & Smith Inc.	2,903
Goldman Sachs & Co.	2,400
Drexel Burnham Lambert Group	2,300
First Boston Corporation	1,486
PaineWebber Group Inc.	1,437
Dean Witter Reynolds	1,344
Bear Stearns & Company	1,320

* Had not yet merged with EF Hutton

Top US Brokerage Firms in 1988 Ranked by Customer Accounts

Firm	*Brokers*	*Customer Accounts*
Merrill Lynch, Pierce, Fenner & Smith Inc.	13,300	5,800,000
Shearson Lehman Hutton Inc.	11,750	4,600,000
Dean Witter Reynolds, Inc.	7,758	2,200,000
Prudential-Bache Securities, Inc.	6,082	1,900,000
Paine Webber Incorporated	4,350	1,870,000
A. G. Edwards & Sons Inc.	3,250	541,000
Thomson McKinnon Securities Inc.	2,400	500,897
Smith Barney, Harris Upham & Co., Inc.	2,311	500,000
Kidder Peabody & Co, Inc.	2,178	520,015
Bear Stearns & Co. Inc.	2,166	145,000

Source: Securities Industry Association

Buying and Selling Stocks

How do you choose a stock?

There's no one method. Simple ways are talking to your broker, reading the newspaper, and tracking stocks' progress in the daily stock tables.

There are, however, two major schools of thought on picking stocks. Many serious investors swear by ***fundamental analysis,*** which involves appraising a company's financial condition and management, and an industry's competitive position. Many investors, however, live and die by ***technical analysis***, which ignores fundamentals and, instead, uses charts based on past performance to identify price trends and cyclical movements of particular stocks, industries or the market as a whole.

Those who feel every factor must be considered study both fundamental and technical information (which probably leaves very little time for their families). Finally, of course, there's the less time-consuming method of throwing darts at the stock page. (It's often argued that this method is as effective as any ever invented).

How do you place an order with your broker?

The most common order is called a ***market order***, asking the broker for the best buy or sell price available in the current market:

Buy (or sell) 100 shares of XYZ Company for me, at the best price you can get.

But let's say you have some educated guesses about market trends and a strategy for dealing with them. You might give your broker more specific guidelines.

If you think the market for a stock is going your way, you can place a ***limit order***. This kind of order says:

Trade for me only if and when you can do better than 42 (or whatever price you decide).

A Broker by any Other Name...

Depending on where you do business, you may find your broker known as:
Financial Consultant *at Merrill Lynch or Shearson Lehman Hutton;*
Institutional Salesman *at Salomon Brothers;*
Securities Salesperson *at Goldman Sachs;*
Account Executive *at Drexel Burnham, Prudential-Bache or Dean Witter;*
Investment Executive *at PaineWebber; or*
Portfolio Salesman *at First Boston.*

Of the biggest brokerage houses, only Morgan Stanley calls a broker simply a ***Broker***.

More ways to choose a stock

Anywhere there is speculation there are "sure-fire" methods for beating the system. The stock market, of course, is no exception. Some of the methods are quite esoteric, if not far-fetched, if the following book titles are any indication.

- *Astrological Warnings and the Stock Market*
- *Investing for Profit with Torque Analysis of Stock Market Cycles*
- *How to Use the Three-Point Reversal Method of Point & Figure Stock Market Tradir*
- *The Stock Digest Price Rate Test Method to Stock Market Success*
- *Granville's New Strategy of Daily Stock Market Timing for Major Profit*
- *Psyche, Sex and Stocks*
- *Tight Money Timing*
- *Psycho-Cybernetics and the Stock Market*
- *Mind over Money*

What is an odd lot trade?

Most stock trading orders refer to ***round numbers*** of shares – multiples of 100. But what of the small investor with a fixed sum of money to invest – say, a gift of $300? The number of shares that $300 will buy is likely to be an ***odd*** number, not a multiple of 100 shares; hence the term ***odd lot*** for this kind of order.

The rules of the trade

Just about every activity has rules, whether it's touch football or stock trading. Here are some trading rules for the New York Stock Exchange and the American Stock Exchange:

- *If two orders are equal, the first order gets priority.*
- *If two orders are equal and simultaneous, the larger order gets priority.*
- *If two orders are equal in all respects... What else? They flip a coin.*

At times though, your educated guesses could be wrong, and the market for a stock could move in the opposite direction. To protect yourself from losing too much in those instances, you could place a ***stop order***. This kind of order says:

If the stock goes as low as 40, (or any price you name) sell my shares and save me from any further losses.

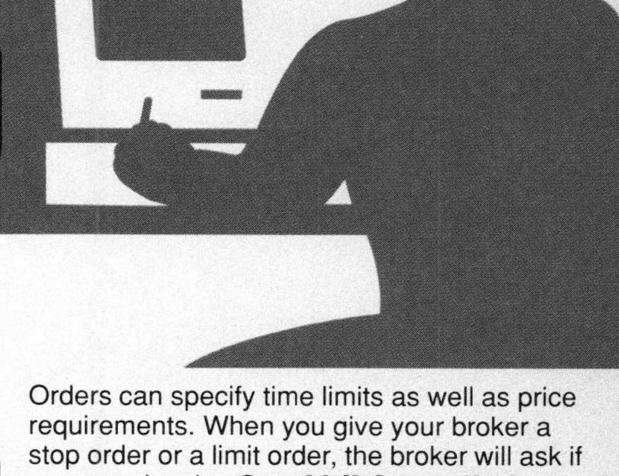

If the market is going up, and you're making money on your stock, you might decide to place a ***limit order to sell*** which says:

Don't sell my stock until you can sell it for 45 (or whatever price you name).

Orders can specify time limits as well as price requirements. When you give your broker a stop order or a limit order, the broker will ask if you want it to be ***Good 'til Cancelled***, or ***GTC*** (the order will stand until either it's filled or you cancel it), or a ***day order*** (it will either be filled that day or cancelled automatically).

What happens when a broker can't fill your order?

What if you place an order at or better than a certain price and your broker can't find a trader willing to make a deal?

This is where the ***specialist*** – the matchmaker of the exchange – comes in. Specialists concentrate on trading particular stocks and stay at the post on the exchange floor where those stocks trade. If a broker can't fill an order immediately, the order will be left with the specialist at the post. The specialist keeps lists of these unfilled orders and, as the market price moves up or down, looks for opportunities to fill each order. In this way, the specialist acts as the broker to the brokers, charging them commissions for every order successfully carried out.

What happens if the specialist can't make a match?

When the ***spread*** between the ***bid*** and the ***ask*** (the gap between the highest price offered by a buyer and the lowest price asked by a seller) is wide, specialists turn into dealers and buy or sell some stock themselves. This has the effect of narrowing the spread and stimulating more trading activity – a good thing for exchange vitality and for specialists as well, since the more busily their stocks trade, the more commissions they can earn.

The Ticker Tape

For over a century, ticker tape was the stockbroker's gospel – a one-inch wide strip of tape spewing steadily from a printer that ticked as it ran, listing the latest price and size of every stock transaction. The computer revolution has changed all that.

How do brokers get their information?

These days, it's tough to find actual ticker tape on Wall Street – or anywhere else. Even the ticker tape parades of lower Manhattan have had to make do with crowds tossing shredded computer printouts and confetti.

On an average day in the 1920s, between one-quarter and one-third of a mile of tape went through the ticker – about 1,500 feet of tape.

When today's stock professionals refer to "the tape", they mean a band of rapidly moving information on a computer or television screen which carries up-to-the-minute stock prices – just as actual ticker tape once did.

Ticker prices first go to brokerage firms and investment professionals. Then, after a fifteen-minute delay, the prices appear on a display board in the broker's office or at home on television via a cable network.

What's replacing the ticker tape?

Today's brokers have a remarkable device on their desks. ***The computerized quote machine*** links them not only to the fast-paced world of modern financial marketplaces, but to substantial analytic resources as well.

In a matter of seconds, brokers can summon the latest data on individual stocks, bonds, mutual funds, commodities and options; on corporations, industries or currencies; on yields, dividends or earnings; on market volume, indexes or averages. They are continuously apprised of the news around the world – virtually as it hits the news wires.

With the help of this desktop quote machine, your broker can provide you with all the information you could possibly need to make informed decisions about your investments.

How do you read the Tape?

The ticker tape displays two rows of information, stacked one on top of the other. On the top row are the stock symbols; ***BP*** for British Petroleum, ***FBC*** for First Boston, Inc. and so on. (There are a number of stock symbol guides to help you decipher the codes. Your broker can tell you where to find one.)

You may find the company symbol followed by what looks like a capital ***P*** and small ***r*** printed together. This ***Pr*** indicates that the stock transaction involved the company's ***preferred*** stock. Often, an additional letter specifies which one of a company's several types of preferred stock was traded. In this sample, ASPr indicates a trade of Armco (symbol AS) preferred stock. AMXPrB refers to the preferred B stock of Amax, Inc. (symbol AMX).

The ***bottom row*** shows the price per share and number of shares involved in each transaction. When just a price appears after the symbol, it indicates that 100 shares have traded. The figure can be misleading, though. Those who read the ticker are expected to know the trading range of the stocks they're watching. If British Petroleum (BP) had been trading between $40 and $50 the 100 shares recorded here will have sold for $46 7/8 per share – not $6 7/8.

When the price is preceded by a number and an ***S***, the number indicates that a multiple of 100 shares was traded. You can see that 2500 shares of Amax preferred B stock (AMXPrB) were traded at $40.50 per share. If a number above 10,000 appears before the S, that number should not be multiplied by 100; it represents the total amount traded. Texaco (TX) had a hefty 200,000 shares traded at $34. A trade of over 10,000 shares is often called a ***block trade***.

```
LTR2s28 1/2 MAD11 1/8 SQD2s26 3/4.3s 7/8 SIM21.2s21.2s21

WS14 1/4 POY3s8 1/4 FGI2s38 ALA.WS.O2s6 5/8 SOD2s5 1/2 TP19 1/2

-----------------------------------------------------------

GM
     L-  72 1/4    O  72 1/2    C   73
     B   72 3/8    H  72 1/2    NC- 3/4
     A   72 1/2    L  72 1/4    V   149        T  10 17
```

On this computer screen, brokers can see the day's activity in a particular stock. In this case, GM is General Motors. ***GM*** is the stock's quote symbol. ***L*** represents the last trade, indicating whether it was at a higher price (+) or a lower price (-) than the previous trade, and the last price. ***B*** shows the current bid price (the buyer's offer), while ***A*** shows the current ask price (the seller's offer).

O, ***H***, ***L*** give the day's opening, high and low trade prices.

C gives the previous day's closing price. ***NC*** shows the net price change from the previous day's close. In this case, GM is down $^{3}/_{4}$ from the previous day's closing price. ***V*** and ***T*** display current volume and time of last trade.

Brokers can retrieve additional information, such as annual high and low and dividend payments at the press of a button on their keyboards.

*22 companies enjoy the prestige of being identified by a single letter of the alphabet – **C** for Chrysler, **S** for Sears, **T** for AT&T. The letters **I**, **O**, **Q** and **W** are not used – I and O look too much like numbers. and Q is reserved for bankrupt companies.*

Sometimes the symbol is followed by an ***ampersand*** (&) and a letter standing for the exchange on which the trade took place. For example, the symbol ***ICN*** for ICN Pharmaceuticals is followed by ***&N***, indicating that this trade took place on the NASDAQ. (the word ***LAST*** means the company halted trading after this trade took place.)

```
MX  UNP   C GLW   PHH   HAL        ICN&N▪LAST  IN
1/8  5   4 3/4  6   6 7/8  5 3/8  1 1/8▪▪▪         24
```

On June 13, 1927, three weeks after his solo flight across the Atlantic, Charles A. Lindbergh returned to receive the greatest welcome New York City has ever bestowed on any hero. Driving up Broadway to City Hall in his parade, Lindbergh was deluged by an estimated 750,000 pounds of saved-up ticker tape and torn-up telephone books.

The flyer was escorted to the grandstand by official greeter Grover Whalen and Mayor Jimmy Walker, who said: "New York is yours. I don't give it to you. You won it. And one other thing. Before you go will you provide us with a new street-cleaning department to clean up the mess?"

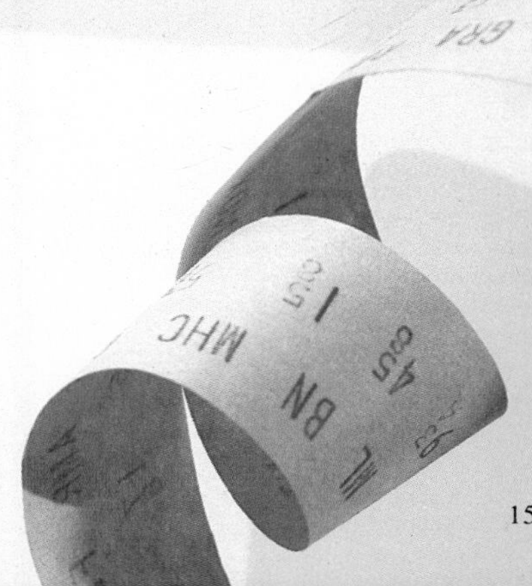

Keeping Tabs on Your Stock

At first glance, stock listings look like an endless sea of numbers. This has more to do with the volume of listings and the use of small type than with the complexity of the information.

To read the listings, remember that stock prices are given in fractions of dollars. Thus 8½ equals $8.50; 8¼ equals $8.25. The fraction ⅛ refers to 12½ cents; and 8⅛ equals about $8.13.

Highest and lowest prices of the stock are shown for the last 52 weeks. Stocks reaching a new high or low for the year are marked with an arrow in the lefthand margin. These figures show you the ***volatility*** of a stock – an indicator of both profit potential and risk. The percentage gain or loss is often more significant than the dollar gain or loss: a $5 change in a $10 stock indicates more volatility than a $5 move in a $30 stock.

For instance, Harcourt Brace Jovanovich, Inc. was more volatile over the past year (swinging 9½ points, or 71%, between 13¼ and 3¾) than was Harris Corp. which moved 18⅛ points between 40⅛ and 22, or roughly 45%.

Cash dividend per share is given in dollars and cents. A dividend is a payment to shareholders of part of a company's profit. This figure is an estimate of the anticipated yearly dividend per share. Hartmarx's yearly dividend is estimated at $1.10 per share. If you owned 100 shares, you'd receive $110 in dividend payments each year, probably in quarterly payments of $27.50.

Sometimes the dividend column for a company is blank, indicating that the company doesn't pay cash dividends.

52 Weeks Hi	52 Weeks Lo	Stock	Sym	Div	Yld %	PE	Vol 100s	Hi	Lo	Close	Net Chg
13¼	3¾	HarBraceJ	HBJ		...	10	2314	12½	11⅞	12¼	+ ⅛
11½	5¾	HarBraceJ pf		1.62t	14.9	...	142	11	10¾	10⅞	− ⅛
25¾	16⅜	Harland	JH	.58	2.7	16	792	21⅞	20⅞	21¼	+ ⅝
29⅞	9¼	HarleyDav	HDI		...	8	444	26⅜	26	26¼	+ ½
17⅜	6⅜	HarmanInt	HAR		...	11	256	16¼	15⅞	16⅛	+ ⅛
29¾	8½	Harnisch	HPH	.20	1.2	22	3021	17⅜	17⅛	17⅛	− ¼
40⅛	22	Harris	HRS	.88	3.2	17	1020	28¼	27	27⅞	+1
37⅞	23½	Harsco	HSC	1.12	3.6	11	417	30⅞	30½	30⅞	+ ¼
33¼	18¼	Hartmarx	HMX	1.10	4.2	13	244	26⅞	26⅜	26½	− ⅜
19⅜	13½	HattersSec	HAT	1.56	9.8	11	2	16	16	16	+ ⅛
33⅝	22¼	HawaiiElec	HE	1.92	6.6	12	495	29	28¾	29	..
9½	6¾	HlthRehab	HRP	1.12	12.3	11	901	9¼	9	9⅛	+ [illegible]
[illegible]	[illegible]	HlthCareProp	HCP	2.59	9.5	15	560	27⅛	26⅞	27⅛	+ [illegible]
										23/32	+ 3[illegible]

Company names are abbreviated, listed alphabetically, and followed by the ticker symbol. Most symbols are closely related to the name of the company – HMX for Hartmarx Corp. – though some may be more related to what the company does. CAF, for instance, is the symbol for Furr's/Bishop's Cafeterias (not shown).

__pf__ or __pr__ following the name of a company refers to __preferred stock__ rather than common stock (stocks listed without Pf or pr are common stock). Preferred stock pays dividends at a fixed rate, and the company's obligation to pay them is stronger than for common stock.

Per cent yield is a way of expressing the stock's current value: it tells you how much ***dividend*** you get for what you pay. The table calculates yield for you; you could do it yourself by dividing the dividend by the ***closing price*** (next to last column). For Hartmarx Corp.'s yield divide $1.10 by 26.5 to get .042 or ***4.2% yield***. Think of it this way: *I will get 4.2% of my purchase price in dividends each year.*

When no dividend has been quoted, of course, the yield cannot be calculated and the yield column will be blank.

__wt__ following the company name means the quote is not for stocks but for __warrants__. A warrant is the right to buy stock during a certain period for a certain price.

P-E Ratio, short for price-earnings ratio, refers to the relationship between the price of one share of stock and the annual earnings of the company. (Since earnings aren't given here, you can't calculate this figure yourself from this chart.)

For La-Z-Boy Chair Corp., the price-earnings ratio has been derived by dividing the ***closing price*** of $15.37 by the company's ***earnings per share*** (about $1.39) to arrive at 11. It's useful to read the P-E ratio as follows: *The price of a La-Z-Boy share is 11 times the company's earnings per share for the most recent four quarters.*

The P-E ratio is a critical piece of information because it expresses the value of a stock in terms of company earnings rather than selling price. The P-E ratios of different stocks can be compared to assess their relative values.

It's important to remember that there's no perfect P-E ratio. Some stocks which have lower earnings will have higher P-E ratios; these are usually growth stocks. On the other hand, an income stock which pays consistently high dividends will tend to have a lower P-E ratio.

Net change compares the closing price given here with the closing price of the day before (given in the previous day's paper). A minus (-) indicates this closing price is lower than the previous day's; a plus (+) means it's higher. This figure shows you what's happened to the stock's price in the last day. Since La-Z-Boy Chair Corp., closing at $15 3/8, was down 1/8 point; you can infer that the closing price quoted the previous day was 15 1/2.

Stocks that show a price change of 5% or more are shown in boldface type. Landmark Bancshares Corp.'s move of 1 1/8 represents a change of 8.1%

...ks Lo	Stock	Sym	Div	Yld %	PE	Vol 100s	Hi	Lo	Close	Net Chg
10¾	LaQuintaPtnr	LQP	2.00	15.1	...	19	13⅜	13¼	13¼	...
13	LaZ Boy	LZB	.48	3.1	11	59	15½	15⅛	15⅜	– ⅛
26	LacledeGas	LG	2.20	7.5	9	105	29⅝	28⅝	29½	+ 1⅛
9⅝	Lafarge	LAF	.40	2.2	10	622	18½	18⅛	18½	+ ¼
4¼	LamsonSes	LMS		...	12	1201	19⅛	18⅝	18⅞	– ⅛
10⅝	**LandBanc**	**LBC**	**.72**	**4.8**	**11**	**365**	**15**	**13¾**	**15**	**+ 1⅛**
12¼	LandsEnd	LE	.15i	.5	23	140	30	29¾	29¾	...
8⅜	LawtonInt	LAW	.52	4.3	15	158	12	11¾	12	– ⅛
9⅞	LeaRonal	LRI	.48	2.9	16	13	16⅜	16¼	16⅜	+ ⅛
20	Lee Ent	LEE	.64	2.3	18	29	28	28	28	...
9½	LeggMason	LM	.24	2.0	16	136	11¾	11⅝	11¾	...
20	LeggetPlat	LEG	.64	2.8	10	32	22⅞	22¾	22¾	+ ¼
10⅝	Lehman	LEM	2.14e	17.3	...	199	12½	12⅜	12⅜	...
3	LeisrTech	LVX		...	4	32	4	3⅞	3⅞	...
[illegible]	[illegible]		2.25	11.8	...	3	19	19	19	+ ⅛
[illegible]	[illegible]				7	326	19¼	19	19⅛	– ⅛

52 Weeks Hi	Lo
38	25
7⅝	3[illegible]
4½	1[illegible]
2½	15[illegible]
23½	11[illegible]
52⅝	41[illegible]
36	11[illegible]
19¾	1[illegible]
22¼	1[illegible]
n 10½	
n 4	
18⅜	[illegible]
26¾	[illegible]
22¼	
15½	
28⅛	
24⅜	

Sales in hundreds refers to the ***volume*** of shares traded on the previous day. Just multiply the figure in this column by 100. For example, 36,500 shares of Landmark Bancshares Corp. stock were traded on this day. Stocks with unusual sales volumes are underlined.

Occasionally a ***z*** appears before the number in this column. This means you should *not* multiply by 100; the figure refers to the actual number traded.

***s** in the left hand column indicates a recent **stock split**. The split may be 2 for 1, 3 for 1 or even 10 for 1. There's no way to tell from the table.*

High, low and close tell you a stock's highest, lowest and closing price for the previous day.

These numbers give you an idea of how widely the price has fluctuated in a single day; usually the differences are small. The largest spread seen here is for Landmark Bancshares stock, which traded for as high as $15 per share and as low as $13 3/4, and closed at $15.

***n** in the left hand column indicates a **new stock**, issued within the last 52 weeks. This doesn't necessarily mean the company listing is new, just that the stock being traded is a new issue.*

Tricks of the Trade

Novice investors may not want to start by selling short, buying on margin, or buying warrants. But it's a good idea to know how the veterans do it.

How does short selling work?

Logic dictates that first you buy stock and then you sell it. But in ***short selling***, you actually sell stock before you buy it. Here's how it works:

You borrow the shares from your broker (for example, 100 shares of XYZ), sell them in the market and receive the money from the sale. Then you wait. Your hope is that the price of the stock will soon drop, because you will eventually have to replace the stock you borrowed – in other words, repay the loan. If later on you can buy the stock for less than you originally sold it, you'll profit.

For example, you sell short 100 shares of XYZ at $8 a share. Two weeks later, you buy the shares of XYZ at $6 a share, give them to your broker and keep the $2 a share difference as your profit.

What is the risk of selling short?

Buying the shares back is called covering the short position. While waiting for the right time to cover the short position, you pay your broker interest on the stock you borrowed. The longer you wait to buy back the shares, the more interest you pay.

The greater risk comes, however, from what happens to the price of the stock. You want the price to fall, but if the price rises you will be forced to pay more to buy it back than you made from selling it.

For example, if you sold XYZ at $8 a share and two weeks later the price was $10, you'd be facing a $2 per share loss. Your decision would then be either to keep waiting and paying more interest, hoping the price will drop back down, or to end the risk by buying back the shares and accepting the loss.

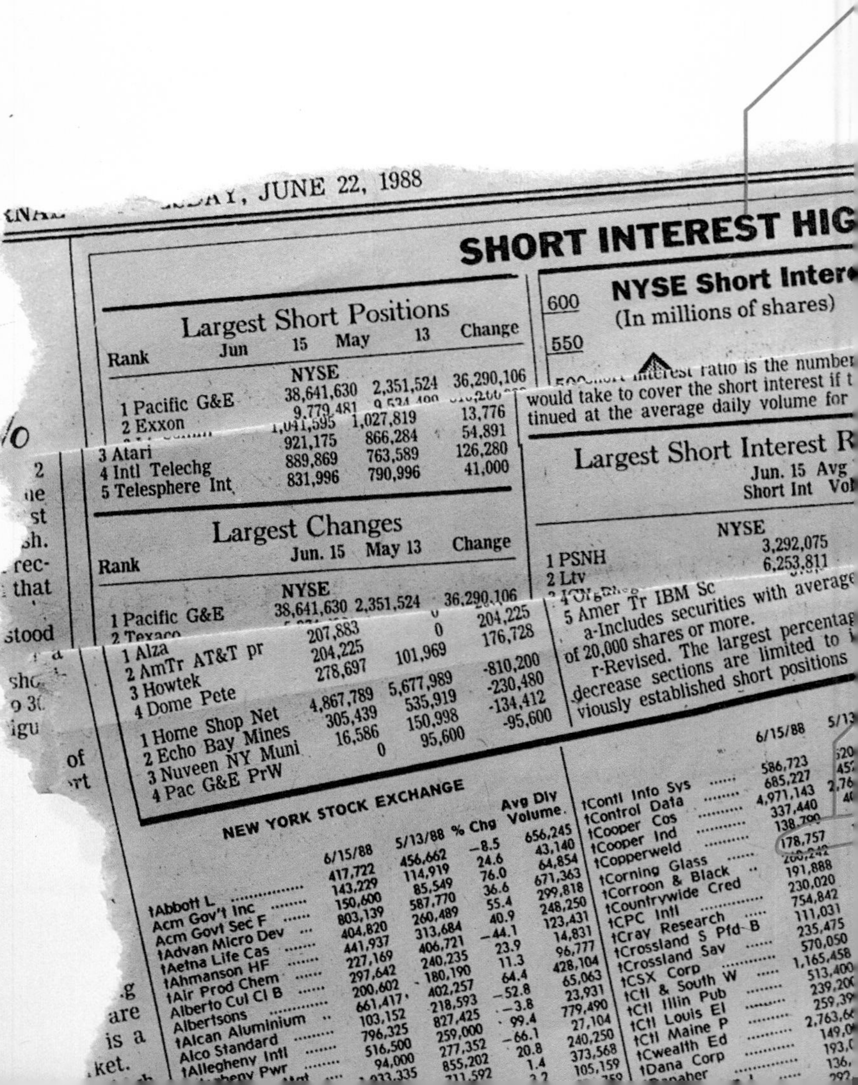

…DAY, JUNE 22, 1988

SHORT INTEREST HIG…

Largest Short Positions

Rank	Jun 15	May 13	Change
NYSE			
1 Pacific G&E	38,641,630	2,351,524	36,290,106
2 Exxon	9,779,481	[illegible]	[illegible]
	1,041,595	1,027,819	13,776
3 Atari	921,175	866,284	54,891
4 Intl Telechg	889,869	763,589	126,280
5 Telesphere Int	831,996	790,996	41,000

Largest Changes

Rank	Jun. 15	May 13	Change
NYSE			
1 Pacific G&E	38,641,630	2,351,524	36,290,106
2 Texaco			
1 Alza	207,883		
2 AmTr AT&T pr	204,225	0	204,225
3 Howtek	278,697	101,969	176,728
4 Dome Pete			
1 Home Shop Net	4,867,789	5,677,989	-810,200
2 Echo Bay Mines	305,439	535,919	-230,480
3 Nuveen NY Muni	16,586	150,998	-134,412
4 Pac G&E PrW	0	95,600	-95,600

NYSE Short Inter…
(In millions of shares)

600
550
500

…short interest ratio is the number … would take to cover the short interest if t… tinued at the average daily volume for …

Largest Short Interest R…

	Jun. 15 Short Int	Avg Vol…
NYSE		
1 PSNH	3,292,075	
2 Ltv	6,253,811	
5 Amer Tr IBM Sc		

a-Includes securities with average … of 20,000 shares or more.
r-Revised. The largest percentag… decrease sections are limited to … viously established short positions

NEW YORK STOCK EXCHANGE

	6/15/88	5/13/88	% Chg	Avg Dly Volume
tAbbott L.	417,722	456,662	−8.5	656,245
Acm Gov't Inc	143,229	114,919	24.6	43,140
Acm Govt Sec F	150,600	85,549	76.0	64,854
tAdvan Micro Dev	803,139	587,770	36.6	671,363
tAetna Life Cas	404,820	260,489	55.4	299,818
tAhmanson HF	441,937	313,684	40.9	248,250
tAir Prod Chem	227,169	406,721	−44.1	123,431
Alberto Cul Cl B	297,642	240,235	23.9	14,831
Albertsons	200,602	180,190	11.3	96,777
tAlcan Aluminium	661,417	402,257	64.4	428,104
Alco Standard	103,152	218,593	−52.8	65,063
tAllegheny Intl	796,325	827,425	−3.8	23,931
tAllegheny Pwr	516,500	259,000	99.4	779,490
	94,000	277,352	−66.1	27,104
		855,202	20.8	240,250
		711,592	1.4	373,568
				105,159

	6/15/88
tContl Info Sys	586,723
tControl Data	685,227
tCooper Cos	4,971,143
tCooper Ind	337,440
tCopperweld	
tCorning Glass	178,757
tCorroon & Black	
tCountrywide Cred	191,888
tCPC Intl	230,020
tCray Research	754,842
tCrossland S Pfd B	111,031
tCrossland Sav	235,475
tCSX Corp	570,050
tCtl & South W	1,165,458
tCtl Illin Pub	513,400
tCtl Louis El	239,20…
tCtl Maine P	259,39…
tCwealth Ed	2,763,6…
tDana Corp	149,0…
	193,…
	136,…

What are warrants?

Warrants are sold by companies intending to issue stock in the future, or by those seeking to raise cash by selling shares held in reserve. For instance, a company planning a new issue might sell a number of warrants for those stocks in advance, to ensure that the new issue will be bought up.

When you buy a warrant, you're paying a small price now for the ***right to buy*** a certain number of shares at a fixed price when the stock is finally issued. Consequently, you'll ***pay now and own later***. You do this only if you think the price of the stock will rise. Suppose, for example, you pay $1 a share for warrants that give you the right to buy shares at $7 when they're issued. If the shares are eventually issued at $10 a share, it will have cost you only $8 ($1 + $7) for a $10 stock.

33¾	24	PacTelesis	PAC	1.76	6.0	12	2959	29½	29⅛	29⅜ – ⅛
37	26¾	PacifiCp	PPW	2.64	7.5	9	323	35⅛	34¾	35 + ¼
36	13⅛	PaineWeb	PWJ	.52	3.2	15	392	16½	16⅜	16⅜ – ⅛
25	12¾	PaineWeb pf		1.37	9.0	...	31	15½	15¼	15¼ ...
5½	2⅜	PanAm	PN	...	...	...	1187	2¾	2⅝	2⅝ ...
1⅞	7/16	PanAm wt			...	...	59	⅝	⅝	⅝ ...
		PanhdlEast	PEL	2.00	7.5	9	1213	26½	26	26½ + ⅜
34¾	18¼	PanhdlEast	PKC		...	14	6	9⅝	9⅜	9⅜ – ⅛
17	5	PanhillKnit	PNS	.16	1.0	18	726	15¾	15½	15½ – ⅛
27¼	10½	PansophSy	PRX	.02e	.2	12	341	13⅜	13	13 – ⅜
26	12⅛	ParPhar	PTC		...	10	24	9½	9⅜	9½ ...
10¾	4¾	ParTech	PDN							5¾ ...

Pan American World Airways, Inc. has issued a ***warrant*** that is trading for about 62 cents (5/8 dollar). Your broker can tell you what a warrant represents, and when the shares it represents will be issued.

Short Interest Highlights shows the companies with the largest amount of short selling in their stock; the largest increases and decreases during the month; and something called "largest short interest ratios", which indicates the number of days it would take to repurchase all the stock sold short, based on that stock's average daily volume for the month. Investors watch short interest to judge what other investors are thinking. For example, an increase in short selling of a stock means investors expect the price to fall.

HTS

Largest % Increases

Rank	Jun. 15	May 13	%
...Bank	104,400	20,566	407.6
AMEX			
1 MacNeal Schw	73,932	11,744	529.5
2 Fur Vault	41,882	12,109	245.9
3 Dome Pete	278,697	101,969	173.3
4 Alza	499,136	245,826	103.0
5 Carnival	82,990	45,494	82.4

Largest % Decreases

Rank	Jun. 15	May 13	%
...		434,485	-14.3
2 Echo Bay M	361,000	5,677,989	-11.6
3 Michaels St	4,867,789	666,315	
4 Home Shop Netw	588,760		
5 Organogene			

	6/15/88	5/13/88	% Chg	Avg Dly Volume
†Inco Ltd.	654,900	802,799	–18.4	586,145
Ingersoll R	322,021	428,778	–24.9	100,386
†Inland Steel	350,264	411,384	–14.9	144,363
†Insilco	210,966	211,351	–0.2	24,663
†Inspirat Resr.	149,604	157,934	–5.3	112,763
†Int Flavors	238,863	128,230	86.3	81,786
†Integrated Res	482,120	447,095	7.8	15,313
Intelogic Tr	440,500	453,678	–2.9	22,309
†Intercoinc	105,814	69,563	52.1	71,095
†Intl Bus Mach	2,978,119	2,457,913	21.2	989,322
†Intl Minerals	629,518	472,930	33.1	210,063
†Intl Paper	1,219,672	1,222,009	–0.2	373,168
†Intl Rectifier	243,445	235,945	3.2	19,290
Ipalco Enterpr	581,300	667,000	–12.8	60,104
†Irving Bank	104,400	20,566	407.6	212,831
†ITT Corp	718,252	721,577	–0.5	364,509
†James River	156,016	143,740	8.5	131,868
John H. Harland	282,015	145,789	93.4	53,650
†Johnson & John	1,075,142	845,346	27.2	415,572
†Johnson Controls	493,604	499,389	–1.2	50,000
†K mart	701,220	702,482	–0.2	319,281
†Kaisertech	126,896	140,697	–9.8	159,704
†Kaneb Svcs	138,220	138,320	–0.1	104,659
Kansas C Pwr Lt	437,500	420,158	4.1	48,136
Kansas Gas&El	676,825	435,408	55.4	466,104
Ind...	188,505	188,335	0.1	7,854
	144,807	169,841	–14.7	43,186
		370,181	9.9	115,436
			295.0	31,200
				60,140

The ***number of shares*** held by short sellers, or the short interest, in Corning Glass was 178,757 on June 15, up from 148,417 on May 15.

% Change shows the percentage rise or fall in short interest volume from one month to the next.

Average Daily Volume indicates the average number of shares sold short each day during the monthly period.

Buying on Margin

When you sell short, you borrow stocks. When you buy on margin, you borrow money at the going rate of interest.

What does buying on margin mean?

You can borrow money from your broker to buy stock if you open a ***margin account*** and sign a contract called a margin agreement. You must also deposit $2,000 in cash or eligible securities (securities your broker considers valuable collateral), which is called the minumum margin requirement. All trades using borrowed money will be conducted through that margin account.

Under the rule called Regulation T, set by the Federal Reserve, you're permitted to borrow up to 50% of the purchase price of stock. You have to pay interest on the loan, but don't have to repay what you borrow until you sell the stock. So, for example:

If you have $2,000 in your margin account and you want to buy 100 shares of XYZ at $20 per share ($2,000)...

Then you could use $1,000 from your margin account and borrow $1,000, with interest, from your broker...

And you would still have $1,000 in your margin account to use toward another purchase on margin.

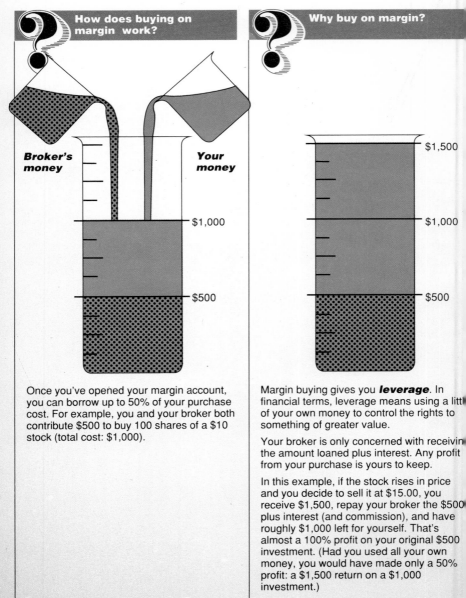

How does buying on margin work?

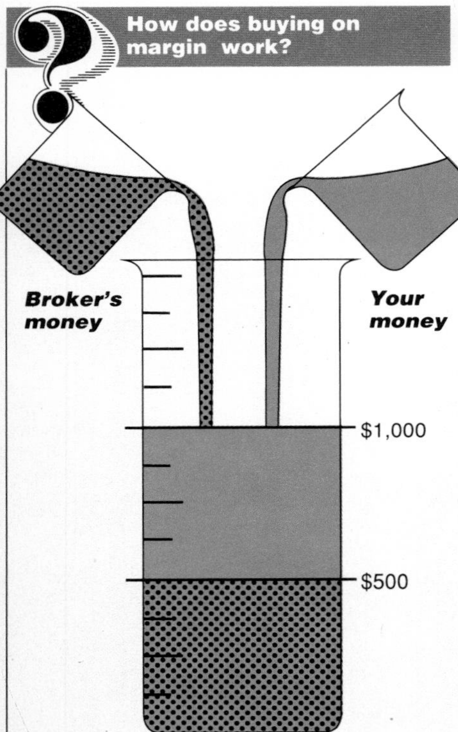

Once you've opened your margin account, you can borrow up to 50% of your purchase cost. For example, you and your broker both contribute $500 to buy 100 shares of a $10 stock (total cost: $1,000).

Why buy on margin?

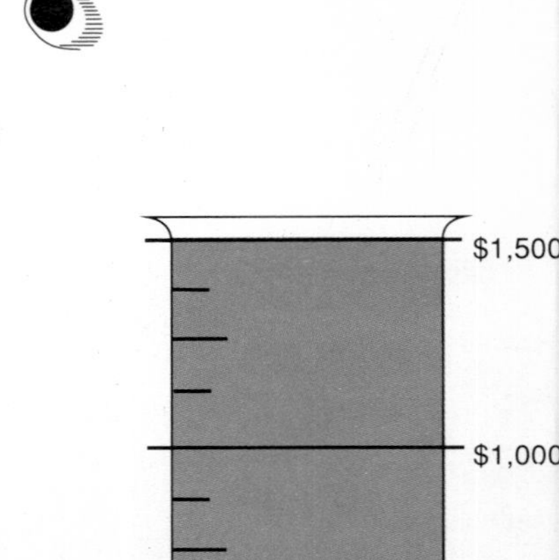

Margin buying gives you ***leverage***. In financial terms, leverage means using a little of your own money to control the rights to something of greater value.

Your broker is only concerned with receiving the amount loaned plus interest. Any profit from your purchase is yours to keep.

In this example, if the stock rises in price and you decide to sell it at $15.00, you receive $1,500, repay your broker the $500 plus interest (and commission), and have roughly $1,000 left for yourself. That's almost a 100% profit on your original $500 investment. (Had you used all your own money, you would have made only a 50% profit: a $1,500 return on a $1,000 investment.)

Margin Calls Create Dilemma For Investors

YOUR MONEY MATTERS

By KAREN SLATER
...aff Reporter of THE WALL STREET JOURNAL

While all stock-market investors are ...eating these days, those who bought ...cks on margin—that is, with borrowed ...ney—are sweating twice as much. ... continue to slide, more ... margin calls ...

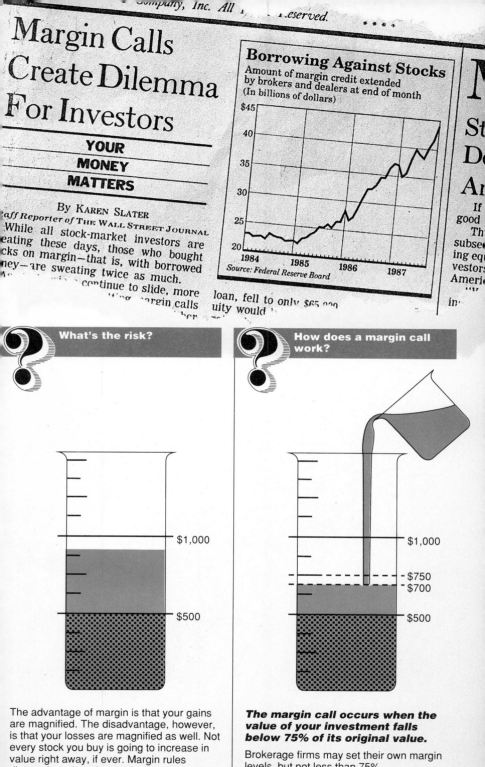

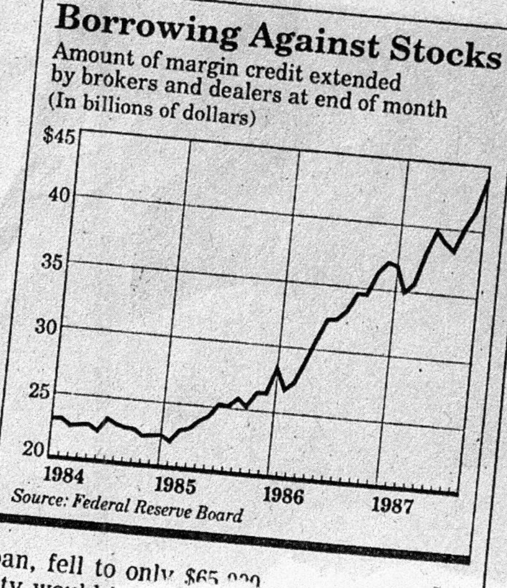

loan, fell to only $65,... uity would ...

What's the risk?

$1,000

$500

The advantage of margin is that your gains are magnified. The disadvantage, however, is that your losses are magnified as well. Not every stock you buy is going to increase in value right away, if ever. Margin rules dictate that when the stock price falls, only the amount ***you*** have invested loses value. The broker's loan amount doesn't change.

Some stock you buy might even lose so much value that selling it won't raise enough money to repay your loan. To protect brokers from this problem, brokers put out a ***margin call.***

The margin call is literally a call from your broker asking you to put more money into your margin account. The Federal Reserve policy governing margin calls is set according to the following formula in the next panel:

How does a margin call work?

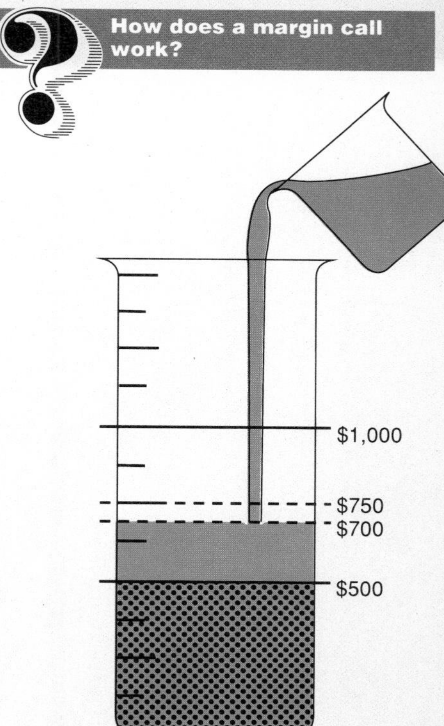

The margin call occurs when the value of your investment falls below 75% of its original value.

Brokerage firms may set their own margin levels, but not less than 75%.

If, for example, the stock value slips from $1,000 to less than $750 – to $700 – the stock is now less than 75% of its original value.

Your broker will call and ask you to deposit at least another $250 ($2.50 x 100 shares) to bring the margin back to its minumum level – to put enough cash into your account to cover your debt. If you don't want to meet the margin call, you must sell the stock, pay back the broker in full and take the loss.

The Stock Exchange

The exchange is the meeting place for buyers and sellers of securities, the modern equivalent of the open-air market.

The origins of the ***New York Stock Exchange***, the most famous of the world's exchanges (shown below), can be traced back to its days outdoors. In 1792, 24 merchants and auctioneers formed its forerunner by pledging to trade stocks every day under a buttonwood tree on Wall Street.

The activity explained on this page applies to trades of more than 1,200 shares. Smaller market orders are wired directly to the specialist's computer and the trade is completed automatically at the current price. This system is called the ***Designated Order Turnaround (DOT)***. Often it fills over 50% of all the orders on the Exchange.

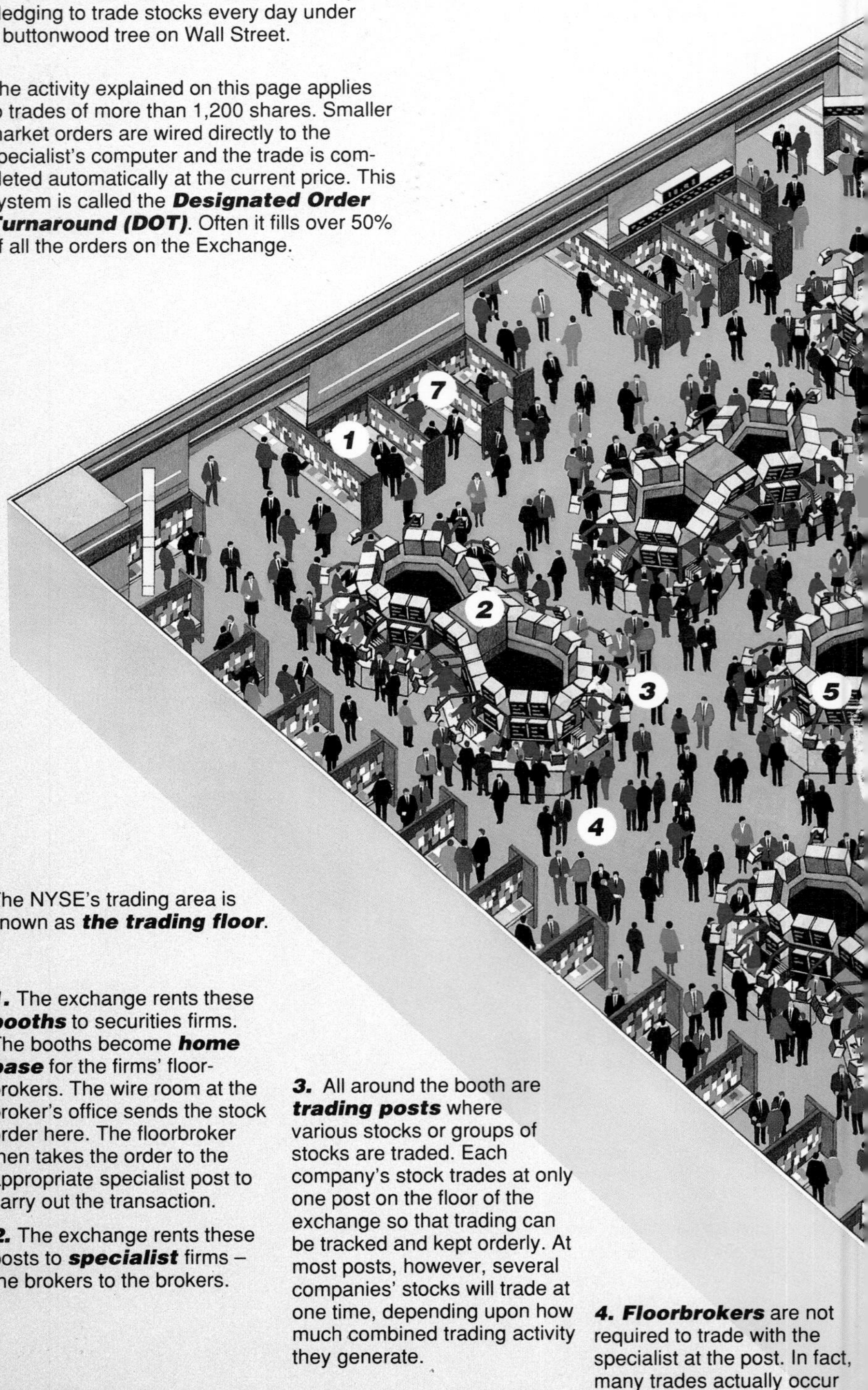

The NYSE's trading area is known as ***the trading floor***.

1. The exchange rents these ***booths*** to securities firms. The booths become ***home base*** for the firms' floorbrokers. The wire room at the broker's office sends the stock order here. The floorbroker then takes the order to the appropriate specialist post to carry out the transaction.

2. The exchange rents these posts to ***specialist*** firms – the brokers to the brokers.

3. All around the booth are ***trading posts*** where various stocks or groups of stocks are traded. Each company's stock trades at only one post on the floor of the exchange so that trading can be tracked and kept orderly. At most posts, however, several companies' stocks will trade at one time, depending upon how much combined trading activity they generate.

4. Floorbrokers are not required to trade with the specialist at the post. In fact, many trades actually occur between two floorbrokers who show up at a post at the same time.

We can say that stock trading happens **auction style**, because in every transaction stock is sold to the highest bidder and purchased from the lowest offerer. Supply and demand determine the prices of stocks. ***The Exchange never establishes a price***. This is not just a matter of custom – it's the rule of the Exchange.

There are 142 of these marketplaces operating in major cities around the world.

5. Post Display Units show the day's information on stocks traded at that post, including the last sale price and order size.

6. After every deal, a reporter shoves a ***mark sense*** card into a ***reporting device***, and the transaction appears on the ticker almost instantly.

7. Confirmation takes place when the floorbroker returns to the firm's booth and sends the trade details over the wire to the broker's branch, confirming that the order has been carried out successfully.

8. At the end of a weary day, during which a floorbroker will walk – and often run – an average of 12 miles, the closing bell will be rung from ***the podium***. (It's also where the opening bell is rung.)

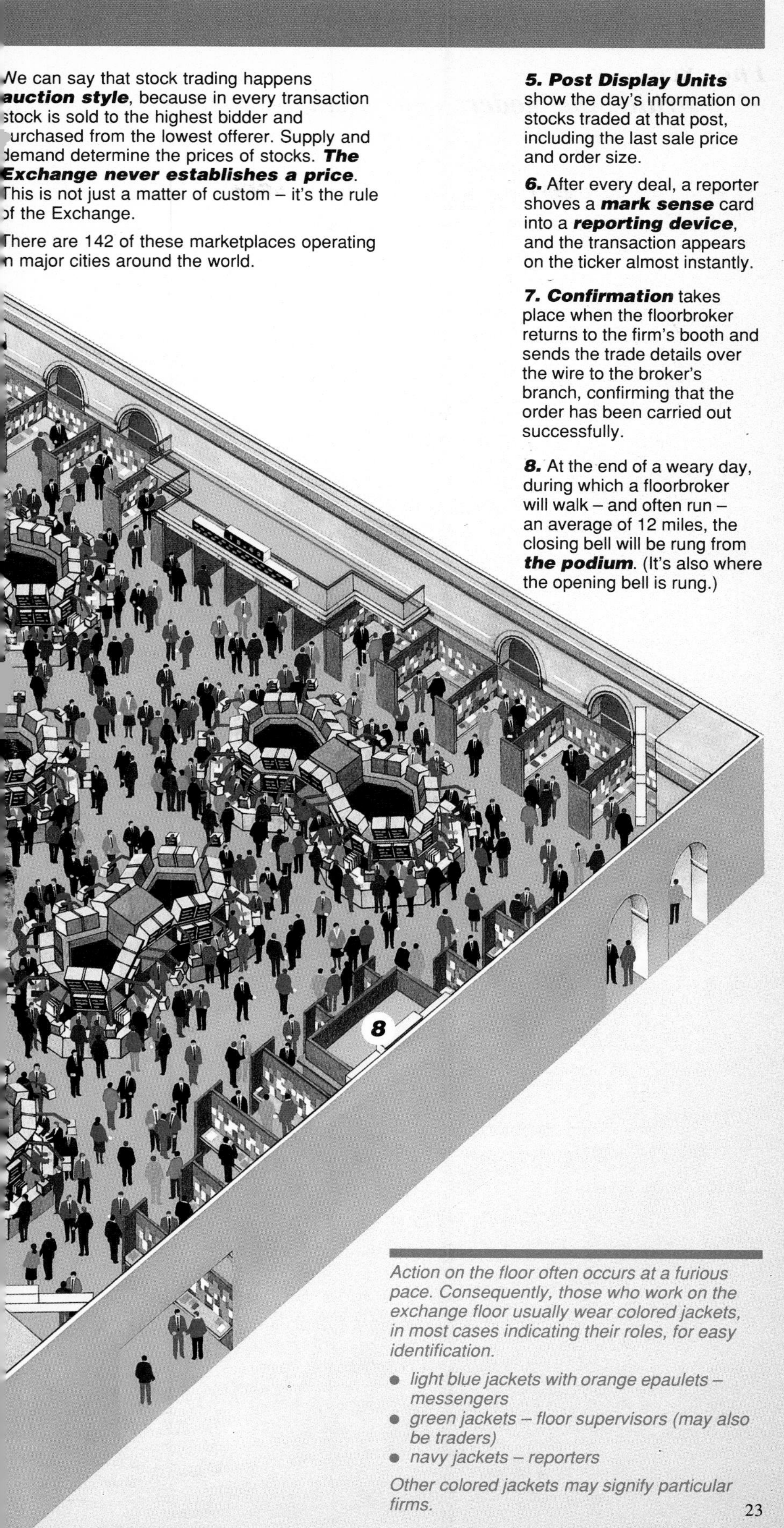

Action on the floor often occurs at a furious pace. Consequently, those who work on the exchange floor usually wear colored jackets, in most cases indicating their roles, for easy identification.

- *light blue jackets with orange epaulets – messengers*
- *green jackets – floor supervisors (may also be traders)*
- *navy jackets – reporters*

Other colored jackets may signify particular firms.

The Stock Market: US Exchanges

In the United States, there are two principal stock exchanges, both located in New York City: the New York Stock Exchange, NYSE, also known as the Big Board, and the American Stock Exchange, AMEX.

Philadelphia can claim the first stock exchange in America, organized in 1790. But when the traders who met every day under the buttonwood tree on Wall Street adopted the name New York Stock Exchange Board in 1817, the most famous stock exchange in the world formally began.

No other exchange was founded to rival the New York Stock Exchange Board until the New York Curb Exchange in 1842. Faithful to its name, this exchange actually traded on streetside until it moved indoors in 1921. In 1953, the Curb Exchange became known by its present name, The American Stock Exchange (AMEX).

The world's oldest stock exchange is London's, officially established in 1773 (although its origins date back a century or more before that). Other exchanges were founded in the following years: Paris – 1802, Tokyo – 1818, Sydney – 1872.

Are there other exchanges?

Even if you own stock listed on the NYSE or AMEX, your brokerage firm may end up selling it for you on one of the 14 regional exchanges located in other cities. These smaller exchanges, like the Pacific, Midwest, Boston and Philadelphia Exchanges, are linked with the two in New York to make finding a buyer and seller faster and easier.

Trading results of stocks listed on both the NYSE and regional exchanges are combined at the end of each day, which is why the NYSE stock page in the newspaper is called ***Composite Trading***. Many small, regional companies, however, are listed only on a regional exchange. The most actively traded of these stocks are listed in the table, ***Other Markets***.

OTHER MARKETS

Selected Stocks; Dually Listed Issues Excluded
Tuesday, June 21, 1988

Toronto (Canadian Funds)
Quotations in Canadian funds.
Quotations in cents unless marked $

Sales	Stocks	High	Low	Close	Chg.
3880	Abti Prce	$22⅝	22½	22½	
4300	Agnico E	$19⅜	19⅛	19¼	+ ⅜
30084	Alt Energy	$17⅛	17	17	− ¼
3586	Alta Nat	$13½	13¼	13⅜	− ⅛
2393	Algoma St	$22	21¾	22	+ ¼
29600	A Barick	$27	26⅝	26⅞	+ ⅛
110228	Atco I f	$9⅜	9	9⅛	− ¼
28201	BCED	375	350	375	+20
2900	BP Canada	$20¾	20¼	20¼	
377060	Bank N S	$14¼	13⅝	14⅛	+ ⅜
1740	Baton	$14½	14½	14½	− ⅛
66626	BCE Inc	$37	36¾	37	+ ¼
		[illegible]	105	105	
			24	24¼	− ¼
			[illegible]¼	19¼	
				[illegible]	− ⅛
					¼

Sales	Stock	High	Low	Close	Chg.
56300	Indal	$9½	9¼	9⅜	+ ⅛
2200	Inland Gas	$11¾	11⅝	11⅝	+ ⅛
220810	I Corona	$9⅞	9⅝	9¾	+ ⅛
90300	Intl Thom	$14⅛	13¾	13¾	− ¼
3417	Interhome	$47¼	46⅞	47	
1236	Ipsco	$17¾	17⅝	17⅝	− ⅛
715	Ivaco A f	$13⅝	13½	13⅝	+ ⅛
8840	Jannock	$18⅝	18½	18⅝	+ ⅛
11523	Labatt	$23	22¾	22⅞	− ⅛
55137	Lacana	$12⅜	12	12¼	
276	Loblaw Co	$11⅛	11	11⅛	+ ⅛
2100	Lumonics	$5¼	5⅛	5¼	
30977	Magna A f	$12¾	12½	12⅝	+ ⅛
300	MDS H A	$26¾	26¾	26¾	− ¼
164500	Mclan H X	$12⅛	11⅞	12	
1870	Maritime f	$15¾	15⅝	15⅝	− ⅛
[illegible]	[illegible] Res	$10⅜	10¼	10⅜	+ ⅛
				[illegible]¾	+ ⅜

Sales	Stock	High	Low
55700	Tex Can	$33⅞	32[illegible]
15150	Thom N A	$28⅛	27[illegible]
559568	Tor Dm Bk	$32⅞	32[illegible]
10608	Torstar B f	$28⅜	28[illegible]
225	Trns Mt	$14	14[illegible]
86168	TrnAlta U	$13⅝	1[illegible]
41334	TrCan PL	$14	1[illegible]
9125	Trimac	400	39[illegible]
63100	Trilon A	$17⅝	[illegible]
46698	Turbo	50	
3810	Unicorp A f	$8	
1996	Un Carbid	$20⅜	
18089	U Entprise	$10	
100	U Keno	$7½	
6500	Wrdair A f	$9⅞	
2500	Wrdair B	$10⅛	
2184	Westmin	$10⅝	
		[illegible]23¾	

Wall Street provided the setting for the first meeting of the New York Stock Exchange, and now lends its name to the financial markets in general. The street got its name from the stockade built by early settlers to protect New York from pirates and from Indians attacking from the north.

Courtesy Museum of the City of New York

NYSE: Gentlemen Only

In the 1870s, while the members of the Curb Exchange – forerunner of the AMEX – whooped and hollered outside, NYSE swells wore top hats and swallowtail coats. In those days, members were encouraged to present a respectable image. Those who remained recalcitrant were fined as follows:

Smoking a cigar – $5.00
Standing on a chair – $10.00
Throwing a paper dart – $10.00
Knocking off a member's hat – 50¢

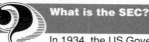

What is the SEC?

In 1934, the US Government created the ***Securities and Exchange Commission***, ***SEC***, to regulate the activities of stock traders.

Composed of five members appointed by the President, the Securities and Exchange Commission sees that the securities markets operate honestly and fairly. When necessary, it enforces the law with sanctions.

The SEC's role can be summed up by stating its two main objectives:

- to see that investors are fully informed about securities being offered for sale; and
- to prevent misrepresentations, deceit and other fraud in securities transactions.

What is the SIAC?

Hidden away in lower Manhattan is a cavernous room that's one of the focal points of AMEX and NYSE stock trading. This little-known room, run by the ***Securities Industry Automation Corporation***, ***SIAC***, stores a phalanx of over 200 mainframe computers, neatly stacked in about 50 refrigerator-sized cabinets, which process all electronic trading. On the day of the market crash of 1987, as well as the day after, these supercomputers handled as many as 60 transactions every second.

NYSE Volume is published every day in ***The Wall Street Journal***. It illustrates at a glance the daily volume of trading on the New York Stock Exchange for running 6-month periods. It can help you analyze trends in the market. It also shows you that the men and women who worked on the floor of the exchange during those days in 1987 put in a full day's work: they averaged 89,466 trades a day – 229 trades every minute.

On March 1, 1988 there were 71,456,000,000 shares of stock registered on the New York Stock Exchange. On the day of the October 1987 market plunge, 608,000,000 shares were traded, 8/10 of one percent of the registered shares. On a typical day 175,000,000 shares trade, just over 2/10 of one percent of the total.

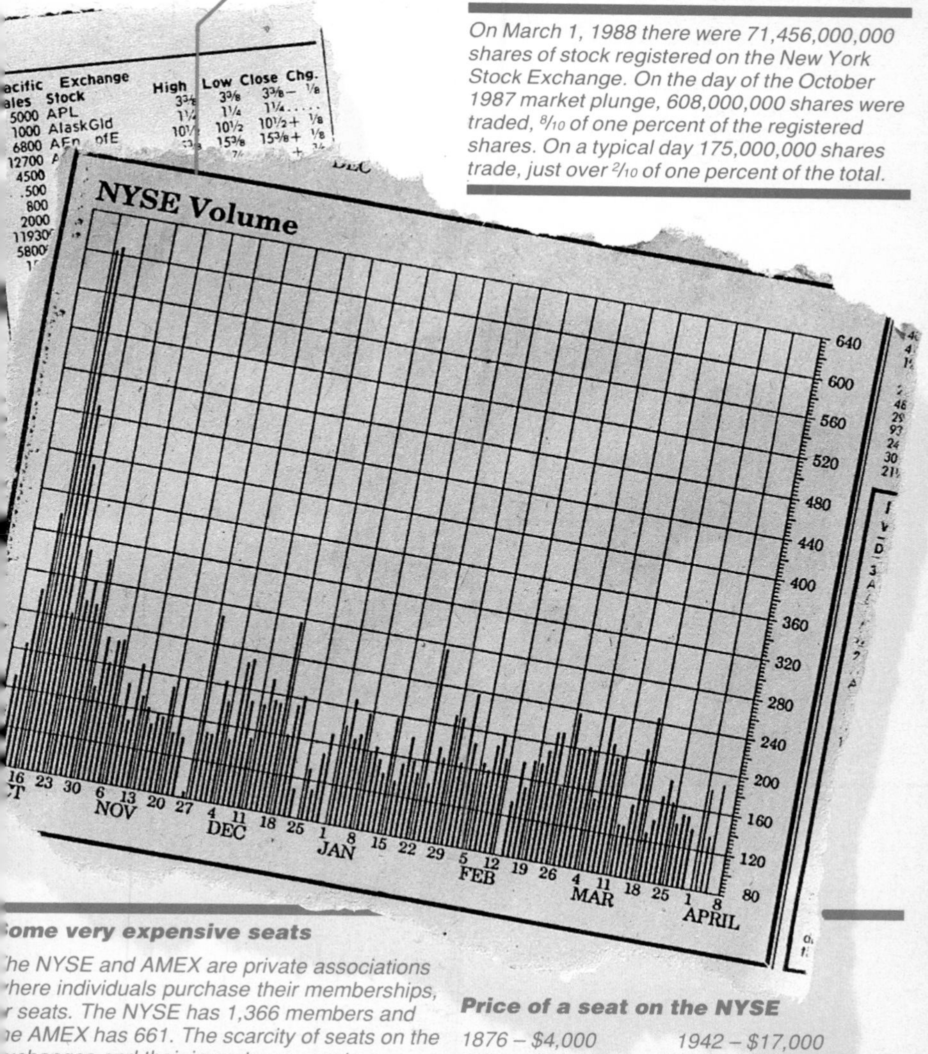

NYSE Volume

ome very expensive seats

he NYSE and AMEX are private associations here individuals purchase their memberships, r seats. The NYSE has 1,366 members and e AMEX has 661. The scarcity of seats on the xchanges and their importance create a ompetitive market for them.

Price of a seat on the NYSE

1876 – $4,000	*1942 – $17,000*
1929 – $625,000	*1987 – $1.1 million*
1930 – $205,000	*1988 – $665,000*

The Stock Market: Over-the-Counter

The great majority of US stocks are not traded at an exchange at all. Instead, they're traded on the Over-the-Counter Market, OTC, an electronic marketplace.

Traders in the OTC market don't deal face-to-face. Their marketplace is as large and wide as the number of desks with brokers at work that day. They see into this marketplace by studying the activity reported on their computer screens. And they trade with other brokers by telephone.

The OTC, however, is far from a chaotic free-for-all. It's a highly sophisticated network, called the *National Market System*, ***NMS***. Its members regulate themselves through an organization called the *National Association of Securities Dealers*, ***NASD***. Appropriately, the name you see heading the newspaper's over-the-counter listings is called ***NASDAQ***, the *National Association of Securities Dealers Automated Quotations.*

How are the OTC stocks listed?

There are so many thousands of stocks traded over-the-counter, listing them all would require nearly all the pages in ***The Wall Street Journal***. Consequently, only the most actively traded issues are listed, and even those are broken down into three separate tables:

- The ***National Market Issues*** table lists the most actively traded OTC stocks. You can find more detailed information about the stocks in this table than any other OTC stocks.

Notice that most companies pay no dividends – in fact, there isn't even a ***dividend*** heading on the table. (Dividends are listed, however, after the ticker symbol.) Few OTC stocks pay dividends because they're generally either small or start-up companies which need to put earnings back into the business.

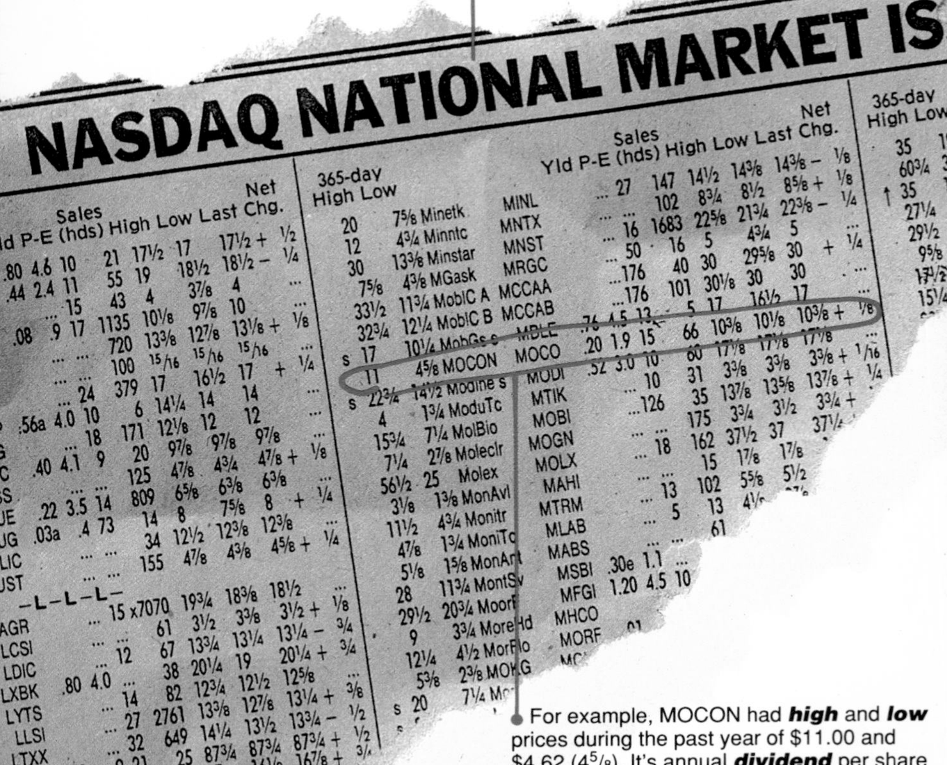

NASDAQ NATIONAL MARKET IS...

	Yld	P-E	Sales (hds)	High	Low	Last	Net Chg.
	.80	4.6	10 21	17½	17	17½	+ ½
	.44	2.4	11 55	19	18½	18½	− ¼
		...	15 43	4	3⅞	4	...
	.08	.9	17 1135	10⅛	9⅞	10	...
	...	...	720	13⅜	12⅞	13⅛	+ ⅛
	...	...	100	15/16	15/16	15/16	...
	...	24	379	17	16½	17	+ ¼
P	.56a	4.0	10 6	14¼	14	14	...
G	...	18	171	12⅛	12	12	...
IC	.40	4.1	9 20	9⅞	9⅞	9⅞	...
SS	...	...	125	4⅞	4¾	4⅞	+ ⅛
UE	.22	3.5	14 809	6⅝	6⅜	6⅜	...
UG	.03a	.4	73 14	8	7⅝	8	+ ¼
LIC	...	...	34	12½	12⅜	12⅜	...
UST	...	...	155	4⅞	4⅜	4⅝	+ ¼
–L–L–L–							
AGR	...	15	x7070	19¾	18⅜	18½	...
LCSI	...	...	61	3½	3⅜	3½	+ ⅛
LDIC	...	12	67	13¾	13¼	13¼	− ¾
LXBK	.80	4.0 ...	38	20¼	19	20¼	+ ¾
LYTS	...	14	82	12¾	12½	12⅝	...
LLSI	...	27	2761	13⅜	12⅞	13¼	+ ⅜
LTXX	...	32	649	14¼	13½	13¾	− ½
LVMHY	.76e	.9 21	25	87¾	87¾	87¾	+ ½
LPAI	...	23	4449	17	16⅛	16⅞	+ ¾
LCLD	.10e	.3 7	5	36½	36½	36½	−
..DF	.20a	1.2 11	270	16½	16¼		
..20	...	31	3238	13⅛	13..		

365-day High	Low	Stock	Sym	Yld	P-E	Sales (hds)	High	Low	Last	Net Chg.
20	7⅝	Minetk	MINL	...	27	147	14½	14⅜	14⅜	− ⅛
12	4¾	Minntc	MNTX	...	...	102	8¾	8½	8⅝	+ ⅛
30	13⅜	Minstar	MNST	...	16	1683	22⅝	21¾	22⅜	− ¼
7⅝	4⅜	MGask	MRGC	...	50	16	5	4¾	5	...
33½	11¾	MobIC A	MCCAA	...	176	40	30	29⅝	30	+ ¼
32¾	12¼	MobIC B	MCCAB	...	176	101	30⅛	30	30	...
s 17	10¼	MobGs s	MBLE	.76 4.5	13	5	17	16½	17	...
11	4⅝	MOCON	MOCO	.20 1.9	15	66	10⅜	10⅛	10⅜	+ ⅛
s 22¾	14½	Modine s	MODI	.52 3.0	10	60	17⅞	17⅞	17⅞	...
4	1¾	ModuTc	MTIK	...	10	31	3⅜	3⅜	3⅜	+ 1/16
15¾	7¼	MolBio	MOBI	...	126	35	13⅞	13⅝	13⅞	+ ¼
7¼	2⅞	Moleclr	MOGN	...	...	175	3¾	3½	3¾	+
56½	25	Molex	MOLX	...	18	162	37½	37	37¼	
3⅛	1⅜	MonAvl	MAHI	...	...	15	1⅞	1⅞		
11½	4¾	Monitr	MTRM	...	13	102	5⅝	5½		
4⅞	1¾	MoniTc	MLAB	...	5	13	4⅛			
5⅛	1⅝	MonAnt	MABS	...	...	61				
28	11¾	MontSv	MSBI	.30e 1.1	...					
29½	20¾	MoorF	MFGI	1.20 4.5	10					
9	3¾	MoreHd	MHCO							
12¼	4½	MorFlo	MORF	.01						
5⅜	2⅜	MOKG	MC..							
s 20	7¼	Mo..								

365-day High	Low
35	19..
60¾	3..
↑ 35	1..
27¼	
29½	
9⅝	
17½	
15¼	

For example, MOCON had ***high*** and ***low*** prices during the past year of \$11.00 and \$4.62 ($4^5/_8$). It's annual ***dividend*** per share is 20¢; its current yield, 1.9%; its ***price-earnings*** ratio, 15. ***Sales volume*** the previous day was 6600 shares. During that day's trading, it sold as ***low*** as $10^1/_8$ per share and as ***high*** as $10^3/_8$ per share, where it closed. This ***net change*** was $^1/_8$ point higher than the previous quoted closing price.

Continued on Page 60

NASDAQ BID AND ASKED QUOTATIONS

Stock & Div	Sales 100s	Bid	Asked	Net Chg.
AA Importing	10	3¾	4¼	...
AdelphiaCm A	104	19½	20¼	− ¼
Advatex Assc	60	3	3½	+ ⅜
AFN Inc	45	9-16	⅝	...
Airsensors	58	2	2 1-16	...
Alex Energy	32	⅞	[illegible]	...

Stock & Div	Sales 100s	Bid	Asked	Net Chg.
Energy Vent	2	10¾	11½	...
Enscor Inc	30	1 5-16	1½	...
EssxCGs 1.20	3	16¼	17	...
Falconbrg Ltd	261	20⅞	[illegible]	...

Stock & Div	Sales 100s	Bid	Asked	Net Chg.
Ovonic Imag	50	2¾	3⅛	...
Ovonic	40	3	[illegible]	...

ADDITIONAL NASDAQ QUOTES

	Bid	Asked
Action Staffing	31-32	1⅛
AdvDisplay Tec	¼	9-32
AdvPrdctsTc A	11-16	13-16
AdvPrdctsTc C	¾	⅞
AdvMedical Pr	1-32	1-16
AdvnNMR Syst	5¾	5⅞
AdvNMRSys wt	5⅜	5⅝
Advanced Prod	2 7-16	2 9-16
AdvPrdctTc ut	10¾	11¾
AdvtgCos ut	5¼	6
AdvisorsCp Tc	¼	5-16
Aerosonic Corp	1 7-16	1½
AFP Imaging	1 3-16	1 5-16
Agouron Pharm	13¾	14½

	Bid	Asked
C&R Clothiers	(z)	(z)
Creative Cmptr	⅛	5-32
Creative Tech	5⅛	5¾
Credo Petrol	1⅜	1⅝
Crown Resourc	2⅛	2 3-16
Cryodynamics	1⅝	1¾
Cumo Resource	1-32	1-16
Cusac Industr	1¼	1⅜
Cyanotech Cp	11-16	23-32
Cybermedic Inc	5-32	3-16
CytRx Bio ut	7⅛	7⅜
CytRx Bio wt	13-16	15-16
CytRx Biopool	1 9-16	[illegible]
CytRx Corp ut	[illegible]	[illegible]
Dallas OilMin	[illegible]	[illegible]

	Bid	Asked
IstecInd Tech	3¾	4
Istecl Tech ut	7½	8½
JackCarl 312Fut	9-32	⅜
JAM Inc	½	15-16
Jayark Corp	⅜	7-16
Jean Philippe	1⅛	1 3-16
Jennifer Convrt	4	4¼
JenniferConv ut	9¾	10¼
JennifrCnv wt	1 11-16	2
JT Moran Fin	5½	5⅝
J2 Communictn	2¼	2¾
Judicate Inc	2½	2 11-16

	Bid	Asked
Raycomm Tran	2⅜	2½
Raytech Corp	1⅜	1¾
RCM Technolg	2 3-16	2¼
RCM TchB ut	2⅜	2⅝
Rea Gold Corp	2 11-16	2 15-16
Renaissn GRX	1⅞	2
Renaissance wt	11-32	⅜
Rent Rite Inc	1 9-16	1⅝
Repco Inc	1¼	1⅝
ReproMed Syst	31-32	1
Research Frnt	7¾	8½
Rexcom System	1-32	3-32

NASDAQ Bid and Asked Quotations presents the second tier of most actively traded OTC stocks. The information provided here includes the stock name & dividend, sales volume, the highest ***bid*** and the lowest ***ask*** of the day, and the net change for the day.

AA Importing pays no dividend, traded 1,000 shares. Buyers were paying $3.75 a share at the close, while sellers were selling at $4.25. The stock was unchanged from the previous day's close.

Additional OTC Quotes shows the OTC stocks that are the least actively traded of all stocks listed in ***The Wall Street Journal*** – yet, they're still more heavily traded than thousands of other stocks in the OTC marketplace. Information on these stocks only includes the highest bid and lowest ask of the day. The number of trades actually conducted at these prices is difficult to quote, given the decentralized nature of OTC trading.

Pink Sheets

Some low-priced, infrequently traded stocks are not listed in the papers because they're not on the NASDAQ system. They may trade only 100 shares (or less) a day; they may trade for literally a fraction of a cent a share. Only brokers receive the daily results for these stocks, on a listing called the pink sheets. In 1988 efforts were being made to computerize these listings

Why do companies list on one exchange over another?

A company able to meet NYSE or AMEX listing requirements gains prestige by listing on those exchanges. Many large and reputable companies, however, choose to stay listed on the OTC; among them are MCI Corp. and Apple Computer Inc. In addition, many banks and insurance companies traditionally list on the OTC. Many companies listed on the NYSE or AMEX are also listed on regional exchanges. None are listed on both NYSE and AMEX, although it's technically feasible.

Requirements for listing on the exchanges

Exchange	Requirements	Type of Company	Number Listed
NYSE	Pre-tax earnings of $2.5 million; 1.1 million shares publicly held with $18 million market value; net tangible assets of $18 million	Oldest, largest best-known companies	1,600
AMEX	Pre-tax income of $750,000; 500,000 shares publicly held; net tangible assets of $4 million	Smaller, younger companies	890
OTC	None for ***pink sheet*** listings; minimal for NASDAQ and National Market Systems issues	Smallest, youngest companies. Many high technology and financial service companies	31,000+

Globalization of Trading

Technology has brought 24-hour trading within the grasp of investors around the world.

The combined power of global markets and electronic trading has created a world where stock prices never sleep – they're always subject to change somewhere in the world. When trading on a stock ends in one city, it can continue in another city, causing the stocks to travel around the world every 24 hours, in a perpetual, circular motion.

Here is a 24-hour chart of the stock market. The horizontal patches represent the hours the markets are open. Reading the chart vertically allows comparison of the trading hours. For example when the Tokyo market opens at 9 AM their time, it's 7 PM in New York. By the time Tokyo closes, it's 1 AM in New York and London will be opening in three hours.

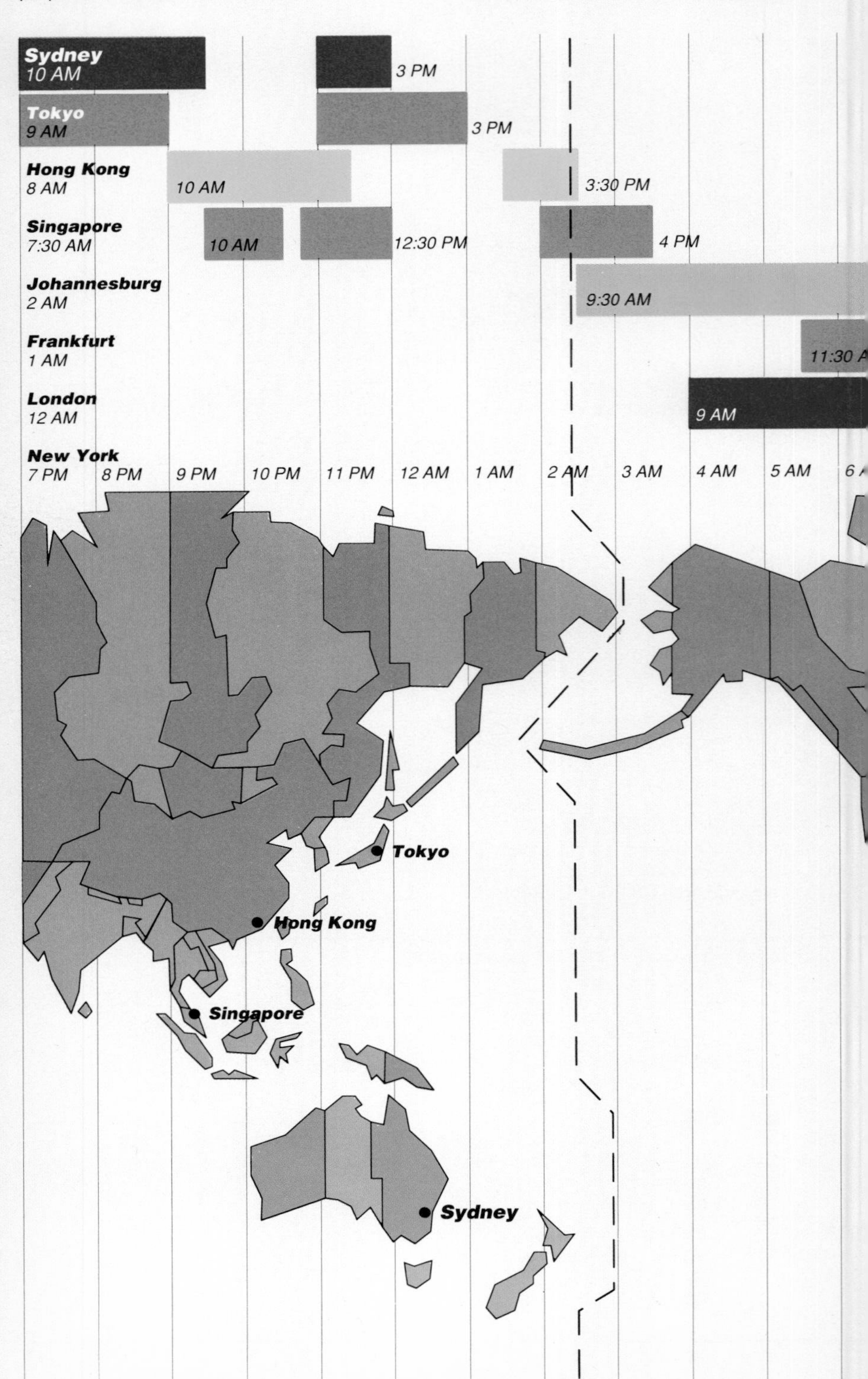

What are Foreign Indexes?

Every day, ***The Wall Street Journal*** lists the performances of the major stock exchanges around the globe. The performances are expressed as ***indexes*** – statistical composites like the NYSE Index or AMEX Index. You can see the day's close, the net change from the previous day, as well as that change expressed in percentage terms. (Notice that only foreign exchanges are listed here.)

Stock Market Indexes

EXCHANGE	TUESDAY CLOSE	NET CHG	PCT CHG
Tokyo Nikkei Average	26315.35	– 19.94	– 0.08
Tokyo First Section	2136.02	– 6.91	– 0.32
London FT 30-share	1382.9	– 3.8	– 0.27
London 100-share	1737.6	– 4.9	– 0.28
London Gold Mines	233.1	– 4.2	– 1.77
Frankfurt FAZ	451.72	+ 0.32	+ 0.07
Zurich Credit Suisse	438.6	+ 2.0	+ 0.46
Paris CAC General	284.6	+ 0.5	+ 0.18
Milan Stock Index	1061	– 5	– 0.47
Amsterdam ANP-CBS General	241.7	+ 0.9	+ 0.37
Stockholm Affarsvarlden	790.4	+ 0.1	+ 0.01
Brussels Stock Index	4805.58	– 34.06	– 0.70
Sydney All Ordinaries	1412.9	– 2.9	– 0.20
Hong Kong Hang Seng	na		
Singapore Straits Times	926.83	+ 9.15	+ 1.00
Johannesburg J'burg Gold	na		
Toronto 300 Composite	3328.31	+ 15.40	+ 0.46
Europe,Australia,Far East	861.9	– 7.0	– 0.81

NA-Not available.

price at which the

Globalization of Trading

The worldwide, continuous market is one reason why stocks often end trading at one price on an exchange and begin the next day's trading at a different price on the same exchange.

Today, what happens on the Tokyo and Hong Kong Exchanges can directly influence what will happen on the London Exchange, which opens about the time trading ends in Tokyo. And what occurs in both those markets overnight (for Americans) can greatly influence events in the New York markets, which open around the time the London markets approach the end of trading.

Not surprisingly, what occurs on the New York markets can directly affect what will happen during the following Tokyo and Hong Kong trading sessions, and the next London session, and so on. Like a perpetual ***domino effect***, the events go spiralling on and on, day after day – investors in each market always eyeing investors in the other markets. The crash of '87 highlighted this relationship, as the charts on the right graphically illustrate.

The Dow Jones World Index has been developed to measure world stock market performance – the global equivalent of the Dow Jones Industrial Average. It helps investors see how international stock markets are responding to each other and to US economic developments.

Foreign Market Quotations appear daily in ***The Wall Street Journal*** for some of the most active stocks traded in other markets around the world. While these quotes appear like any US market quote, be sure to note the currency involved. Most quotes for foreign stocks appear in the currency in which they are traded – not in American dollars.

...dustries surged 44 yen to 129 and Denki ... shares, Daimler ... to 644 marks ($36...

FOREIGN MARKETS

Tuesday, June 21, 1988

TOKYO (in yen)

	Close	Prev. Close
ANA	1800	1850
Aiwa	820	824
Ajinomoto	3270	3350
Alps Elec	1790	1790
Amada Co	1220	1230
Ando Elec	3750	3800
Anritsu	2470	2480
Asahi Chem	1150	1160
Asahi Glass	2010	2050
Bank of Tokyo	1580	1570
Bk of Yokohama	1600	1590
Banyu Pharm	1430	1450
Bridgestone	1450	1460
Brother Ind	835	840
C. Itoh	873	878
CSK	5300	5300
Canon Inc	1180	1230
Canon Sales	3300	3400
Casio Computer	1230	1210
Chubu Pwr	3250	3270
Chugai Pharm	1660	1690
Odakyu Railway	1090	1080
Ohbayashi Corp	964	975
Oji Paper	1400	1430
Oki Elec Ind	915	915
Okuma Mach	1050	1040
Olympus Optical	1110	1130
Ono Pharm	6190	6150
Onoda Cement	931	930
Orient Finance	1450	1460
Osaka Kiko	697	692
Pioneer Electron	3020	3060
Renown	980	998
Ricoh Co	1240	1260
Royal Co	2790	2800
Secom	6480	6600
SMK	798	810
Sankyo Co	2030	2050
Sanrio	4790	4700
Sanwa Bank	2620	2680
Sanyo Elec	635	645
Sapporo Brewery	1760	1780

LONDON (in pence)

	Close	Prev. Close
Allied-Lyons	439	435
Amstrad	205	199
Argyll Group	191	195
Assoc Brit Foods	292	292
Barclays	413	408
Bass	796	796
BAT Industries	429	425
Beecham	475	459
Blue Circle	412	413
BOC Group	406	402
Boots	218	214
Borland	118	120
Bowater Indus	398	398
BPB Indus	295	296
Brit & Com	260	258
British Aero	398	392
British Airways	149	146
British Gas	192	188

FRANKFURT (in Marks)

	Close	Prev. Close
AEG	208.3	207.
Allianz	1389	138
BASF	261.3	257.
Bayer	292	287.9
Byr Vereinsbk	331	326
BMW	525	521.5
Commerzbank	223.5	219
Continental	252.7	251
Daimler Benz	644	632.5
Degussa	339	338
Deutsche Bank	434	426
Dresdner Bank	248.5	242
Hochtief	445	440.5
Hoechst	266	263.3
Karstadt	430	422
Kaufhof	383	389
Linde	684.5	679
Lufthansa	148	142.2

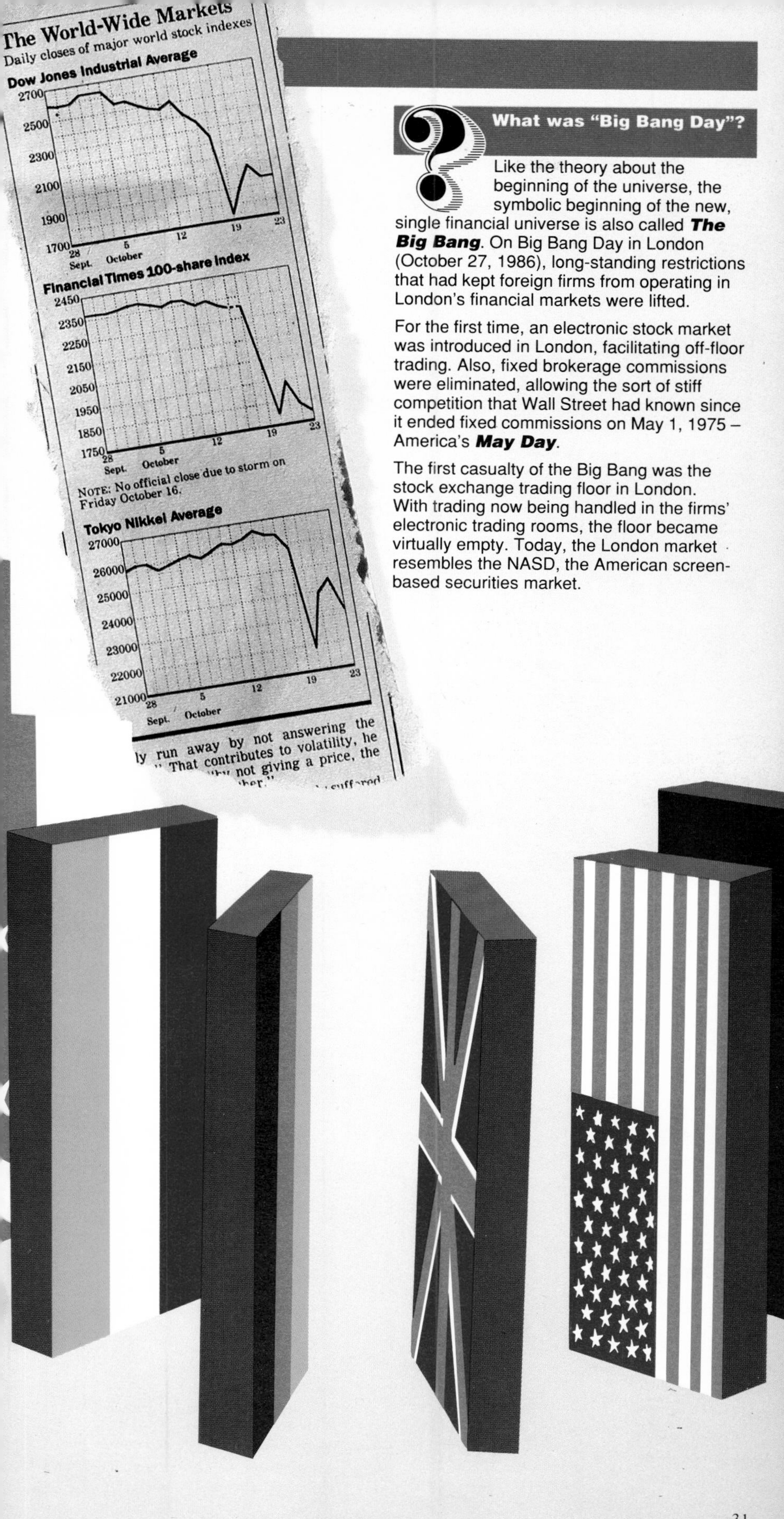

What was "Big Bang Day"?

Like the theory about the beginning of the universe, the symbolic beginning of the new, single financial universe is also called ***The Big Bang***. On Big Bang Day in London (October 27, 1986), long-standing restrictions that had kept foreign firms from operating in London's financial markets were lifted.

For the first time, an electronic stock market was introduced in London, facilitating off-floor trading. Also, fixed brokerage commissions were eliminated, allowing the sort of stiff competition that Wall Street had known since it ended fixed commissions on May 1, 1975 – America's ***May Day***.

The first casualty of the Big Bang was the stock exchange trading floor in London. With trading now being handled in the firms' electronic trading rooms, the floor became virtually empty. Today, the London market resembles the NASD, the American screen-based securities market.

Spotting Trends: The Dow Jones

The stock market is like some huge, enigmatic creature under continuous, intense scrutiny.

Industrials Gain 25.24 to 2109.17 After Swinging Over Wide Range

ABREAST OF THE MARKET

No matter what the stock market does, people want to know how it did it, why it did it, and why it didn't do something else. Because the stakes are so high, we analyze stock market activity in every way imaginable – we want to know highs and lows, and how the market has performed over the last day, week, month, six months, year, five years, ten years, etc. The goal of all these calculations is to anticipate the future activity of stocks based on their history.

What is the Dow Jones Average?

One indicator stands alone as the most accepted – and remarkably reliable – indicator of market health: the Dow Jones Industrial Average. In fact, when people say, "The market was up 10 points today," they mean the Dow Jones Industrial Average rose 10 points. That's how closely ***the Dow*** is tied to the overall market.

The Dow itself is just a formula based on the stock prices of 30 major industrial companies. The formula adds up the stocks' prices and then divides by a certain number to derive the average. Consequently, the higher priced stocks will have a greater effect on the average.

Why is the Dow such a good indicator? The 30 companies were chosen from sectors of the economy most representative of our country's lifeblood. So, if you want to keep your finger on the pulse of our nation's companies, keep your eye on the Dow.

There are actually four Dow Jones Averages, two of which monitor specific industries:

Name of average	*Area of concentration*
Dow Jones Industrial Average	30 industrial companies
Dow Jones Transportation Average	20 airlines, trucking companies, and railroads
Dow Jones Utility Average	15 gas, electric, power companies
Dow Jones 65 Composite Averages	all 65 companies in the other three

The companies, often referred to as ***components***, are listed in ***The Wall Street Journal.***

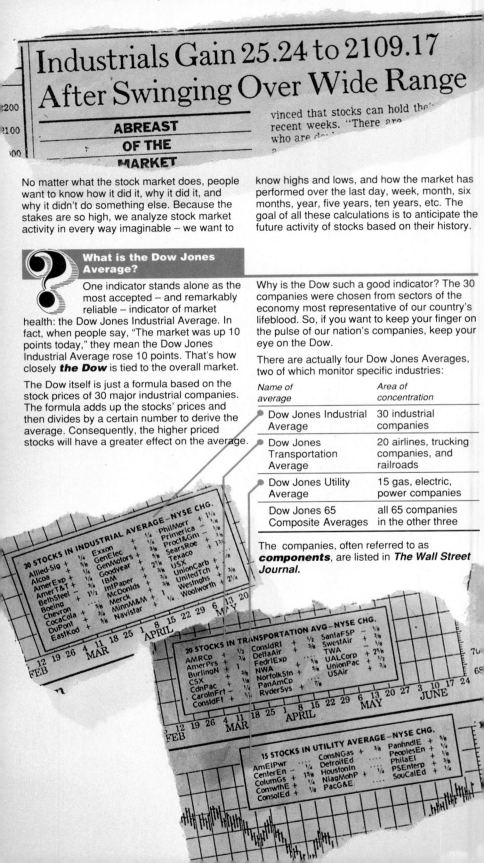

30 STOCKS IN INDUSTRIAL AVERAGE–NYSE CHG.

Allied-Sig, Alcoa, AmerExp, AmerT&T, BethSteel, Boeing, Chevron, CocaCola, DuPont, EastKod, Exxon, GenElec, GenMotors, Goodyear, IBM, IntPaper, McDonlds, Merck, MinnM&M, Navistar, PhilMorr, Primerica, Proct&Gm, SearsRoe, Texaco, USX, UnionCarb, UnitedTch, Westinghs, Woolworth

20 STOCKS IN TRANSPORTATION AVG–NYSE CHG.

AMRCp, AmerPrs, BurlingN, CSX, CdnPac, CarolnFrt, ConsldFt, ConsldRl, DeltaAir, FedrlExp, NWA, NorfolkSTn, PanAmCp, RyderSys, SantaFSP, SwestAir, TWA, UALCorp, UnionPac, USAir

15 STOCKS IN UTILITY AVERAGE–NYSE CHG.

AmElPwr, CenterEn, ColumGs, ComwlthE, ConsolEd, ConsNGas, DetroitEd, HoustonIn, NiagMohP, PacG&E, PanhndlE, PeoplesEn, PhilaEl, PSEnterp, SouCalEd

Why watch the Dow?

The Dow Jones Industrial Average and other stock indexes can be useful to an investor in two ways. First, they track the long-term ups and downs to help investors judge what the market is doing and when to buy and sell. Second, if an investor's particular stock doesn't follow a rise in the Dow over time, the investor may question the health of that stock.

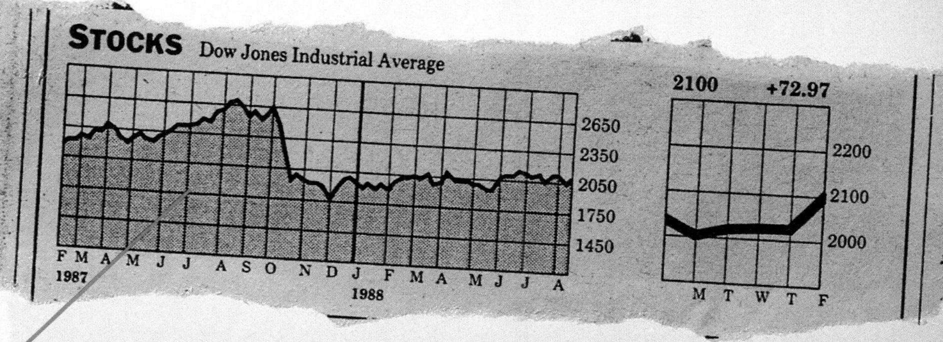

Every day in ***The Wall Street Journal*** you can find this chart showing the Dow over a two-year period. The right-hand chart details the past five days.

How do they figure the averages?

The Dow Jones average looks a lot higher than an average stock price. That's because it's figured according to a special formula. Instead of adding up the stock prices and then dividing by the number of stocks, as they did initially, Dow calculators divide by a much lower number – in 1988, the number was .754 – which has been adjusted for distortions caused by numerous stock splits over the years. That means the Dow Jones Average makes sense only in relation to what it was yesterday, last month or last year.

If you're curious, you can find the ***divisor*** used for each Dow Jones Average listed as a footnote to the charts of the Dow Jones Averages in ***The Wall Street Journal***.

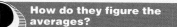

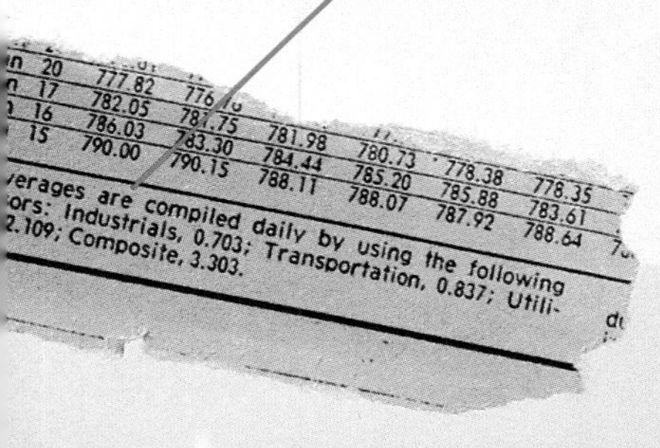

n 20 777.82 776
n 17 782.05 781.75 781.98 780.73 778.38 778.35
16 786.03 783.30 784.44 785.20 785.88 783.61
15 790.00 790.15 788.11 788.07 787.92 788.64

verages are compiled daily by using the following
ors: Industrials, 0.703; Transportation, 0.837; Utili-
2.109; Composite, 3.303.

What's the history of the Dow Jones Average?

One day in 1884, Charles Dow made a list of the average closing prices of 11 representative stocks – 9 railroads, 2 manufacturing firms. He published it in the forerunner of the paper he would later establish with his partner Eddie Jones: ***The Wall Street Journal***. By 1896, the Journal was publishing the Average on a regular basis. The original 11 "representative" stocks were:

- Chicago & North Western
- Delaware Lackawanna & Western
- Lake Shore Line
- New York Central
- St. Paul
- Northern Pacific pfd.
- Union Pacific
- Missouri Pacific
- Lousiville & Nashville
- Pacific Mail
- Western Union

Charles Dow worked continually toward creating an index comprised completely of industrial stocks. After 12 years of deletions, additions and substitutions, he published the first list of industrial stocks in 1896. Those original industrials were:

- American Cotton
- American Sugar
- American Tobacco
- Chicago Gas
- Oil Distilling & Cattle Feeding
- General Electric
- Laclede Gas
- National Lead
- North American
- Tennessee Coal & Iron
- US Leather pfd.
- US Rubber

Who decides which stocks will comprise the Dow; which are to be dropped and which are to be added? The top news editors of ***The Wall Street Journal*** are solely responsible.

The Five Biggest Up and Five Biggest Down Moves of the Dow Jones

Date	Change	% Change	Date	Change	% Change
October 6, 1931	+12.86	+14.87	October 19, 1987	- 508.00	-22.61
October 30, 1929	+28.40	+12.34	October 28, 1929	- 38.33	-12.82
September 21, 1932	+7.67	+11.36	October 29, 1929	- 30.57	-11.73
October 21, 1987	+186.84	+10.15	October 6, 1929	- 25.48	-9.92
August 3, 1932	+5.06	+9.52	December 18, 1899	-5.57	-8.72

Spotting Trends: The Dow over Time

Why does the stock market rise and fall?

The market as a whole does well when many people invest; it suffers when investment activity is down. A number of factors influence why and whether people buy stocks.

Some of these factors are economic: productivity levels in the economy, interest rates and exchange rates. Ample money supply stimulates investments of all kinds; tight money holds them down. Changes in tax rates can also have an impact on stock-buying patterns.

In addition, investors often consider the influence of social or political factors upon economic stability. The unsettling economic effect of domestic unrest, pending elections or international conflict can make investors cautious and slow down stock market activity.

What is meant by Bulls and Bears?

The market goes through cycles, trending upward for periods of time, then reversing itself, and vice versa. ***A rising period is known as a bull market*** – bulls being the market optimists who cause prices to rise. ***A bear market is a falling market***, where the pessimists are driving prices lower. The stock market is a constant struggle between the bulls and the bears, both groups tugging in opposite directions.

Popular notions abound regarding the origin of these labels. One common myth is that the terms reflect the animals' methods of attack – bears attack by sweeping their paws downward while bulls toss their horns upward. A useful mnemonic, but not the true origin.

The term ***bear*** is derived from ***bear skin jobbers*** who had a reputation for selling bear skins before the bears were caught. Gradually, the term ***bear*** came to mean speculators who agreed to sell shares they did not own. These bears would agree to sell a stock at a certain price if they felt the price was about to drop. Then they would quickly buy the stock at its lower price and sell it for the previously agreed higher price. Of course, the bears were gambling on a price drop.

Because bull and bear baiting were once popular sports, ***bulls*** came to mean the opposite of bears. Bulls were those who bought heavily expecting a stock price to go up.

• **1897** *First full year of the Dow Jones Averages*
• **1907** *Rich man's panic occurs; stock market plummets*
• **1910** *NYSE creates listing requirements*
• **1914** *Market closes for 3 months when war is declared*
• **World War I**
• **1929** *Stock Market crash! Black Tuesday sets off the Great Depression which lasts 10 years. Before the crash a seat on the stock market sold for $625,000.*
World War II •
1897
1900
1905
1910
1915
1920
1925
1930
1935
1940

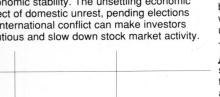

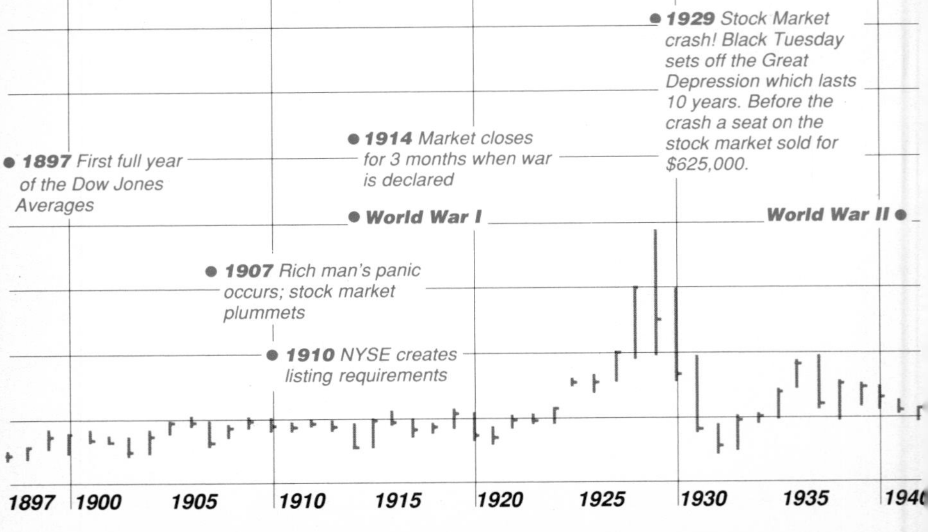

Great Bull and Bear Markets in History

Sometimes market trends last a long time, even years. Overall, though, ***bull markets usually continue for longer periods of time than bear markets.*** This doesn't mean, however, that markets usually rise farther than they fall: it just means that drops in the market tend to happen quickly while rises tend to take a long time. You might say, in fact, that the stock market seems to move according to the rules of gravity; you can fall 1,000 feet very quickly but, climbing 1,000 feet takes quite a bit more stamina.

high

close (year end)

low

2700
2600
2500
2400
2300
2200
2100
2000
1900
1800
1700
1600
1500
1400
1300
1200
1100
1000
900
800
700
600
500
400
300
200
100

● **Viet Nam War**

● ***1978*** *Inter-Market Trading System,* ***ITS****, links the regional exchanges with the NYSE and AMEX*

● ***1953*** *New York Curb Exchange becomes the American Stock Exchange.*

1945 1950 1955 1960 1965 1970 1975 1980 1985

Market Indicators

Knowing when to buy and when to sell – timing – is crucial to making money in the stock market.

Are there other ways to measure the market?

Market indicators and activity reports are scrutinized today more than ever. Because the Dow Jones Averages are based on so few companies, the need arose in recent years for other indexes formulated from broader bases. ***The Wall Street Journal*** provides performance information on all the major indexes, including the previous day's activity, the previous 12-month's performance and the month's performance.

The NYSE Composite Index includes all stocks traded on the New York Stock Exchange.

The ***Dow Jones Averages, S&P 500,*** and ***NYSE Composite Index*** reflect activity on the New York Stock Exchange.

The Standard & Poor's 500, or S&P 500, as it's commonly called, is widely used as an indicator of stock market trends. Standard & Poor's was first introduced in 1957 and incorporates a broad base of 500 stocks. Some stocks exhibit a greater influence over the market than others. The S&P 500 compensates for this by giving greater weight to some stocks in its calculations.

Like the Dow Jones 65 Composite Average, the Standard & Poor's 500 is broken into smaller industry segments which are monitored separately. These segments are 400 industrial companies, 20 transportation companies, 40 utilities, and 40 financial companies.

The NASDAQ National Market System Composite Index monitors stocks traded over-the-counter. ***NASDAQ*** stands for *National Association of Securities Dealers Automated Quotations*. The over-the-counter market is more speculative overall, and has more start-up companies, particularly in high technology and financial services. An increase in NASDAQ activity shows investor enthusiasm for small stocks and a willingness to take risks on the future of the economy.

The AMEX Market Value Index measures the performance of over 800 companies listed on the American Stock Exchange. Other major indexes of interest to traders in American securities include the Value-Line Index; the Financial Times (of London) Industrial Index; the Nikkei Stock Average (which measures the Tokyo Exchange securities); and the Wilshire 5000, the broadest index, incorporating all the NYSE and AMEX issues, as well as many traded in the OTC markets.

1987

STOCK MARKET DATA B

Major Indexes

HIGH	LOW (12 MOS)		CLOSE	NET CH
DOW JONES AVERAGES				
2722.42	1738.74	30 Industrials	2109.17	+ 25.24
1101.16	661.00	20 Transportation	x868.13	+ 11.2
213.79	160.98	15 Utilities	182.14	+ 1.9
992.21	653.76	65 Composite	x785.20	+ 9.
NEW YORK STOCK EXCHANGE				
187.99	125.91	Composite	153.29	+
231.05	149.43	Industrials	185.62	+
80.22	61.63	Utilities	72.58	+
168.20	104.76	Transportation	136.01	+
165.36	107.39	Finance	129.38	+
STANDARD & POOR'S INDEXES				
336.77	223.92	500 Index	271.67	+
393.17	255.43	Industrials	313.87	
274.20	167.59	Transportation	211.38	
121.11	91.80	Utilities	110.58	
32.56	20.39	Financials	24.51	
NASDAQ				
455.26	291.88	Composite	387.7	
488.92	288.30	Industrials	402.7	
475.78	333.66	Insurance	396.	
510.24	365.63	Banks	454	
195.37	124.98	Nat. Mkt. Comp.	167	
187.94	110.21	Nat. Mkt. Indus.	15	
OTHERS				
365.01	231.90	AMEX	3	
1926.2	1232.0	Fin. Times Indus.		
28342.46	21036.80	Nikkei Stock Avg.	27	
289.02	181.09	Value-Line(geom)		
3299.44	2188.11	Wilshire 5000		

Most Active Issues

	Volume	Cl
NYSE		
Texaco Inc	3,971,800	
IBM	2,113,600	
Exxon Corp	1,671,500	

Price Percentage G

NYSE — Clos

ONEOK Inc, Saul, Qual, Beve, Max, IPCO, Wyle, Whee, Black, Manv

NAS: Bell, Am, Onc, Wel, Vi

Diodes Inc, Vanguard Tec

Volume Pe

NYSE: Orange-CoInc, FirstBoston, SonatInc, MurrayOhio, Montedison, SWEnergy, Heilig-Meyers, FortHoward, GiantGroup, SPSTechn, ToroCo

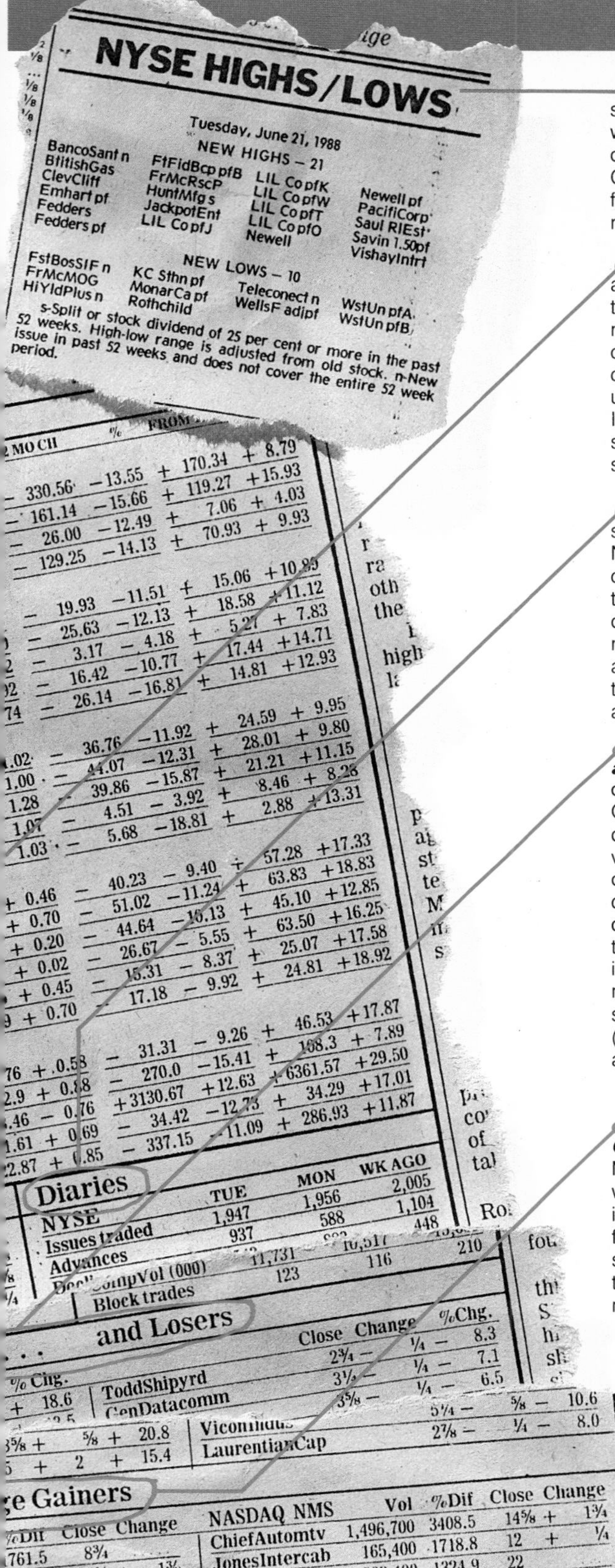

NYSE HIGHS/LOWS

Tuesday, June 21, 1988

NEW HIGHS – 21

BancoSant n, BritishGas, ClevCliff, Emhart pf, Fedders, Fedders pf, FtFldBcp pfB, FrMcRscP, HuntMfg s, JackpotEnt, LIL Co pfJ, LIL Co pfK, LIL Co pfW, LIL Co pfT, LIL Co pfO, Newell, Newell pf, PacifiCorp, Saul REst, Savin 1.50pf, VishayIntrt

NEW LOWS – 10

FstBosSIF n, FrMcMOG, HiYldPlus n, KC Sthn pf, MonarCa pf, Rothchild, Teleconect n, WellsF adjpf, WstUn pfA, WstUn pfB

s-Split or stock dividend of 25 per cent or more in the past 52 weeks. High-low range is adjusted from old stock. n-New issue in past 52 weeks and does not cover the entire 52 week period.

Diaries

NYSE	TUE	MON	WK AGO
Issues traded	1,947	1,956	2,005
Advances	937	588	1,104

and Losers

	Close	Change	%Chg.
ToddShipyrd	$2\frac{3}{4}$ –	$\frac{1}{4}$ –	8.3
GenDatacomm	$3\frac{1}{2}$ –	$\frac{1}{4}$ –	7.1
	$3\frac{5}{8}$ –	$\frac{1}{4}$ –	6.5
Viconindus	$5\frac{1}{4}$ –	$\frac{5}{8}$ –	10.6
LaurentianCap	$2\frac{7}{8}$ –	$\frac{1}{4}$ –	8.0

...ge Gainers

NASDAQ NMS	Vol	%Dif	Close	Change
ChiefAutomtv	1,496,700	3408.5	$14\frac{5}{8}$ +	$1\frac{3}{4}$
JonesIntercab	165,400	1718.8	12 +	$\frac{1}{4}$
GartnerGroup	503,100	1324.9	22	
ManitowocCo	161,400	1319.0	$20\frac{3}{4}$ –	$\frac{1}{4}$
MetroAirlines	240,300	1261.6	6	
ViratekInc	329,600	1233.1	$14\frac{3}{4}$ +	$2\frac{1}{4}$
TalmanHmFed	232,200	1170.4	$6\frac{7}{8}$ –	$\frac{1}{8}$
AMEX				
SynalloyCorp	120,900	1307.6	$6\frac{3}{8}$ +	$\frac{1}{4}$
Regal-Beloit	182,500	968.4	$18\frac{1}{2}$	
GundleEnvrm	141,100	921.9	$21\frac{1}{2}$ –	$\frac{1}{4}$
WestnInvReTr	74,800	818.0	$18\frac{1}{2}$	
	111,200	709.8	$32\frac{1}{4}$ +	$1\frac{3}{8}$

NYSE highs/lows summarizes those companies which experienced highest – or lowest – prices of the year. Champagne suppliers and florists watch this column regularly.

Most Active Issues are the stocks most actively traded during the day. The number of shares which changed hands during the course of the day is listed under the heading "volume." It's not uncommon to have stocks trade several million shares in one day.

Diaries provides a snapshot of the activities of the NYSE, AMEX and OTC and compares today's price with the price of one day ago and one week ago. It includes the number of stocks which advanced and declined, those that remained unchanged, and new highs and lows.

Percentage Gainers and Losers lists the few dozen NYSE, AMEX, and OTC stocks which increased or decreased dramatically in value. This chart concentrates on the greatest percentage changes rather than actual dollar changes. This means that a \$15 stock which increased \$5 (33%) might make the list when a \$75 stock which increased \$7 (6.6%) would not. Big losers also appear in this listing.

Volume Percentage Gainers lists the NYSE, NASDAQ and AMEX stocks whose share trading increased most dramatically from the previous day. ***Vol*** shows the number of shares traded. ***% Dif*** shows how much trading increased.

Two Crashes

Until 1987, there had been only one great stock market collapse in twentieth century American history.

The Crash of '29 occurred on October 29, 1929. The Dow closed at 230.07 after plummeting roughly 30 points, an astounding one-day movement for its time. After having reached an all-time high of 469.49 on September 19th, the Dow had taken a 51% nosedive.

On October 19, 1987, however, the stock market suffered its second major collapse of the twentieth century. This time, the stock market dropped into a free fall that didn't end until the Dow had lost 508 points. Only two months earlier, the Dow had set another all-time high at 2722.42 but after the crash, the Dow ended 34% lower at 1738.74.

Which day was a greater one-day loss? On October 29, 1929, the Dow closed 12.8% lower than it started. The drop on October 19, 1987 was 22.6%.

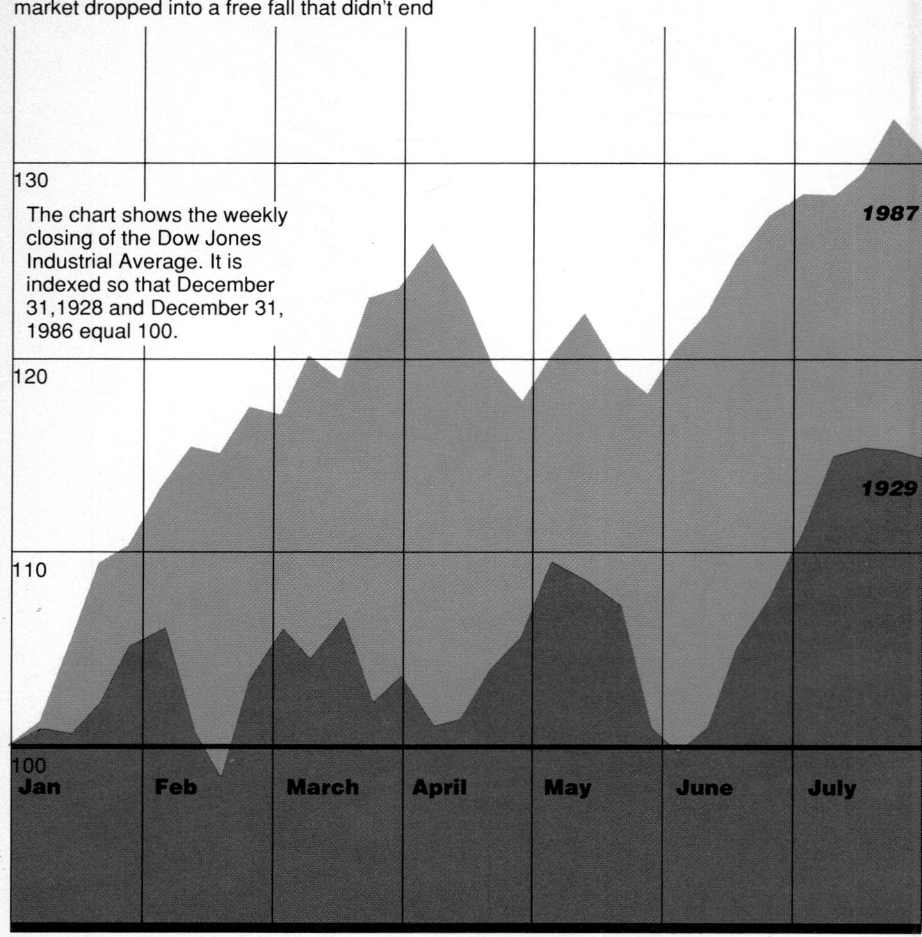

The chart shows the weekly closing of the Dow Jones Industrial Average. It is indexed so that December 31,1928 and December 31, 1986 equal 100.

How Blue Chip Companies Fared in the Two Great Crashes

1929	*opening price*	*closing price*	*loss*	*% loss*
AT&T	266	232	-34	12.7
E. I. DuPont	108	91 1/4	-16 3/4	15.5
Eastman Kodak	222 7/8	181	-41 7/8	18.7
General Electric	297 1/2	250	-47 1/2	15.9
NCR	94	75	-19	18.0
Sears Roebuck	127	111	-16	12.5

1987	*opening price*	*closing price*	*loss*	*% loss*
AT&T	30	23 5/8	-6 3/8	21.2
E. I. DuPont	98 1/2	80 1/2	-18	18.2
Eastman Kodak	90 1/8	62 7/8	-27 1/4	30.2
General Electric	50 3/4	41 7/8	-8 7/8	17.4
NCR	69 7/8	59 1/2	-10 3/8	14.8
Sears Roebuck	41 1/2	31	-10 1/2	25.3

Record trading volumes

On the day of the great crash of '29, over 9,212,000 shares were traded, though that wasn't the greatest volume of its time.

Compare the 1929 figures with those from 1987: the day of the market meltdown produced a new record volume of 604.3 million shares. The day after the meltdown produced another record.

Trading date	*Shares traded*
Oct. 25,1929: previous record	*12.9 million*
Oct. 29, 1929: crash	*9.2 million*
Oct. 30, 1929	*16.4 million*
Jan. 23, 1987: previous record	*302.4 million*
Oct. 19, 1987: crash	*604.3 million*
Oct. 20, 1987	*608.1 million*

The overloaded ticker

The ticker services maintained by the NYSE have not fared particularly well during the days of overwhelming trading. By 2:30 pm on October 25, 1929, the ticker had fallen 147 minutes behind in reporting trades. Preparations were immediately made to manage up to 18 million shares a day.

Despite tremendous technological leaps and preparations for outstanding volume days, the NYSE still couldn't handle the surprisingly huge volume on October 19, 1987. By day's end the ticker had fallen approximately three hours behind in reporting actual trading.

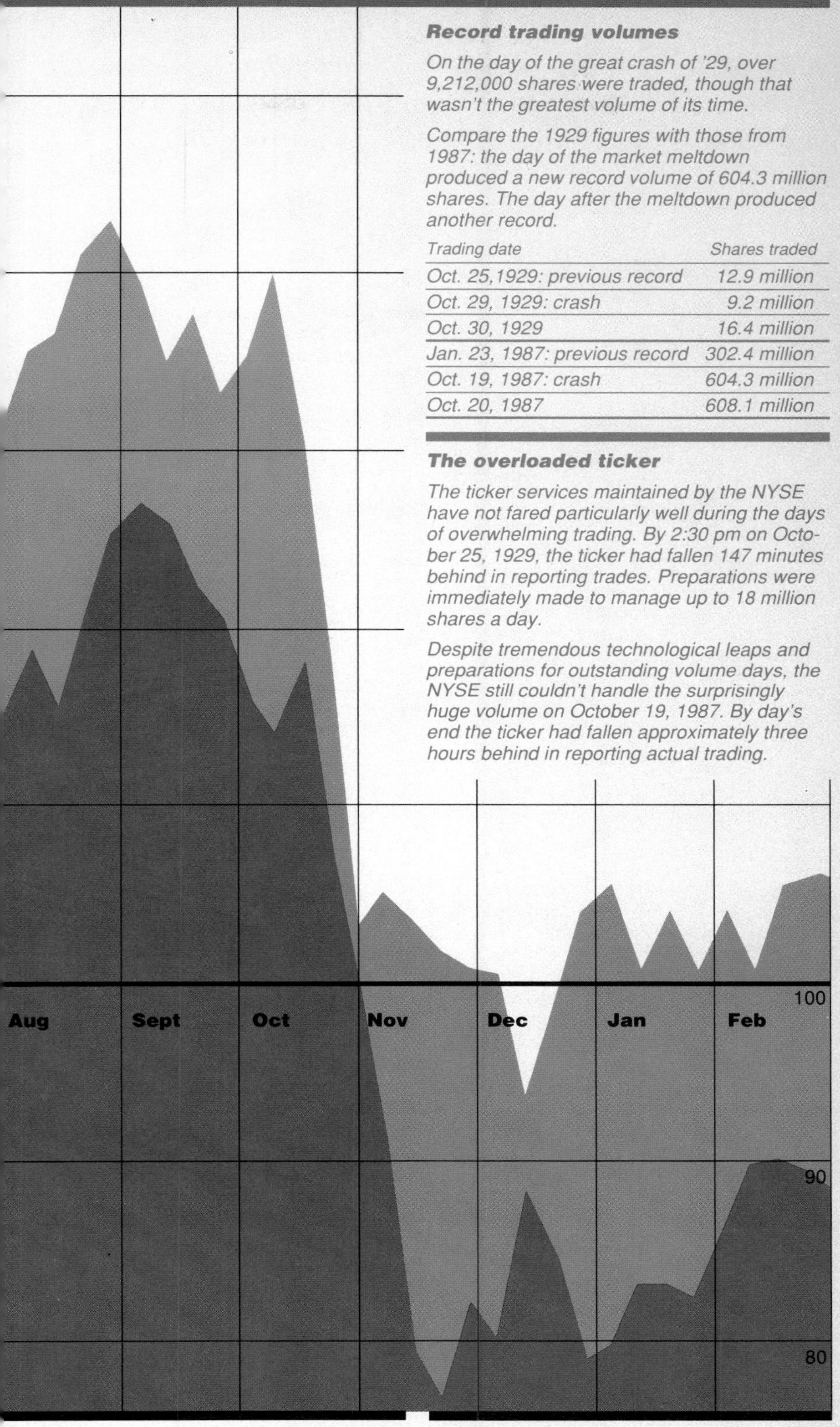

The biggest percentage loser in the '87 crash: US Home Corp. lost $2^3/_8$ points to close at $1^5/_8$ for a total loss of 59.4%.

Despite all the talk of losses, there were some big gainers as well, primarily in the precious metals industry. The two biggest gainers in the '87 crash: Newmont Gold, up 10.5%; Callahan Mining, up 7.4%.

Loss in value

On October 29, 1929, the stock market lost $14 billion of value – at that time, a staggering amount of the wealth of the nation's investors.

The crash that occurred on October 19, 1987, was no less staggering for its day, losing over $500 billion in value.

Evaluating Companies

As an investor, you'll want to do more than watch the stock tables and the Dow to see what other investors are thinking and doing. You'll want to form your own judgements about the companies you invest in.

One way you can follow your company's financial condition is by reading the financial pages. Every day, ***The Wall Street Journal*** offers lists of companies that have released earnings reports or dividend announcements.

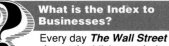

What is the Index to Businesses?

Every day ***The Wall Street Journal*** publishes an index to the companies mentioned in the day's articles. Scanning the index is a quick way to see if anything significant is affecting a company you're trying to follow.

How do you read the Digest of Earnings?

A company's earnings are its profits, reported four times per year. Theoretically, this is considered the most important single factor influencing stock prices. Earnings are the scorecard by which companies are judged to be successful or not. Earnings increases also make dividend increases possible and thus make the stock more attractive.

You can read the column from left to right as follows:

Name of company is listed, followed by a ***code*** for where the stock is traded: American Medical trades on the NYSE. Comparisons are made between the current quarter and that of a year ago. Gross income is listed as ***revenues*** for service companies and as ***sales*** for manufacturing companies. ***Net income*** is the profit made for the time quarter. ***Share earns Net income*** is the net income divided by number of shares. If this is not the first quarter, the same information for the year-to-date is given also.

What is the Corporate Dividend News?

Dividend changes, like changes in earnings, may have a direct influence on stock prices – and then again they may not. In any case, you'll want to keep close track of your company's dividend policies.

Companies make dividend announcements several weeks before the dividends are paid.

You can read the columns from left to right as follows:

The Name of company announcing a dividend and type of stock, in this case American Water Works preferred stock. ***Q*** indicates that this is a quarterly dividend (*M* indicates monthly). The dollar amount of ***dividend per share*** is given next; here it's 31¼¢. From this you can tell that the annual dividend for this stock is $1.25 per share.The ***Payable date*** – when dividend will be issued – is shown followed by the ***Record date***. Dividends will be paid to people who were on record as share owners on this date.

A ***stock split*** occurs when a company issues more stock, lowering the price per share.

Ex-Dividend means, literally, ***without dividend***. It signifies that a dividend has been declared within the past four days. A current purchaser of the stock will not receive a dividend until the next payment is declared.

INDEX TO BUSINESSES

This index of businesses mentioned in today's issue of The Wall Street Journal is intended to include all significant references to parent companies. In news stories inside the paper, first references to these companies appear in boldface type. References are indexed, but not boldfaced, in articles on page one, the editorial pages, the leisure and arts page and the first page of the second section. The index doesn't cite companies listed solely in the Digest of Earnings, which appears today on page 51.

Page numbers listed here refer to the pages where the stories begin.

DIGEST OF EARNINGS REPORTS

AMERICAN MEDICAL INT'L (N)

Quar May 31:	1988	1987
Revs	$760,590,000	$689,332,000
Net inco	33,715,000	31,650,000
Shr earns:		
Net inco ...	.41	.36
9 months:		
Revs	2,176,524,000	2,019,410,000
Income	a80,246,000	88,233,000
Extrd chg ...	b33,900,000	....
Acctg adj ...	c50,700,000	....
Net inco	97,046,000	88,233,000
Avg shrs	86,741,000	92,493,000
Shr earns:		
Income	.98	1.01
Net inco ...	1.17	1.01

a-Includes a gain of $20,400,000 on sale of a subsidiary, less a charge of $20,000,000 from the disposition of certain facilities. b-From repurchase of debt. c-Credit; cumulative effect on prior periods of an accounting change for income taxes.

BUSINESS CARDS TOMORROW (O)

Year Feb 29:	1988	1987
Revenues	$6,393,530	$5,065,633
Net inc...	...540	a978,076
Sh...		

ABBREVIATIONS

A partial list of frequently used abbreviations: Net inv inc (net investment income); Loss dis op (Loss from discontinued operations); inco cnt op (income from continuing operations.)

HUMANA INC. (N)

Quar May 31:	1988	1987
Revenues ...	$891,143,000	a$744,471,000
Net income .	63,820,000	52,274,000
Shr earns:		
Net income	.64	.53
9 months:		
Revenues ...	2,531,068,000	a2,169,228,000
Income	168,828,000	135,371,000
Extrd chg ...	b16,133,000	....
Acctg adj ...	c16,214,000	....
Net income .	168,909,000	135,371,000
Shr earns:		
Income	1.71	1.38
Net income	1.71	1.38

a-Restated. b-From early extinguishment of debt. c-Credit; cumulative effect on prior periods of an accounting change.

PIER I IMPORTS INC. (N)

Quar May 28:	1988	1987
Sales	$97,149,000	$79,698,000
Net income	5,378,000	4,296,000
Shr earns:		
Net income .	.17	a.14

a-Adjusted to reflect a three-for-two stock split paid in July 1987.

QUAKER FABRIC CORP. (A)

13 wk May 28:	1988	1987
Sales	$22,756,900	$27,473,800
Loss	744,700	c269,400
Extrd cred. ...	....	a171,000
Net loss	744,700	c440,400
Shr earns:		
Loss	....	c.16
Net loss	....	c.26

a-Tax benefit from tax-loss carry-forwards. c-Income.

QUALITY FOOD CENTERS (O)

12 wk Jun 11:	1988	1987
Sales	$50,940,000	$43,263,000
Income	1,562,000	1,035,000
Extrd chg	....	891,000
Net income	1,562,000	144,000
Avg shares	4,763,000	4,546,000
Shr earns:		
	33	.23
		.03

...erations Friday.

CORPORATE DIVIDEND NEWS

Dividends Reported April 6

Company	Period	Amount	Payable date	Record date
REGULAR				
American Water Works ...	Q	.17	5–16–88	4–29
Amer Water Works 5%pf .	Q	.31¼	6– 1–88	5–13
Amer Water Wrks 5%pref .	Q	.31¼	6– 1–88	5–13
Dollar General Corp	Q	.05	5– 9–88	4–21
Golden Enterprises	Q	.07	4–27–88	4–18
Horizon Bancorp	Q	.40	5– 1–88	4–15
Horizon Bancorp adjpf	Q	.53¾	5– 1–88	4–15
Kimball Intl clB	Q	.11	7–15–88	6–25
Murphy Oil Corp	Q	.25	6– 1–88	5–16
Pacific Enterprises	Q	y.87	5–16–88	4–20
y-Incorrectly reported under old company name in previous edition.				
Phillips-Van Heusen	Q	.07	6–13–88	5–13
Rite Aid Corp	Q	.18½	4–25–88	4–18
Southwestern Energy Co ..	Q	.14	5– 5–88	4–20
Transcontl GasPL$2.50pf ..	Q	.62½	5– 1–88	4–15
Transcontl GasPL$6.65pf ..	Q	1.66¼	5– 1–88	4–15
Transcontl GasPL$8.64pf ..	Q	2.16	5– 1–88	4–15
IRREGULAR				
ICN Biomedicals Inc	–	.03	5– 1–88	4–20
Neiman-Marcus Group	–	.05	4–29–88	4–18
FUNDS–REITS–INVESTMENT COS–LPS				
Amer Tr AT&T Pr SrA	–	.173	5– 9–88	4–20
Amer Tr AT&T Units SrA	–	.173	5– 9–88	4–20
Evergreen Total Return ..	Q	h.27	4–11–88	4– 7
Houston Oil Trust	M	h.01735	4–25–88	4–15
Mass Financial Bd Fd	M	h.09½	4–15–88	4– 6
Mass Fincl GovtGuarSecs	M	h.073	4–15–88	4– 6
MassFinlGovtSecsHiYld	M	t.096	4–15–88	4– 6
t-Payment consists of 4.4 cents from capital gains and 5.2 cents from income.				
Mass Fincl High Inco Tr ..	M	h.061	4–15–88	4– 6
MassFinclMngdHiYldMuni	M	h.07	4–15–88	4– 6
MassFinclMngdMuniBdTr .	M	h.061	4–15–88	4– 6
Mass Fincl MST Mass	M	h.061	4–15–88	4– 6
Mass Fincl MST Md	M	h.057	4–15–88	4– 6
Mass Fincl MST NC	M	h.061	4–15–88	4– 6
Mass Financial MST SC ...	M	h.06½	4–15–88	4– 6
Mass Fincl MST Virginia .	M	h.06	4–15–88	4– 6
Mass Finl MST WV	M	h.064	4–15–88	4– 6
Mass Finl High Inco II	M	h.081	4–15–88	4– 6
New York Tax Exempt ...	M	.056	5– 2–88	4–15
Newhall Resources	Q	.15	6– 6–88	4–22
Sabine Royalty Trust	M	.12818	4–29–88	4–15
STOCK				
EnergyNorth Inc	–	a	8–22–88	8– 8
a-Three-for-two stock split subject to shareholder approval.				
Jaco Electronics Inc	–	10%	5–10–88	4–28
Vintage Group Inc	–	n	5– 6–88	4–29
n-Distribution of one share of Questline Corp for every 10 shares held.				

INCREASED

Company	Period	Amounts New	Amounts Old	Payable date	Record date
Baton Broadcasting	S	b.12	b.10	5– 2–88	4–15
Bramalea Ltd	S	b.21½	b.18	8– 2–88	7–20
EnergyNorth Inc	Q	.33	.31	6–15–88	6– 1
Houston Indus	Q	.74	.72	6–10–88	5–16

Company	Period	Amount	Payable date	Record date
FOREIGN				
Cheung Kong (Hldgs)ADR	F	p	6–21–88	5–18
p-Approximately $.016 per Depositary Share.				
Waterford Glass Grp ADR	F	w	6–14–88	4–29
w-Approximately $.270 per Depositary Share.				
Waterford Gls ADR unit ..	F	v	6–14–88	4–29
v-Approximately $.324 per Depositary Share.				
INITIAL				
Bank of Stamford	–	.05	5–15–88	4–15

A-Annual; Ac-Accumulation; b-Payable in Canadian funds; F-Final; G-Interim; h-From income; k-From capital gains; M-Monthly; Q-Quarterly; S-Semi-annual.

* * *

Stocks Ex-Dividend April 8

Company	Amount	Company	Amount
ACM Govt Income	.16½	MSI Data Corp	c
American Medical Int'l	.18	c-3-for-2 ...	

Bonds

A bond certificate is simply an IOU. It certifies that you have loaned money to a government or corporation and describes the terms of the loan.

-85
7-
BOWATER INCORP
12 3/8% SINKING FUND DEBENTURE DUE
Bowater Incorporated, a corporation
the "Company," which term includes any suc
received, hereby promises to pay to
or registered assigns, the principal sum
S P E C I M
purpose.
In Witness Whereof, the
BOWATER INCORPORATED CORPORATE SEAL 1964 DELAWARE
Dated:
By
Attest:
Secretary
TRUSTEE'S CERTIFICATE OF AUTHENTICATION
This is one of the Debentures referred to in the within-mentioned Indenture.
CHEMICAL BANK,
as Trustee
By
Authorized Office
SPECIMEN
SPECIMEN
SPECIMEN
SPECIMEN

As with stock certificates, measures are taken to foil counterfeiters. Bonds are printed on safety paper with ***planchettes*** and employ geometric engravings to make reproduction difficult.

Most bonds are issued with three essential pieces of information:

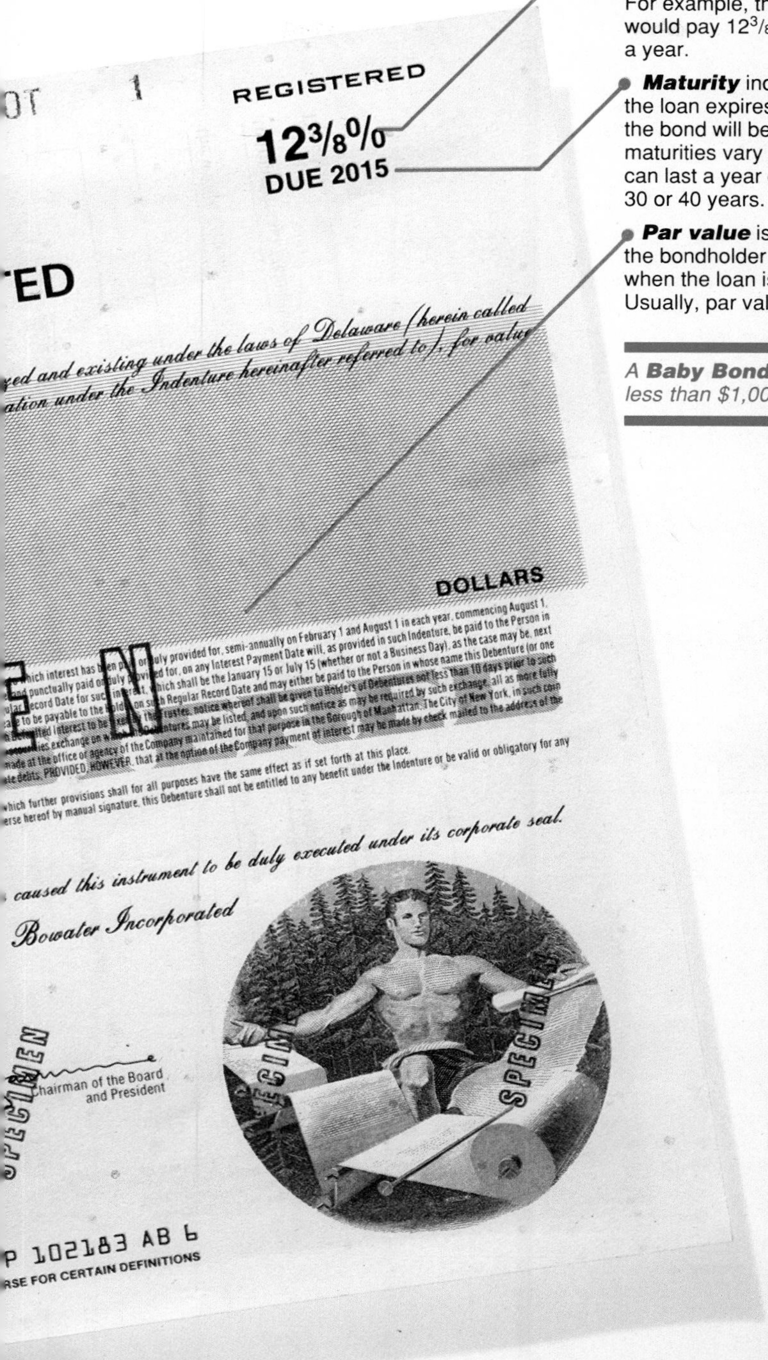

- ***Interest rate*** is the percentage of par value that will be paid in interest to the bondholder on a regular basis. For example, this $1,000 bond would pay $12^{3}/_{8}$%, or $123.75 a year.
- ***Maturity*** indicates when the loan expires (is "due") and the bond will be retired. Bond maturities vary widely; loans can last a year or continue for 30 or 40 years.
- ***Par value*** is the amount the bondholder will be repaid when the loan is over. Usually, par value is $1,000.

*A **Baby Bond** is a bond with less than $1,000 par value.*

In the 1980s, individual investors have been buying bonds in record numbers. In 1985, individuals held $11,149.8 billion worth of bonds and $273.2 billion worth of bond funds. The total budget for the United States Government during the same year was approximately $1,024.3 billion.

Why Are There Bonds?

Bonds are crucial to raising the funds needed to build bridges, repair roads, construct factories and provide essential services to our society.

In the financial world, there are two kinds of securities: debt and equity. When you buy stock, you gain ***equity*** in the company and become a part-owner. When you buy bonds, you own ***debt*** and become a creditor because you have loaned money to the company or government.

A Bond is an IOU

Individuals lend money to institutions, governments, agencies, corporations, etc. in exchange for…

bonds, issued by the ***institutions***, etc. as proof of the loan agreement, plus regular interest payments.

As with most loans, the borrower pays ***interest*** to the lender. A bondholder usually receives regular interest payments from the issuer of the bonds. Unlike stock dividend payments, which change along with company profit levels, interest payments on a bond are usually fixed.

Stocks and bonds are often mentioned in the same breath, but they're very different kinds of investments. Stocks certainly are more glamorous and get most of the press. The ups and downs of the stock market – not bond prices – are the stuff of dramatic nightly news. But the bond market, in terms of dollar volume traded, is many times larger than the stock market.

Bonds may seem less glamorous than stocks because, for years, their prices fluctuated less dramatically. And, unlike stock dividends, interest payments don't increase when a company is profiting. Perceptions may change, however because recently bond prices have fluctuated as much if not more than stock prices.

Should a company go bankrupt, bondholders would have first claim on remaining assets, followed by holders of preferred stock and, last, by holders of common stock.

Some uses of revenue from long-term bond sales in 1987

Airports	$ 1,206,400,000
Education	13,129,300,000
Electric/Hydro power	10,711,000,000
Fire stations	84,000,000
General govt. purposes	18,230,400,000
Health	12,551,500,000
Housing	12,024,800,000
Malls/shopping centers	38,300,000
Parks/zoos/beaches	293,400,000
Parking facilities	372,800,000
Sports complexes	125,600,000
Tennis/golf	20,100,000
Unknown	7,000,000

What is a bond issue?

When companies or government agencies need to raise cash, they will offer the public a deal. It's called ***floating an issue***.

In essence, the issuer tests the market to see if it can raise enough cash at an acceptable interest rate. A common expression for testing something is "Let's see if it will float." Thus, *floating an issue*.

We'll pay you 8% a year for 15 years if you'll lend us some money. We're looking for loans in denominations or ***units*** of $1,000. Overall, we're looking to raise $20 million.

OK, we like that deal, compared to other investments. Your credit reputation is good, meaning you probably won't default on your payments. And we think the deal pays a good rate of return.

Who Issues Bonds?

Only corporations can issue stocks, but bonds can be issued by corporations or governments.

Municipal governments

States, cities, counties and towns issue bonds to pay for a wide variety of publicly beneficial projects – schools, highways, stadiums, sewage systems, bridges, and many others.

Federal government

The US Treasury floats debt issues to pay for a wide range of federal government activities. A large part of the US deficit is made up of outstanding Treasury securities.

Federal government agencies

Bonds issued by federal agencies are indirect obligations of the US government. Some of the most well-known are those issued by home mortgage associations (for example, ***Ginnie Maes – GNMAs***). Other agencies issuing bonds include the Federal Housing Administration and the Tennessee Valley Authority.

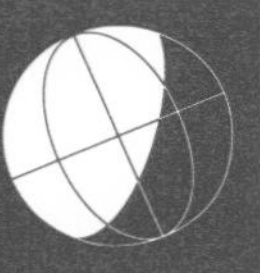

Foreign governments and corporations

Many foreign companies and governments issue bonds specifically to US investors. While many "yankee bonds" are denominated in US dollars, some are available in other currencies.

Corporations

For corporations, bonds are a primary way of raising capital. The money raised pays for expansion, modernization, and operating expenses as well. Corporate bonds have become much more important during the 1980s, particularly because corporations have needed to borrow huge amounts of money to finance their takeovers of other corporations.

How do bondholders make money?

The beauty of bonds is steady income. When you invest in a bond, you can expect to receive regular, fixed interest payments for as long as you hold the bond – unless the issuer goes broke.

You may hear a bond's interest referred to as its ***coupon***. That's because some bond certificates come with detachable coupons, each one representing a scheduled interest payment. (Until recently, all bonds were issued in this form.) With these bonds, you actually clip a coupon and send it in at the appropriate time to receive your interest payment.

Bonds with coupons are called ***bearer bonds***, because they are assumed to belong to whomever possesses ("bears") them – the same way we think about dollar bills. Today, however, most bonds are ***registered*** in the holder's name and have no coupons. Instead, the issuer automatically sends the interest payments to the holder listed on its records.

What Is a Bond Worth?

Two factors usually determine a bond's value: 1) how much you'll earn from it compared to what you could earn from other investments, and 2) how sure you can be that the borrower will repay the loan when it comes due.

How long can you own a bond?

Every bond has a predetermined lifetime, a ***date of maturity*** upon which the bond expires and the borrower must repay the loan in full. The date is right on the bond and in the bond's newspaper listing. (Only a tiny fraction of the bonds issued are listed in the newspaper.) This full repayment is called the ***par value*** (what the bond will be worth at maturity). And whoever owns the bond at that time will receive the repayment.

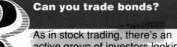

Can you trade bonds?

As in stock trading, there's an active group of investors looking to buy previously issued bonds. The market for these bonds, where their selling prices fluctuate, is called the ***secondary market***.

*In Britain, government bonds are called **gilts** – short for **gilt-edged investments**.*

*The **Liberty Bonds** which helped win World War I were traded on the New York Stock Exchange. They raised $16 billion for the war effort.*

Why do bond prices change?

Changes in ***interest rates*** affect the price of a bond. Issuers of bonds offer to pay investors a rate of interest which is competitive with other bond rates at the time. As a result, the rate on a *new* bond is usually similar to other interest rates: the prime rate, mortgage rates, personal loan rates, etc.

After a bond is issued, however, interest rates in the economy may change – making the rate on the issued bond (which can't change) more or less attractive to investors. If the bond is paying more interest than generally available elsewhere, investors will be willing to pay more to own it. If the bond is paying less, the reverse is usually true.

In general, consequently, interest rates and bond prices fluctuate like two sides of a seesaw. As the table below illustrates, when interest rates drop, the value of existing bonds usually goes up; when interest rates climb, the value of existing bonds usually falls.

Let's say, for example, that XYZ Corporation floats a new issue of bonds offering $6^3/_4$% interest. You, the bond buyer, decide this is a good rate compared to what else you could invest in. So you buy some bonds at full price (par value), $1,000 per bond.

Three years later, interest rates in general are up. If new bonds costing $1,000 are paying 8% interest, no buyer is going to pay you $1,000 for your $6^3/_4$% XYZ bond. To sell, you'll have to offer your bonds at a ***discount*** to induce buyers to own a bond with lower than the going rate.

Now consider the reverse situation. If new bonds selling for $1,000 offer only a $5^1/_2$% interest rate, you'll be able to sell your $6^3/_4$% XYZ bonds for more than you paid – say, $1,200 per bond – since buyers will be willing to pay a ***premium*** to obtain the higher interest rate.

A Bond's Interest Rate vs. Its Price

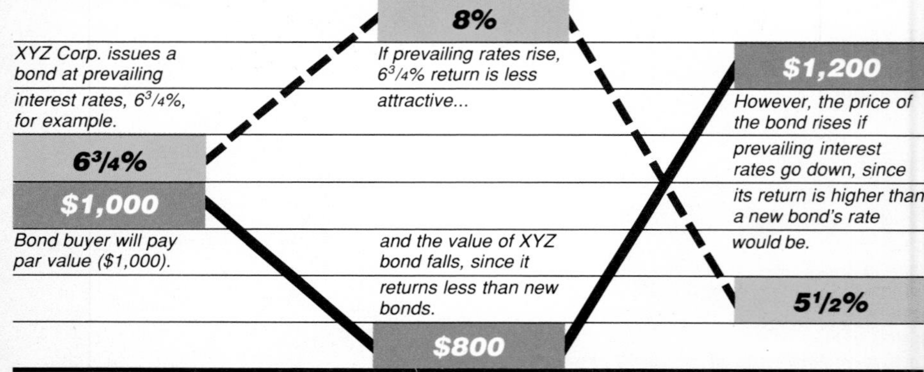

8%
XYZ Corp. issues a bond at prevailing interest rates, 6³/₄%, for example.
If prevailing rates rise, 6³/₄% return is less attractive...
$1,200
However, the price of the bond rises if prevailing interest rates go down, since its return is higher than a new bond's rate would be.
6³/₄%
$1,000
Bond buyer will pay par value ($1,000).
and the value of XYZ bond falls, since it returns less than new bonds.
5¹/₂%
$800

What Does Yield Mean?

A bond's **yield** is not the same as its interest rate.

The term "yield" describes what you'll actually earn from a bond, based on a simple calculation. Investors determine bond values largely by comparing yields. Dividing the amount of money a bond will pay in interest by the price of the bond gives you a bond's yield.

Figures for current yield are offered in most bond charts and tables and are phrased as *percentages.* For example, if a bond's yield is given as 12%, it means: "Your interest payments will be 12% of what you'll pay for the bond today." You will receive a 12% return on your investment.

You can also see yields on bonds issued by ***The World Bank,*** which borrows money from investors and loans it to underdeveloped countries. Below is a portion of a bond table taken from ***The Wall Street Journal***. A look at the complete table shows yields on bonds issued to raise funds for government subsidized mortgages, assistance to farmers and other government programs.

Student Loan Marketing

Rate	Mat	Bid	Asked	Yld
9.63	5-88	100.9	100.13	6.33
11.70	7-88	101.2	101.6	6.57
7.90	7-89	100.5	100.15	7.48
12.85	9-89	106.19	107.5	7.37
13.15	9-90	107.1	107.19	7.33
10.90	2-90	105.19	105.25	7.55
6.95	8-90	97.25	98.3	7.84
7.90	9-90	99.27	100.5	7.83
8.45	12-90	101.3	101.9	7.90
7.38	2-91	98.27	99.5	7.96
8.55	5-91	100.29	101.7	7.39
7.75	6-91	98.31	99.9	8.00
7.60	6-91	98.15	98.25	8.02
5.60	8-91	92.26	93.4	8.00
8.00	8-91	99.19	99.29	8.03
8.25	6-92	99.13	99.31	8.25
9.25	9-92	102.23	103.1	7.85
8.80	12-92	100.31	101.9	8.46
		108.8	108.14	8.41
			?5.15	8.46
				?45

Bond yields are listed every day in ***The Wall Street Journal***. This chart shows the yields on bonds bought by investors to help the government provide student loans.

How do you calculate yields?

Yield is not the same thing as the interest rate. In fact, yield may be higher or lower than the bond's interest rate. If, for instance, a bond costs $1,000 and pays 8% interest, you'd receive $80 a year from this bond...it would yield 8%.

If, however, a year later, the bond loses value and it's sold for $800, the new buyers would still receive the $80 a year – but, since they only paid $800, the yield for them would be 10%.

On the other hand, should the bond be sold next year at a premium, say $1,200, the $80 a year interest would only be a yield of 6²/₃%.

What is yield to maturity?

An even more precise measure of value is ***yield to maturity***. This figure takes into account the interest rate in relation to the price; the purchase price versus the par value; and the number of years left until maturity. So, if the par value of a bond is $200 more than you paid, that eventual profit will be added to your interest in calculating the yield to maturity.

Yield to maturity isn't easy to calculate yourself – it's computed according to a complicated formula – and it doesn't appear in all bond tables. Nevertheless, you should know a bond's yield to maturity before you make a decision to buy. Your broker can provide you with this information.

How Yield Fluctuates

Yield from a bond with an interest rate of 8%:	*Interest Payment*	*Yield*
If you buy it at **par — $1,000:**	$80.00	**8%**
If you buy it at a **discount** price of **$800:**	$80.00	**10%**
If you buy it at a **premium** price of **$1,200:**	$80.00	**6²/₃%**

The Language of Bonds

Newspaper announcements and articles about bonds can be hard to understand if you're not familiar with some common bond features and terminology.

Bills, Notes or Bonds ?

Bills, notes and bonds are all IOUs from either a government or corporation. They differ according to their maturity period – the length of time until they become due. ***Bills*** mature in 1 year or less, ***notes*** in 1–10 years, and ***bonds*** in over 10 years.

Municipalities and corporations only issue notes, bonds and debentures – never bills.

During times of volatile interest rates, investors often turn to Treasury bills with their short maturities, to avoid being locked into a rate for a long time.

What's a debenture...and what isn't?

Despite its technical sound, the term ***debenture*** (de•ben´cher) has a simple meaning. It refers to any bond which is backed only by the good credit of the organization issuing it. In other words, the issuer doesn't put up any specific assets to assure repayment of the loan. As a bond buyer, you rely on the issuer's ***full faith and credit*** as your only assurance of being paid the interest and principal on your loan.

This isn't as risky as it may seem. When issued by reliable institutions, debentures are usually relatively safe investments.

What is a subordinated bond?

Remember, buying a bond makes you a money lender to the organization. You are a creditor. When you buy a subordinated bond, it means that the organization will be obligated to pay its debts to some other creditors before paying you. Your rights are subordinated to the rights of some others.

The bonds with higher claims are called ***senior*** securities. Subordinated bond payments can be made only after the more senior obligations have been met.

What are asset-backed bonds?

Some bonds are backed by specific assets. The most common are ***mortgage-backed bonds***. For these, the issuer promises to mortgage property, if necessary, to repay the loan. Other kinds of bonds are backed by ***equipment*** or by collateral trusts – security holdings from other institutions.

What are floating-rate bonds?

Floating-rate bonds have periodically adjustable interest rates.

This announcement is under no circumstances to be construed as an offer to sell or as a solicitation of an of
The offering is made only by the Prospectus.

NEW ISSUE

$250,000,000

PENNZOIL COMPA

Debentures due April

Copies of the Prospectus may be ob
such of the undersigned or othe

Merrill Lynch Capital Mar
The First Boston Corpora
Salomon Brothers I

This is neither an offer to sell nor a solicitation of an offer to buy these securities.
The offer is made only by the Prospectus and the related Prospectus Supplement.

$200,000,000

ASSOCIATES CORPORATIO
OF NORTH AMERICA

Medium Term Senior Notes, Series
and
Medium Term Subordinated Notes, Se

New Issue

NZ$100,000,000

A Subsidiary of Transamerica Corporation

Transamerica Financial Corpo

Floating Rate New Zealand Dollar Notes Due 1991

Price 100%
(plus accrued interest, if any, from date of delivery)

Prudential-Bache Capital Funding
Bear, Stearns & Co. Inc.
Daiwa Securities America Inc.
Kidder, Peabody & Co.
Incorporated

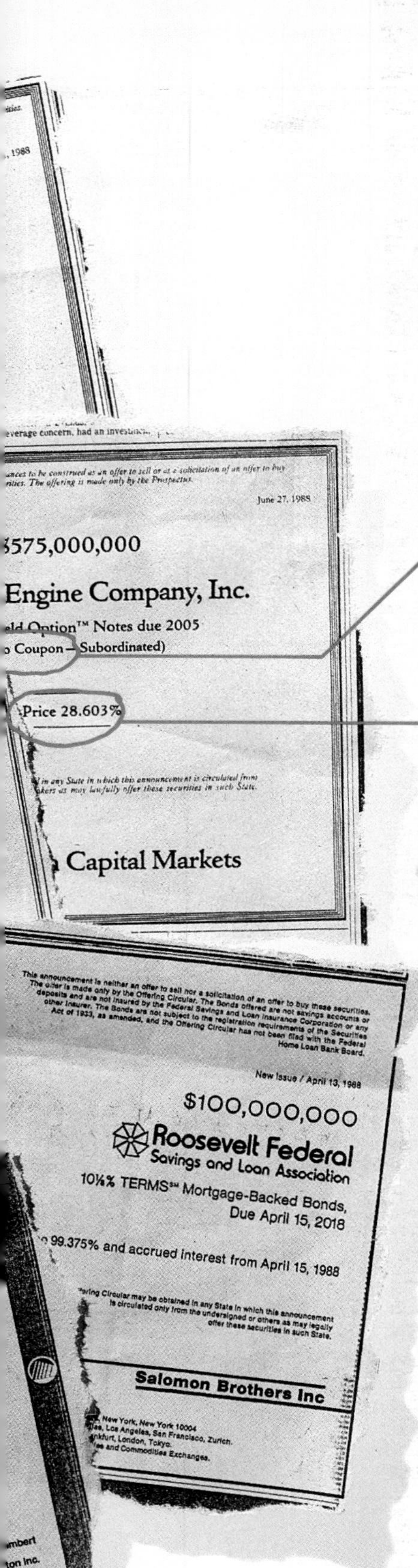

June 27, 1988

$575,000,000

Engine Company, Inc.

Option™ Notes due 2005

Coupon – Subordinated)

Price 28.603%

Capital Markets

This announcement is neither an offer to sell nor a solicitation of an offer to buy these securities. The offer is made only by the Offering Circular. The Bonds offered are not savings accounts or deposits and are not insured by the Federal Savings and Loan Insurance Corporation or any other insurer. The Bonds are not subject to the registration requirements of the Securities Act of 1933, as amended, and the Offering Circular has not been filed with the Federal Home Loan Bank Board.

New Issue / April 13, 1988

$100,000,000

Roosevelt Federal Savings and Loan Association

10⅛% TERMS℠ Mortgage-Backed Bonds, Due April 15, 2018

99.375% and accrued interest from April 15, 1988

Salomon Brothers Inc

What is a convertible bond?

When you buy a convertible bond, you receive interest payments for a while, but you also have the option to convert your bonds into company stock as repayment of the loan instead of cash. The terms of conversion – when you'll be allowed to make the conversion, and how much stock each bond can be exchanged for – are always specified at the time you buy the bond.

What is a zero-coupon bond?

Zero-coupon bonds are a relatively recent innovation – and an increasingly popular one. ***Coupon***, in bond jargon, means interest. Therefore, a zero-coupon bond is one that pays *no* interest while the loan is outstanding. Instead, interest ***accrues*** (builds up) and is paid all at once at maturity.

You buy zero-coupon bonds at prices far lower than par value, called ***deep discounts***. When the bond matures, you receive all the accrued interest plus your original investment, which together add up to the bond's par value.

This sounds great for the issuer, but not so great for you. So, why have zeroes become so popular?

Investors like to buy zeroes because they can buy more bonds for their money. And issuers like zeroes because they can keep and use their money longer than if they were required to make periodic interest payments. The one potential drawback, though, is that investors have to pay taxes on the interest they *would have received* had a periodic payment been made. The only exception is for purchasers of tax-free zeroes, such as municipal zero-coupon bonds.

What are callable bonds?

Many bonds come with a string attached: the issuer may ***call*** the bonds – pay off the debts – any time after a certain number of years. Issuers may want to call a bond if interest rates drop; then they can pay off the debt and issue new bonds at a lower rate. (It's the same idea as refinancing your house to get a lower interest rate and make lower monthly payments.) This process is called ***redemption*** – redeeming the bonds. If only some of the bonds of a specific issue are to be redeemed, those to be called are chosen by lottery.

You'll see announcements by issuers redeeming bonds in major newspapers like ***The Wall Street Journal***.

Often, the announcement will mention a ***sinking fund***. The sinking fund is a reserve of cash put aside by the issuer expressly for the purpose of redeeming some bonds periodically.

To protect bondholders counting on long-term steady income, call provisions usually specify that bonds can't be called until after a certain number of years, usually five or ten.

The World of Bonds

		Usual trading amount	Usual maturity period
	**Corporate Bonds** Corporate bonds have become increasingly important and prominent over the past decade because individuals have invested heavily in them. As of 1987, about 80% of all the money borrowed by corporations was accomplished through bond issues.	**$1000** (occasionally *baby bonds* issued at $100 or $500).	**Short-term: 1-5** yrs (some financial corporations). **Intermediate-term: 5-10** yrs (many banks). **Long-term:10-20** yrs (utilities and industrials).
	**Municipal Bonds** There are more than one million municipal bonds to choose from. This is many times more than the available corporate stock and bond issues, and the market is growing fast. Municipal bonds are issued by all political entities smaller than the federal government to finance all kinds of new construction, from schools to turnpikes.	**$5000** (brokers often ask for a multiple of this as a minimum investment).	**Varies** widely, from one month to thirty years. Usually includes *serial* maturities, meaning that a predetermined amount of interest as well as principal is repaid each year.
	**T-Bonds and T-Notes** These long-term debt issues of the Federal government are of paramount importance both to the government and to investors, who trade them actively and in tremendous volumes. Treasury securities are no longer issued as engraved certificates. They exist as bookkeeping entries in the records of the Treasury Department itself (through a system call ***Treasury Direct***) or in the records of commercial banks.	**$1000** (also issued in $5000; $10,000; $100,000; and $1 million amounts).	Bonds – **over 10** yrs Notes – **2-10** yrs
	**T-Bills** Treasury bills are the largest component of what is called the money market – the market for short-term debt securities. Not only are they valuable investments, they are a major tool of the Federal Reserve in controlling the money supply.	**$10,000** (also issued in amounts up to $1 million).	**3** months **6** months **1** year
	**Agency Bonds** The most popular and well-known of these are the bonds of mortgage associations, nicknamed **Ginnie Mae, Fannie Mae** and **Freddie Mac.** But many federal agencies also issue bonds to raise money.	**Varies** widely, from $1000 to $25,000 and up.	**Varies** widely, from 30 days to 20 years.

How traded	Rated	Tax exemptions for interest	Call provisions	General investment characteristics
By brokers, either on an exchange or OTC.	By all major rating services.	None.	Often included.	**More risky** than government bonds; but very little risk with highly rated bonds. **Higher yields** than government bonds. **Bought in large quantities** (often, round lots of $100,000).
Entirely by brokers, OTC. Often, investment bankers underwrite whole issues, buying in bulk and reselling to dealers.	Yes, by major services.	Exempt from federal taxes In some cases, exempt from all taxes.	Sometimes callable.	**Lower interest rates** than comparable corporate bonds, **because of tax-exemption.** Especially attractive to high tax-bracket investors, who benefit from tax-exemption feature.
New issues: at any Federal Reserve Bank, through auction system. **Outstanding issues:** active OTC market handled by securities dealers.	Not rated, since considered risk-free.	Exempt from state and local taxes.	Usually not callable.	Highly **liquid**; active secondary market. **Maximum safety** of principal, since backed by Federal government itself. Relatively **low** rate of **return.**
New issues: auction at any Federal Reserve Bank . **Outstanding issues:** active OTC market handled by securities dealers.	Not rated, since considered risk free.	Exempt from state and local taxes.	Not callable.	Excellent **short-term** *parking places* for cash. No periodic interest payments. Instead, interest consists of the difference between a discounted buying price and the par amount paid at maturity. Sold in **high denominations**, thus less accessible to small investors unless as part of a fund.
By brokers, OTC; or bought and sold directly by investors, through banks.	Some issues rated by some services.	**Ginnie Mae, Fannie Mae, Freddie Mac:** fully taxable interest **Other agencies**: interest exempt from state and local taxes.	Not callable.	Marginally **higher risk and higher interest** than Treasury issued government bonds.

How Do Bonds Rate?

Rating services inform investors about the risks involved in buying the bonds of a particular issuer.

How can you measure risk?

When you buy a bond, how can you be sure you'll be paid the interest and principal? What's the chance that the issuer will fail to repay you?

Most bond buyers turn to ratings services for the answers. The best known are ***Standard & Poor's*** and ***Moody's***. These companies measure the financial stability of the issuer rather than the market attractiveness of the bond. Their sole concern is to inform investors about the risks involved in buying the bonds of a particular issuer.

It might seem that bonds backed by mortgages or equipment are safer investments than ***debentures*** (bonds backed only by the borrower's good word). A major factor investors consider, however, is the rating a bond receives from the ratings services. A debenture issued by a highly rated institution may, in fact, be less risky than a mortgage-backed bond issued by a low-rated organization – simply because the likelihood for repayment may be better.

Why are ratings important?

Aside from indicating an issuer's ability to repay your loan, a credit rating will influence the yield on a new bond issue.

In general, the higher a bond's rating, the lower its interest rates will tend to be. Issuers of higher-rated bonds don't need to offer high interest rates; their credibility will attract investors. But issuers of lower-rated bonds will offer higher rates to induce investors to take the potentially greater risk.

What are Junk Bonds?

Junk bonds are corporate bonds with low-grade investment ratings – meaning a greater than average likelihood that the issuer will fail to repay its debt – or no ratings at all. The highly-publicized mergers and takeovers of the 1980s inundated the market with junk bond issues: corporations wishing to take over another company would sell junk bonds to the public and, with the cash they raised, buy up the shares of the other company.

Moody's and Standard & Poor's Rating Codes

These rating systems are similar, although not identical. The chart is a key to reading the ratings:

Moody's	***S & P's***	***Meaning***
Aaa	**AAA**	Bonds of the best quality, offering the smallest degree of investment risk. Issuers are exceptionally stable and dependable.
Aa	**AA**	Bonds of high quality by all standards. Slightly higher degree of long-term investment risk.
A	**A**	Bonds with many favorable investment attributes.
Baa	**BBB**	Bonds of medium-grade quality. Security appears adequate at present but may appear unreliable over the long term.
Ba	**BB**	Bonds with speculative element. Moderate security of payments; not well safeguarded.
B	**B**	Cannot be considered a desirable investment. Small long-term assurance of payments.
Caa	**CCC**	Bonds of poor standing. Issuers may be in default or in danger of default.
Ca	**CC**	Bonds of highly speculative quality; often in default.
C	**C**	Lowest rated class of bonds. Very poor prospects of ever attaining investment standing.
–	**D**	In default.

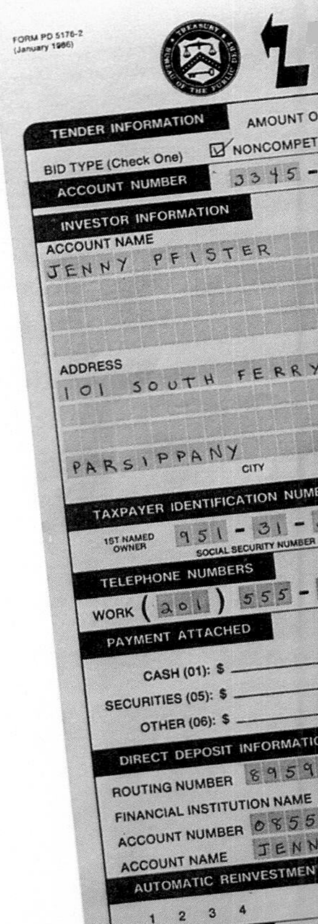

FORM PD 5176-2
(January 1986)

TENDER INFORMATION
AMOUNT OF
BID TYPE (Check One) ☑ NONCOMPETI
ACCOUNT NUMBER 3345 -
INVESTOR INFORMATION
ACCOUNT NAME
JENNY PFISTER
ADDRESS
101 SOUTH FERRY
PARSIPPANY
CITY
TAXPAYER IDENTIFICATION NUMB
1ST NAMED OWNER 951 - 31 -
SOCIAL SECURITY NUMBER
TELEPHONE NUMBERS
WORK (201) 555 -
PAYMENT ATTACHED
CASH (01): $
SECURITIES (05): $
OTHER (06): $
DIRECT DEPOSIT INFORMATIO
ROUTING NUMBER 8959
FINANCIAL INSTITUTION NAME
ACCOUNT NUMBER 0855
ACCOUNT NAME JENN
AUTOMATIC REINVESTMEN
1 2 3 4
AUTHORIZATION

You can buy bonds through your broker. Many US Government bonds, though, can be bought directly through banks. Commissions vary widely, so it pays to shop around.

Where do brokers buy bonds for their clients?

Mostly, already-issued bonds are traded ***over the counter*** (OTC) – a term that today really means ***over the phone***. Dealers of bonds across the country are connected via electronic display terminals that give them the latest information on bond prices. A broker buying a bond consults a terminal to find out which dealer is currently offering the best price, then calls that dealer to negotiate.

The New York Stock Exchange and American Stock Exchange, despite their names, also list a large number of bonds. Their ***Bond Rooms*** are the scene of the same kind of brisk auction-style trading that occurs on the stock trading floor.

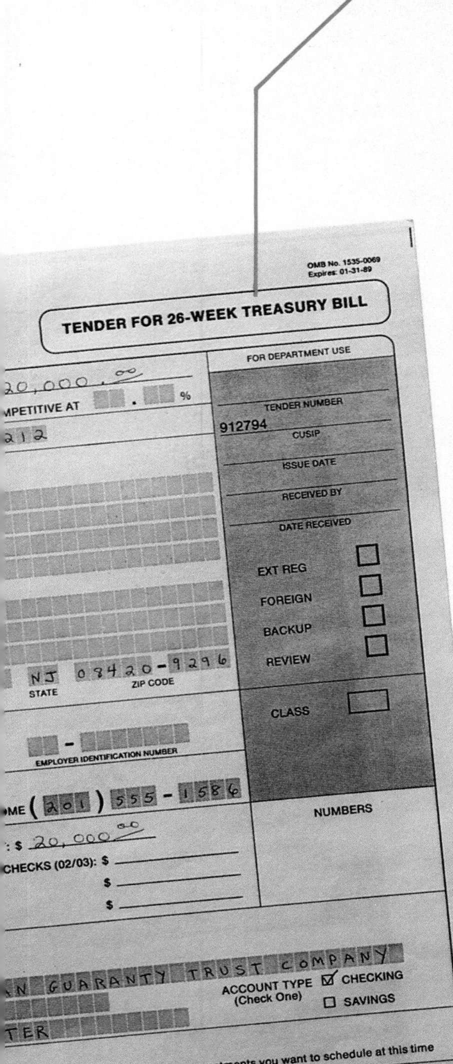

OMB No. 1535-0069
Expires: 01-31-89

TENDER FOR 26-WEEK TREASURY BILL

FOR DEPARTMENT USE

20,000.00

MPETITIVE AT . %

TENDER NUMBER

912794

212

CUSIP

ISSUE DATE

RECEIVED BY

DATE RECEIVED

EXT REG ☐

FOREIGN ☐

BACKUP ☐

REVIEW ☐

NJ 08420-9296

STATE ZIP CODE

CLASS ☐

EMPLOYER IDENTIFICATION NUMBER

ME (201) 555-1586

NUMBERS

: $ 20,000.00

CHECKS (02/03): $

$

$

N GUARANTY TRUST COMPANY

ACCOUNT TYPE (Check One) ☑ CHECKING ☐ SAVINGS

TER

e number of sequential 26-week reinvestments you want to schedule at this time

the Privacy and Paperwork Reduction Acts, see the accompanying instructions.

o the provisions of Department of the Treasury Circulars, Public Debt Series Nos. 1-86 and 2-86 and the by the Department of the Treasury.

ertify that the number shown on this form is my correct taxpayer identification number and that I am not g because (1) I have not been notified that I am subject to backup withholding as a result of a failure to , or (2) the Internal Revenue Service has notified me that I am no longer subject to backup withholding. I nformation provided on this form is true, correct and complete.

7/12/88
DATE

The Treasury Bill (T-Bill) Auction Process

1. Jenny has $20,000 to invest. She wants a safe, short-term instrument, and chooses T-bills. Instead of paying a broker's commission, she decides to buy the bills herself, directly from the government.

2. The US Treasury offers 26-week Treasury bills for sale every Monday. On Monday, March 23rd, it will sell $13 billion worth of the bills.

3. At her local bank, Jenny receives the form for submitting ***a tender*** (an offer) to buy 26-week Treasury bills. She fills out the form, stipulating that she wants two bills. Every Treasury bill has a par value of $10,000, so she includes a check for $20,000.

4. Across the country, institutional investors (pension funds, mutual funds, etc.) want to buy T-bills at next Monday's auction. Planning to buy at least $500,000 worth, they're entitled to participate in the auction as competitive bidders. Their bids must arrive by 1:00 pm Monday, the auction deadline, and state how much less than $10,000 they'd be willing to pay for each T-bill. (All T-bills are sold at less than par and then redeemed at par. Unlike most bond transactions, the difference between price paid and par is interest, not capital gain.) ABC, Inc. offers to pay $9800 per bill; XYZ, Inc. bids $9900; and PDQ, Inc. comes in at $9600.

5. All tenders, competitive and non-competitive, received by the Federal Reserve before the deadline are forwarded to the Treasury Department in Washington.

6. The Treasury accepts bids beginning with those closest to $10,000 until its quota is filled. This raises the most revenue possible from the auction with the least possible debt.

7. On Monday afternoon, the Treasury announces that its cut-off point was $9,800. News services report the information that afternoon, and some bidders learn that they've bought T-bills, while others learn they've asked to pay too little and have been denied.

8. The Treasury takes the average accepted bid and informs all non-competitive bidders, like Jenny, that this average, $9,850, is their price for the T-bills. It refunds Jenny the extra $300 ($150 x 2 T-bills) she sent in.

9. Six months later, when Jenny's T-bills come due, she receives a check for $20,000 from the Treasury. The $300 is the interest she's earned, which translates into a 3% annual return.

Keeping Tabs on Corporate Bonds

Both the New York Stock Exchange and the American Stock Exchange list a large number of corporate bonds for trading. Quotes for these bonds are listed in daily tables in* The Wall Street Journal. *The table below is for the New York Exchange. Tables for the American Exchange are read the same way.

The ***name*** shows the company or organization issuing the bond. These abbreviations can differ from the abbreviations for the same companies in the stock tables. Some are easily guessed (Gdyr for Goodyear, for instance) or even fully spelled-out (Exxon and Hills); you may need a key to help you decipher others.

The last two digits show the year in which the bond's principal will be paid off, or ***mature.*** It's understood that the first two digits are either 19 or 20. For example, Gulf Resources' 10⅞ bond will come due in 1997; their 12½ bond, not until 2004.

+ 2 − 5	Bonds	Cur Yld	Vol	Close	Net Chg.	Bonds
− ¾	DukeP 9½05	9.8	45	96⅞	− ⅝	Gdyr 7.35s97
+ ¼	DukeP 8⅜06	9.6	23	87⅜	+ ⅜	Grace 4¼90
− 1	DukeP 8⅛07	9.6	14	84⅜	− ¾	GrnTr dc8¼95
+ 1⅛	DukeP 10⅛09	10.1	191	100	− 1	Greyh 6½90
− 1¾	EKod 8⅝16	10.3	365	84	− ¾	GreyF 16⅛92
+ ½	Enron 10¾98	10.7	5	100½	− 1½	GreyF zr94
+ ⅛	Ens 10s01	cv	33	103	− 1	GroIr 13⅝03
+ ¼	EnvSys 6¾11	cv	10	69¼	− ¼	GrowGp 12½9
− ⅛	Equitc 10s04	cv	22	72¼	− ½	GrowGp 8½06
− ⅝	EssxC 6s12	cv	25	74½	− ½	Grumn 9¼09
...	Exxon 6s97	7.6	98	79¼	− ¾	GlfWn 7s03A
...	Exxon 6½98	8.0	40	81⅝	+ ¼	GlfWn 7s03B
− 1	Exxon 6½89	6.6	13	98⅝	− ⅛	GlfRes 10⅞97
− 1½	ExxP 6⅝98	7.4	21	90⅛	+ ⅜	GlfRes 12½04
− ½	FMC 7½01	9.3	11	80¼	...	Harns dc12s04
+ ¾	Frch 9¾98	11.5	6	85	+ 1⅞	Hills 8¾02
				87¾	...	Holidy 10½94
						Holidy 11s99

This is the set ***interest rate*** for this bond issue. Many companies, of course, have bonds outstanding from a number of bond issues, floated at different times and with different rates. See for example DukeP (Duke Power) with bonds from four different issues quoted.

Bond interest always refers to a percentage of ***par value***, which is the amount the issuer will repay the bondholder when the bond comes due. The par value of most corporate bonds is $1000. Thus, for EnvSys (Environmental Systems) the interest rate of 6¾% means 6.75% of $1000, or $67.50. The interest payment for this bond will always be $67.50 per year.

The ***s*** which sometimes appears after the interest rate is not a meaningful symbol. It's used simply to separate the interest rate figures from the following figures; usually, it appears when the interest rate doesn't include a fraction and may be confused with the numbers following (see, for example, its use after Exxon's interest rate of 6%).

The ***yield*** is critical, since it describes the bond's current value. For example, the yield for the Exxon 6% bond listed here is 7.6%. You can read this as follows: *Your interest payments will be 7.6% of what you'll pay for the bond today.*

You can see that some yield figures are higher than the bond's interest rate, while others are lower. Enron's yield of 10.7% is slightly lower than its interest rate of 10¾%; the yield of Exxon's bond, listed as 7.6%, is higher than its interest rate of 6%.

Net change represents the difference between the closing price of the previous trading day and the closing price of the day before that. It appears as a fraction and always refers to a fraction of ***par value***. For example, Goodyear was ***up 5/8 point***, which means the closing price given here is 5/8% of par value greater than the closing price given the previous day. Since par is $1000, you know that the closing price shown here is $6.25 (5/8% of 1000) more than the last closing price. This closing price is given as 86 5/8, or $866.25; therefore, the last closing price must have been $860.

Net price changes almost always reflect interest rate changes. If bond prices are down from the previous day – as are the majority shown here – you can guess that interest rates rose. When most bond prices are up, you know that interest rates fell.

Vol	Close	Net Chg.
20	86 5/8	+ 5/8
2	101	...
100	84 1/2	− 1/8
5	144 1/2	− 22 1/8
10	106 3/8	+ 1 3/8
7	50 1/4	− 3/4
3	101 1/2	+ 7/8
5	98 5/8	+ 1/8
56	97 1/2	− 4 1/2
31	101	...
185	75	− 1/8
1	75 1/2	...
10	92 1/2	...
2	96 1/2	...
1	100 3/8	+ 7/8
10	97	...
137	97 5/8	− 1/4
64	93 7/8	
60	78 3/[illegible]	

Bonds	Cur Yld	Vol	Close	Net Chg.
Maxxm 13 5/8 92	15.1	35	90 1/8	− 3/8
McCro 6 1/2 92	cv	2	62	...
McCro 7 1/2 94N	12.4	5	60 1/2	...
McDInv 8s11	cv	10	82	+ 1
McDnl zr94	...	40	59 5/8	− 1/8
McKes 9 3/4 06	cv	7	146 1/2	...
Mead 6s12	cv	10	91 1/2	− 1/2
Melln 6 3/4 89t	6.8	5	99 1/2	...
Melln 8.6s09	10.7	27	80 1/8	− 3 1/4
Melln 7 1/4 99	8.6	1	84	...
MerLy zr06	...	729	23 3/4	...
MerLy zr91	...	25	74 1/2	...
MesaCap 12s96	12.1	60	99 1/2	− 1/2
MichB 7 3/4 11	9.9	10	78 5/8	− 1 7/8
MichB 9.6s08	9.9	10	97 1/4	− 3/4
MichB 9 1/8 18	10.0	50	91	− 3/8
MKT 5 1/2 33f	...	10	63	...
MPac 4 1/4 05	7.9	7	54	...
[illegible]	...	41	48 7/8	...
	...	11	48 7/8	...
	...	45	49 7/8	− 1/8
				1/4

Bond ***volumes*** are not isted in terms of number of ssues sold, but in terms of dollar worth. The volume figure ells you how many thousands of dollars were traded the previous day. You can read he figure by adding three zeroes. Thus, $10,000 worth of Hills bonds were traded the previous day – small in comparison with the Holiday 10 1/2% issue, which saw $1,137,000 worth of bonds raded.

zr appearing instead of an interest-rate figure means that this bond is a zero-coupon bond. Since zero coupons pay no periodic interest, allowing the interest to accrue until maturity, no figure is given here.

Municipal Bonds

There are hundreds of thousands of* muni's *issued.* The Wall Street Journal *quotes prices for only some large, representative bonds.

Coupon rate is the interest rate. It is given as a percentage of par value. Thus, the bond issued by the Lower Colorado River Authority of Texas, with its interest rate of 7%, offers an annual interest payment of 7% of $1,000, or $70.

Maturity date is the date the bond will be paid off and retired. This Lower Colorado bond will come due on January 1, 2009. You can see that muni's are often long-term bonds; all those listed here have maturities in the 21st century.

Yield represents the yield to maturity. Lower Colorado's 8.19% yield to maturity is on the high side of the bonds quoted here.

TAX-EXEMPT BONDS

Monday, June 13, 1988

Here are representative current prices for several active tax-exempt revenue and refunding bonds, based on large institutional trades. Changes are rounded to the nearest one-eighth. Yield is to maturity.

Issue	Coupon	Mat.	Price	Chg.	Bid Yld.
Baltimore Co Md Ser 88	7.750	07-01-16	100 1/8	+ 1/8	7.74
Bergen Co Utl/NJ waste	7.750	03-15-13	99	+ 1/8	7.84
Cal Pub Works Board	6.625	09-01-09	87	+ 1/4	7.88
Calif Pub Cap Fin Imp	8.100	03-01-18	101 1/8	+ 1/8	8.00
Chgo Ill. Air Rev Ser A	8.200	01-01-18	98 1/8	+ 1/2	8.37
Ga. Muni Elec Auth	7.800	01-01-20	98 1/8	+ 1/4	7.96
Ga. Muni Elec Auth Ref	8.125	01-01-17	99	+ 1/4	8.22
Grand Rv Dam Auth Okla	7.000	06-01-06	88 1/2	+ 1/4	8.22
Grand Rvr Dam Auth Okla	7.000	06-01-10	87 1/8	+ 1/8	8.27
Harris Co. Tex	8.125	08-15-17	96 1/2	+ 1/4	8.44
Hillsborough Co Fla Wtr	8.300	08-01-16	100 1/2	+ 1/4	8.25
Intrmtn Pwr Agcy Utah	7.000	07-01-15	89	+ 1/8	8.00
L.A. Cnty Hlth Fac Cal.	7.500	03-01-08	95 1/8	+ 3/8	7.98
L.A. Dept Wtr & Pwr El.	7.900	05-01-28	100 1/8	+ 1/4	7.89
L.A. Harbor Dept Calif.	7.600	10-01-18	96 3/4	+ 1/8	7.88
Los Ang Co Transp Comm	8.000	07-01-18	100 [illegible]	+ [illegible]	[illegible]
Lower Colo Riv Auth Tex	7.000	01-01-09	88 1/8	+ 1/4	8.19
Mass Industrial Fin Agy	8.125	10-01-17	99 1/4	+ 1/4	8.19
Md. Hlth & Higher Ed.	7.500	07-01-20	96 1/2	+ 1/4	7.80
Metro Wash Airprts Auth	8.200	10-01-18	100 7/8	+ 1/4	8.12
N Carolina Eastrn Muni	8.000	01-01-21	97 1/4	+ 3/8	8.24
[illegible]arolina MPA #1	7.625	01-01-14	96 1/4	+ 3/8	7.97
[illegible]lina MPA #1	7.875	01-01-19	97	+ 1/2	8.15
[illegible]i Pwr Agcy	7.250	01-01-21	88 3/8	+ 3/8	8.29
[illegible]	6.750	07-01-06	88 1/4	+ 1/8	7.98
[illegible]	[illegible]000	07-01-07	89 5/8	+ 1/8	7.96
[illegible]	[illegible]0	06-15-18	98 1/2	+ 1/8	7.94
[illegible]	[illegible]	[illegible]1-17	100 1/4	+ 1/4	8.10
[illegible]	[illegible]	[illegible]	[illegible]6 3/4	+ 1/8	8.3
[illegible]	[illegible]	[illegible]	[illegible]	+ 1/8	8.08
[illegible]	[illegible]	[illegible]	[illegible]	[illegible]	7.86

Price is given as a percent of par. Thus, the Lower Colorado bond closed at 88 1/8% of $1,000, or $881.25.

Change from the previous day's closing price is quoted as a percent of par value, just as with corporate bonds. Lower Colorado's price was 1/4th of a point (in percentage terms, .25%) more than the previous quoted price. You can calculate this as follows: .25% of $1,000 is $2.50.

Each week **The Wall Street Journal** *offers information on an index of some 500 municipal bonds.*

During the past week, the average yield of muncipal bonds rose .02% from 8.13% to 8.15%.

Figures are then broken down for two categories of municipal bonds, ***revenue bonds*** (backed only by revenues from the specific project being financed) and ***general obligation bonds*** (backed by the general credit of the issuing organization). As you can see, the average yields of the revenue bonds are higher than those of general obligation bonds. This is because revenue bonds, being less securely backed, involve somewhat more risk and, therefore, higher yields as compensation.

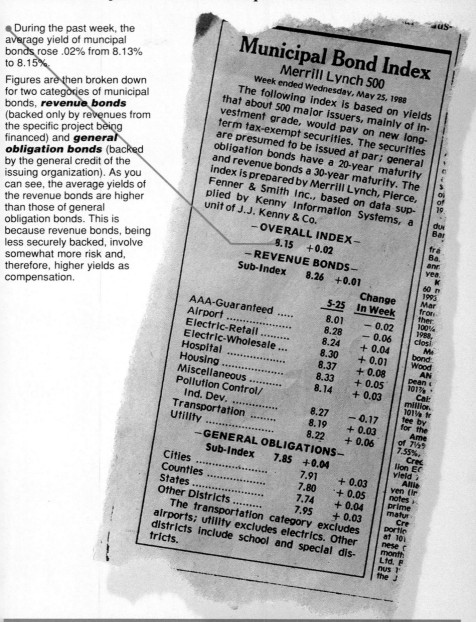

Municipal Bond Index

Merrill Lynch 500

Week ended Wednesday, May 25, 1988

The following index is based on yields that about 500 major issuers, mainly of investment grade, would pay on new long-term tax-exempt securities. The securities are presumed to be issued at par; general obligation bonds have a 20-year maturity and revenue bonds a 30-year maturity. The index is prepared by Merrill Lynch, Pierce, Fenner & Smith Inc., based on data supplied by Kenny Information Systems, a unit of J.J. Kenny & Co.

—OVERALL INDEX—

8.15 +0.02

—REVENUE BONDS—

Sub-Index 8.26 +0.01

	5-25	Change In Week
AAA-Guaranteed	8.01	− 0.02
Airport	8.28	− 0.06
Electric-Retail	8.24	+ 0.04
Electric-Wholesale ...	8.30	+ 0.01
Hospital	8.37	+ 0.08
Housing	8.33	+ 0.05
Miscellaneous	8.14	+ 0.03
Pollution Control/ Ind. Dev.	8.27	− 0.17
Transportation	8.19	+ 0.03
Utility	8.22	+ 0.06

—GENERAL OBLIGATIONS—

Sub-Index 7.85 +0.04

Cities	7.91	+ 0.03
Counties	7.80	+ 0.05
States	7.74	+ 0.04
Other Districts	7.95	+ 0.03

The transportation category excludes airports; utility excludes electrics. Other districts include school and special districts.

The Top Ten Money-Raising States

The states with the largest populations raised the most money from long-term bonds in 1987.

1.	California	$11,779,200,000
2.	New York	10,308,200,000
3.	Texas	8,673,000,000
4.	Florida	5,367,200,000
5.	Pennsylvania	4,603,800,000
6.	Illinois	4,368,000,000
7.	Louisiana	4,062,300,000
8.	New Jersey	3,601,000,000
9.	Ohio	2,906,700,000
10.	Georgia	2,897,900,000

Industrial states were the most frequent issuers of long-term bonds in 1987.

		bonds issued
1.	California	548
2.	Texas	503
3.	Minnesota	479
4.	Illinois	380
5.	Michigan	369
6.	Pennsylvania	330
7.	New York	298
8.	New Jersey	243
9.	Wisconsin	227
10.	Ohio	220

T-Bonds, T-Notes. . .

Treasuries are the most prominent – and most highly regarded – of all the bonds. In fact, in times of economic trouble, owning Treasuries is considered almost as safe as holding cash in your hand.

Bonds and Notes are presented in one table in ***The Wall Street Journal***. They are listed in order of their maturity date.

● ***Interest rate*** is the percentage of par value paid as annual interest. An ***s*** after the rate is not a symbol; it simply refers to the way the numerical words are spoken, as in *ten and three-fourths percent.*

● ***Bid and asked prices*** for Treasury issues are quoted as *bid* and *asked* instead of high, low and closing, as with corporate bonds traded on exchanges. Treasury issues are traded over-the-counter, in thousands of private, one-on-one telephone transactions. So it's not possible to determine the exact prices of the last transactions. The best information available for these issues is the highest price being ***bid*** (offered) by buyers, and the lowest price being ***asked*** by bond sellers, at mid-afternoon of the trading day.

Note that the decimals in these figures refer to 32nds, not 100ths, because bonds trade in increments of 32nds. For example, the first bond quoted here gives a bid price of 100.2. This means the highest price bid was $100+2/32$nds % of par. You can calculate this as follows: If par is $1000, 100% of this is $1,000. Now for the fraction: $2/32$% of $1,000 is $62\frac{1}{2}$ cents. Add the two figures together (dropping the $1/2$ cent) to arrive at $1,000.62 – the highest price bid. The asked price was $1,001.87: $1,000 plus $6/32$% of $1,000 or $1.87.

* * *

TREASURY BON

Wednesday, April 6, 1988

Representative Over-the-Counter quotations based on transactions of $1 million or more as of 4 p.m. Eastern time.

Decimals in bid-and-asked and bid changes represent 32nds; 101.1 means 101 1/32. a-Plus 1/64. b-Yield to call date. d-Minus 1/64. k-Nonresident aliens exempt from withholding taxes. n-Treasury notes. p-Treasury note; nonresident aliens exempt from withholding taxes.

Source: Bloomberg Financial Markets

Treasury Bonds and Notes

Rate	Mat. Date		Bid	Asked	Bid Chg.	Yld.
13¼	1988	Apr n.	100.2	100.6	– .1	4.39
6⅝	1988	Apr p.	99.29	100	.1	6.44
8¼	1988	May n.	100.3	100.6	....	6.24
7⅛	1988	May p.	100.1	100.4	– .1	6.12
9⅞	1988	May n.	100.8	100.11	– .1	6.31
10	1988	May p.	100.9	100.12	– .1	6.14
7	1988	Jun p.	100.3	100.6	+ .1	6.06
13⅝	1988	Jun n.	101.17	101.20	....	6.25
6⅝	1988	Jul p.	99.30	100.1	....	6.45
4	1988	Jul n.	101.31	102.2	....	6.10
	1988	Aug p.	99.24	99.27	....	6.49
	[illegible]	Aug p.	100.30	101.1	– .1	6.46
			101.9	[illegible]		[illegible]

Rate	Mat. Date	
7⅛	1989	Apr p.
14⅜	1989	Apr n.
6⅞	1989	May p.
9¼	1989	May n.
8	1989	May n.
11¾	1989	May n.
7⅜	1989	Jun p.
9⅝	1989	Jun p.
7⅝	1989	Jul p.
14½	1989	Jul n.
7¾	1989	Aug p.
6⅝	1989	Aug p.
13⅞	1989	Aug n.
8½	1989	Sep k.
9⅜	1989	Sep p.
11⅞	1989	Oct n.
7⅞	1989	Oct p.
6⅜	1989	Nov p.
10¾	1989	Nov n.
12¾	1989	Nov p
7¾	1989	Nov p
7⅞	1989	Dec p
8⅜	1989	Dec
7⅜	1990	Jan
10½	1990	Jan
	1990	Feb.

● ***Maturity date*** is the year and then month the bond or note will be paid off and retired.

● A ***p*** signifies a note exempt from withholding tax for foreign bondholders; ***n*** is a note without this qualification.

This distinction is made differently for T-bonds. A ***k*** after the maturity date signifies a bond exempt from withholding tax for foreign owners; no notation means a bond without this qualification.

● ***Bid change*** represents the percent of change between the bid price given here and the bid price given in the table of the day before. Decimals represent 32nds instead of 100ths. For example, the bid price of 100.2 ($100^2/32$nds) is .1 lower ($1/32$nd lower) than the bid price quoted the day before. The bid price quoted the day before, therefore, must have been 100.3.

● ***Yield*** *(to maturity)* shows the long-term value of the bond. Too complicated to calculate yourself, this figure takes into account both current yield and the difference between the price you pay and the sum you'll be paid back at maturity.

Notice that, in general, the yield increases as the maturity date is farther away. This is because bondholders demand a higher yield to compensate for tying up their money for longer periods.

Treasury bill quotes are presented in a separate section of the table. As with notes and bonds, the maturity date is given first. All the maturity dates here are within the same year, since T-bills are short-term securities.

NOTES & BILLS

Bid	Asked	Bid Chg.	Yld.
99.27	99.31	....	7.15
106.30	107.2	– .3	7.08
99.18	99.22	– .1	7.16
102.9	102.15	– .2	6.88
100.26	100.30	+ .1	7.12
104.23	104.27	....	7.10
100.4	100.8	+ .2	7.15
102.20	102.24	– .1	7.23
100.11	100.15	....	7.23
108.19	108.23	+ .1	7.18
100.16	100.20	....	7.26
99.3	99.7	....	7.23
108.8	108.12	....	7.26
101.15	101.19	....	7.34
102.23	102.27	....	7.31
106.9	106.13	....	7.35
100.21	100.25	+ .1	7.33
98.13	98.17	+ .1	7.36
104.30	105.2	+ .2	7.34
107.31	108.3	+ .1	7.30
100.14	100.18	+ .1	7.37
100.17	100.21	+ .1	7.45
101.9	101.13	....	7.48
[illegible]	[illegible]	[illegible]	7.44
[illegible]	[illegible]	[illegible]	[illegible]48

Rate	Mat. Date		Bid	Asked	Bid Chg.	Yld.
10 3/8	2007-12	Nov	112.21	112.27	+ 1	8.97
12	2008-13	Aug	128	128.6	+1.3	8.96
13 1/4	2009-14	May	139.30	140.4	+1.5	8.98
12 1/2	2009-14	Aug k	133.11	133.17	+1.4	8.95
11 3/4	2009-14	Nov k	126.21	126.27	+1.6	8.92
11 1/4	2015	Feb k	124.16	124.22	+1.4	8.83
10 5/8	2015	Aug k	118.15	118.21	+1.3	8.81
9 7/8	2015	Nov	110.17	110.23	+1.1	8.83
9 1/4	2016	Feb k	104.6	104.12	+ .28	8.82
7 1/4	2016	May k	83.18	83.24	+ .23	8.82
7 1/2	2016	Nov k	86.6	86.12	+ .25	8.81
8 3/4	2017	May k	99.7	99.13	+ .28	8.81
8 7/8	2017	Aug k	100.28	101.2	+ .27	8.77

U.S. Treas. Bills

Mat. date	Bid (Discount)	Asked (Discount)	Yield
-1988-			
4-14	6.00	5.88	5.97
4-21	6.52	6.40	6.5[illegible]
4-28	5.09	4.97	5.05
5- 5	5.83	5.76	5.87
5-12	6.02	5.95	6.07
5-19	5.96	5.89	6.01
[illegible]	5.89	5.82	5.95
[illegible]	5.94	5.87	6.01
[illegible]	[illegible]	[illegible]	[illegible] 07

Mat. date	Bid (Discount)	Asked (Discount)	Yield
-1988-			
8- 4	6.13	6.06	6.27
8-11	6.02	5.95	6.16
8-18	6.05	5.98	6.20
8-25	6.01	5.94	6.16
9- 1	6.13	6.06	6.30
[illegible]- 8	6.20	6.13	6.38
[illegible]-15	6.19	6.12	6.38
[illegible]-22	6.22	6.15	6.42
[illegible]-29	6.26	6.19	6.47
1[illegible]	6.17	6.1[illegible]	[illegible]

Bid and asked prices are presented differently for T-bills than for T-bonds and T-notes. That's because T-bills do not pay regular interest payments. Instead, they're sold at a ***discount***, a price lower than par value. At maturity, the T-bill holder is paid back full par value. The difference between the discount price paid and the par value received constitutes the interest. For example, if you pay $9,500 for a $10,000 T-bill, you're paying 5% less than you'll be paid back.

Dealers trade in T-bills by bidding and asking ***discount percents***. For example, for the first bill quoted here, the highest bid offered was 6.00% – meaning someone has offered to buy this bill at a 6% discount – in other words, to pay 94% of par value for the bill. Since par value for T-bills is usually $10,000, this was an offer to pay $9,400.00 for the bill (put another way, an offer to make $600.00 on the bill). The lowest price asked was for a discount of 5.88%. This is the same as asking for a price of 94.12% of par, or $9,412.00.

Yield represents yield to maturity; just as with T-bonds and T-notes, it tells you the comparative value of the issue.

Federal Agency Bonds

Federal agencies have many bond issues outstanding, each one with a different interest rate and maturity date.

Some of these bonds are actually issued by government-sponsored enterprises. These agencies were originally owned by the Treasury, but now are publicly owned. The government doesn't guarantee repayment, although the bonds are issued under the Treasury's supervision.

FHL Federal Home Loan Mortgage Corporation (Freddie Mac)

FHLB Federal Home Loan Bank

FNMA Federal National Mortgage Association (Fannie Mae)

FLB Federal Land Bank

The other agency bond issuers are actually federal agencies whose debts are US Government guaranteed.

FHA Federal Housing Administration

FHDA Farmers Home Administration

GNMA Government National Mortgage Association (Ginnie Mae)

SLMA Student Loan Marketing Administration (Sallie Mae)

TVA Tennessee Valley Authority

Export-Import Bank

Federal Farm Credit Bank

Maritime Administrations

What kinds of mortgage-related bonds are there?

Mortgage-backed bonds are issued by mortgage lending institutions, which use the money raised for a variety of purposes.

Mortgage pool pass-through issues are shares in pools of mortgages which have been sold by the lending institutions to a trustee, who repackages them and sells shares. If you own this kind of issue you will receive payments consisting of both interest and return of principal, since that is the way mortgages are paid off. The mortgage payments made by homeowners are *passed through* to you, the behind-the-scenes lender.

GOVERNMENT AGENCY ISSUES

Wednesday, April 6, 1988

Mid-afternoon Over-the-Counter quotations usually on large transactions, sometimes $1 million or more. Decimals in bid-and-asked represent 32nds; 101.1 means 101 1/32. a-Plus 1/64. b-Yield to call date. d-Minus 1/64. Source: Bloomberg Financial Markets

FNMA Issues

Rate	Mat	Bid	Asked	Yld
10.45	4-88	100	100.3	[illegible].91
10.50	5-88	100.9	100.12	6.12
10.50	6-88	100.18	100.22	6.31
9.40	8-88	100.25	100.29	6.59
16.38	8-88	103.1	103.8	6.48
8.55	9-88	100.18	100.24	6.72
13.20	9-88	102.15	102.19	6.93
9.50	10-88	101.7	101.10	6.83
[illegible]	10-88	102.22	102.28	6.89

Fed. Home Loan Bank

Rate	Mat	Bid	Asked	Yld
10.15	4-88	100.3	100.6	6.11
10.38	4-88	100.2	100.6	6.32
7.38	5-88	100	100.3	6.49
10.15	5-88	100.11	100.15	6.37
7.25	6-88	100.1	100.4	6.55
8.80	6-88	100.13	100.16	6.36
10.80	6-88	100.24	[illegible]	[illegible]
9.15	7-88	[illegible]		
6.90	7-88	[illegible]		
[illegible]	8-88			

Federal Farm Credit

Rate	Mat	Bid	Asked	Yld
10.25	4-88	100.2	100.5	5.65
12.65	4-88	100.4	100.8	5.40
6.75	5-88	99.30	100.1	6.22
7.38	5-88	99.31	100.2	6.27
6.45	6-88	99.29	100	6.41
7.20	6-88	100	100.3	6.41
8.00	6-88	100.4	100.7	6.35
6.70	7-88	99.30	100.1	6.56
7.60	7-88	100.4	100.7	6.52
11.50	7-88	101.5	101.11	6.55
11.70	7-88	101.9	101.13	6.53
7.00	8-88	100	100.3	6.61
6.60	9-88	99.26	99.29	6.80
12.88	9-88	102.8	102.12	6.69
7.00	10-88	99.30	100.2	6.86
11.50	10-88	102.7	102.11	[illegible]
7.50	12-88	[illegible]		

Prices are quoted as *bid and asked,* as they are for Treasury issues. For the first *Federal Home Loan Bank* issue quoted here, the highest price bid was 100 3/32 , or $1,000.94; the lowest price asked was 100 6/32 or $1,001.875.

Also, as with Treasury issues, the decimals in price figures refer not to 100ths but to 32nds. Thus, .1 equals 1/32nd.

This bond's ***yield to maturity*** is 6.11%. Why is this figure – representing the bond's long-term value – so much lower than its interest rate of 10.15%? Because the maturity date is just days away (this chart is dated 4/6/88), meaning that the buyer will receive very little interest for the price he pays, before the bond is retired. The 6.11% interest is what the investor would have made over a full year – not what he'll make in the few days left until maturity.

As an example, look at the ***Federal Farm Credit Bank*** bonds quoted here. The second bond, with an interest rate of 12.65%, matures in April 1988. The highest price bid was 100.40. Read this as 100 4/32% of par. If par is $1,000, this price would be $1,001.25. The lowest price asked was 100.80, or 100 8/32%, of par.

For many people, bonds mean US savings bonds.

Unlike the other kinds of bonds discussed in this section, savings bonds are not marketable bonds. They can be bought only from the government and cannot be traded among investors. So they are somewhere between an investment and a savings instrument...but they remain an important and popular choice for millions of individual Americans.

In one way, savings bonds are the original zero-coupon bonds: you buy them at a discount from par value and, upon maturity, the government pays you the full face amount.

For example, if you've ever bought a $50 savings bond as a wedding or baby gift, you might recall paying about $37.50 for it. During the 10-year maturity period, the government paid no interest on the bond; however, the person who received the gift was able to redeem it for $50 upon maturity.

Savings bonds continue to earn interest even after their maturity date.

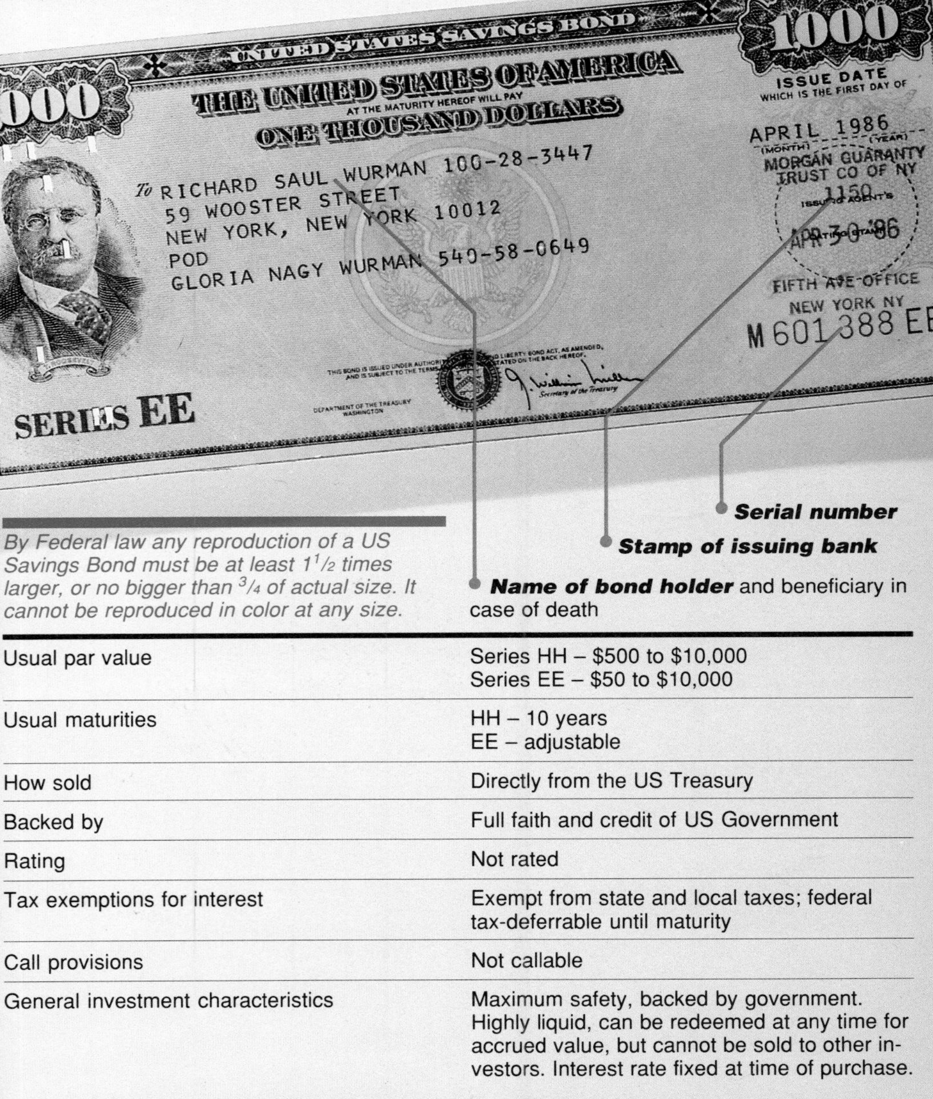

By Federal law any reproduction of a US Savings Bond must be at least 1½ times larger, or no bigger than ¾ of actual size. It cannot be reproduced in color at any size.

Usual par value	Series HH – $500 to $10,000 Series EE – $50 to $10,000
Usual maturities	HH – 10 years EE – adjustable
How sold	Directly from the US Treasury
Backed by	Full faith and credit of US Government
Rating	Not rated
Tax exemptions for interest	Exempt from state and local taxes; federal tax-deferrable until maturity
Call provisions	Not callable
General investment characteristics	Maximum safety, backed by government. Highly liquid, can be redeemed at any time for accrued value, but cannot be sold to other investors. Interest rate fixed at time of purchase.

What were War Bonds?
With the attack on Pearl Harbor, America initiated savings bonds called ***war bonds*** *to enlist the aid of the public in funding the war effort. Marketing and publicity for these bonds were staggering. There were regular radio shows sponsored by the Treasury. And each radio network produced its own weekly* ***Radio Bond Days*** *on which stars asked listeners to buy more bonds.*

Department stores created spectacular window displays with war bond themes and urged customers to take change in war stamps. Volunteers canvassed house to house. There was even a program called Schools at War promoting purchases and teaching the need to conserve resources during wartime.

Silver screen star ***Carole Lombard*** *died in a plane crash on her way home from a War Bond rally in Indianapolis on January 16, 1942.*

Mutual Funds

A mutual fund is a collection of stocks, bonds, or other securities purchased by a group of investors and managed by a professional investment company.

How popular are mutual funds?

They've been around for more than 60 years. Developed in 1924, they grew slowly at first. In the 1980s, however, the world of stocks and bonds became increasingly complex, and mutual fund investing took off.

Every mutual fund distributes to shareholders ***quarterly and annual reports*** which give a breakdown of the assets owned by the fund when the report was issued. Usually, by the time shareholders receive the report, some assets have been sold and others purchased.

The ***type of securities*** this fund owns. This fund invested 97.5% of its money in common and convertible preferred stocks. The other 2.5% was invested in Treasury bonds (not shown here).

The report lists the portfolio's ***stocks by industry*** and the percentage of the overall portfolio these stocks comprise.

The column to the left of the ***name of the stock*** shows the ***number of shares*** held.

The column on the right of the name shows the ***value of the holdings***. If you divide the value by the number of shares, you'll know the stock price on the day this report was prepared.

(b) or ***(c)*** after the name of a stock refers to footnotes, at the end of the portfolio listing, where additional information is given.

Portfolio of Investments Owned

August 31, 1987

Common Stocks and Convertible Preferre

Number of Shares	
Computer Equipment (24.9%)	
60,000	Apple Computer, Inc.
35,000	COMPAQ Computer Corp.**(b)**
25,000	Cray Research, Inc.**(b)**
30,000	Digital Equipment Corp.**(b)**
90,000	Gerber Scientific Inc.
55,000	Hewlett-Packard Co.
50,000	Mentor Graphics Corp.**(b)**
25,000	NCR Corp.
75,000	Norsk Data A.S. Class B, ADR**(c)**
50,000	Prime Computer, Inc.**(b)**
55,000	Stratus Computer, Inc.**(b)**
30,000	Sun Micro Systems, Inc.**(b)**
50,000	Tandem Computers Inc.**(b)**
110,000	Unisys Corp.
25,000	Xerox Corp.
Computer Services/Software (19.8%)	
60,000	Autodesk, Inc.**(b)**
70,000	Comdisco, Inc.
85,000	Computer Associates Interna Inc.**(b)**
70,000	Computer Sciences Corp.**(b**
75,000	General Motors Corp. Class
110,000	Lotus Development Corp.**(**
50,000	Oracle Systems Corp.**(b)**
80,000	Pansophic Systems, Inc.
50,000	Reuters Holdings PLC AD
40,000	SHL Systemhouse Inc.**(b**
100,000	Telerate, Inc.

Who runs the funds?

Investment companies, brokerage houses and some financial institutions operate mutual funds. And, although they're legally prohibited from operating funds themselves, many banks also offer their customers the opportunity to invest through affiliations with mutual fund companies.

Unofficial Mutual Funds

Until the 1930s, small investors were at millionaires' mercy. Many millionaires pooled their money, bought huge blocks of particular stocks, drove prices sky high, then promptly sold out...leaving the overpriced stocks to tumble in the hands of unwary investors. Today, every aspect of mutual fund trading is tightly regulated.

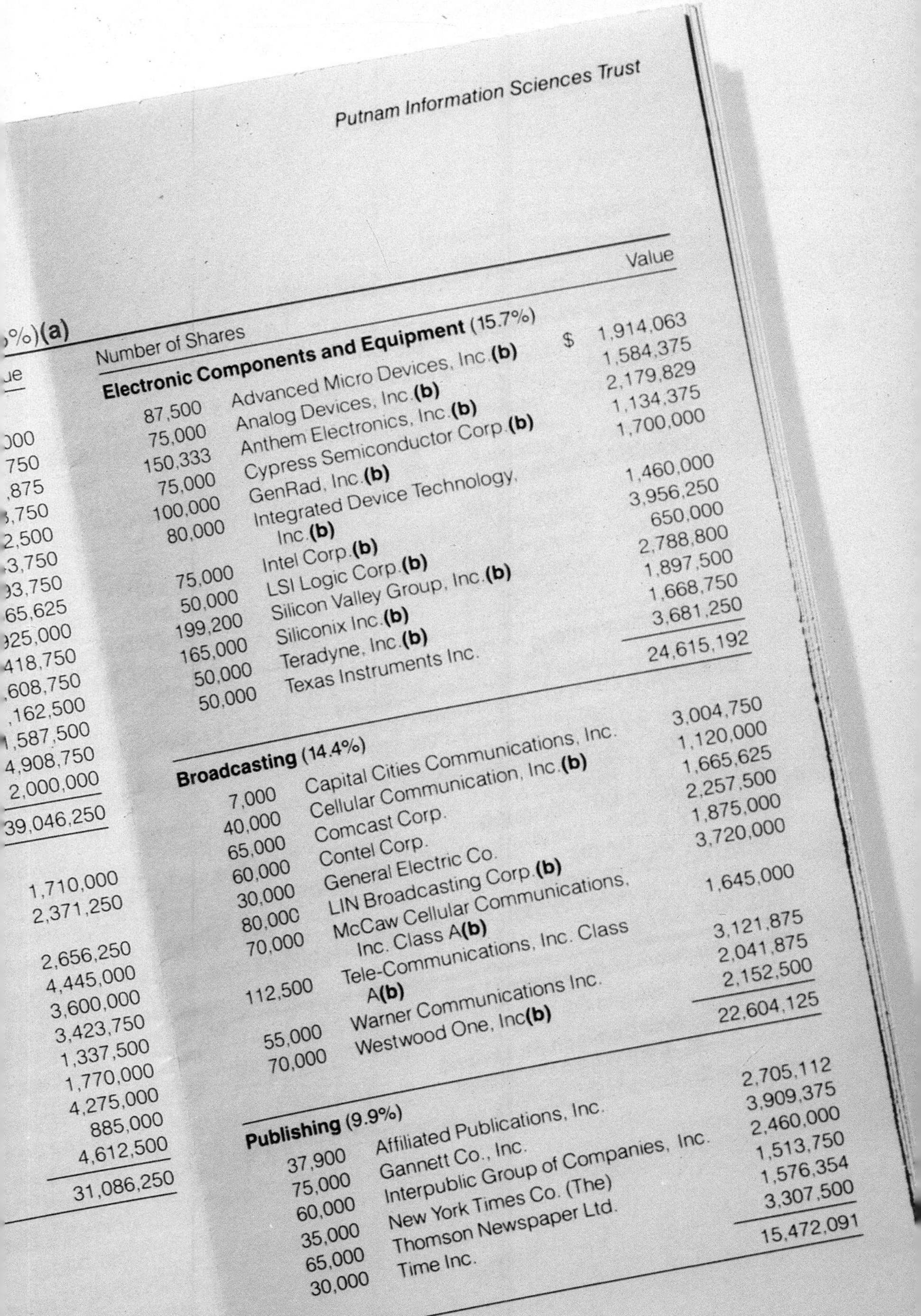

%)**(a)**

ue

000
750
,875
,750
2,500
3,750
93,750
65,625
925,000
418,750
,608,750
,162,500
1,587,500
4,908,750
2,000,000
39,046,250

1,710,000
2,371,250

2,656,250
4,445,000
3,600,000
3,423,750
1,337,500
1,770,000
4,275,000
885,000
4,612,500
31,086,250

Putnam Information Sciences Trust

Number of Shares		Value
	Electronic Components and Equipment (15.7%)	
87,500	Advanced Micro Devices, Inc.**(b)**	$ 1,914,063
75,000	Analog Devices, Inc.**(b)**	1,584,375
150,333	Anthem Electronics, Inc.**(b)**	2,179,829
75,000	Cypress Semiconductor Corp.**(b)**	1,134,375
100,000	GenRad, Inc.**(b)**	1,700,000
80,000	Integrated Device Technology, Inc.**(b)**	1,460,000
75,000	Intel Corp.**(b)**	3,956,250
50,000	LSI Logic Corp.**(b)**	650,000
199,200	Silicon Valley Group, Inc.**(b)**	2,788,800
165,000	Siliconix Inc.**(b)**	1,897,500
50,000	Teradyne, Inc.**(b)**	1,668,750
50,000	Texas Instruments Inc.	3,681,250
		24,615,192
	Broadcasting (14.4%)	
7,000	Capital Cities Communications, Inc.	3,004,750
40,000	Cellular Communication, Inc.**(b)**	1,120,000
65,000	Comcast Corp.	1,665,625
60,000	Contel Corp.	2,257,500
30,000	General Electric Co.	1,875,000
80,000	LIN Broadcasting Corp.**(b)**	3,720,000
70,000	McCaw Cellular Communications, Inc. Class A**(b)**	1,645,000
112,500	Tele-Communications, Inc. Class A**(b)**	3,121,875
55,000	Warner Communications Inc.	2,041,875
70,000	Westwood One, Inc**(b)**	2,152,500
		22,604,125
	Publishing (9.9%)	
37,900	Affiliated Publications, Inc.	2,705,112
75,000	Gannett Co., Inc.	3,909,375
60,000	Interpublic Group of Companies, Inc.	2,460,000
35,000	New York Times Co. (The)	1,513,750
65,000	Thomson Newspaper Ltd.	1,576,354
30,000	Time Inc.	3,307,500
		15,472,091

How Mutual Funds Work

The money you invest in a mutual fund is pooled with other investors' money.

When you invest, you buy shares in a particular fund, not the mutual fund company itself. The aggregate money invested in the fund is then used to trade in a variety of stocks, bonds, or a combination of both. And each mutual fund share you own represents participation in all those stocks or bonds.

You can't trade fractions of stocks – unless you trade through a mutual fund. Mutual funds allow you to invest or withdraw however much you want, regardless of fractions:

	you have	*it costs*	*you get*
stock A	$530	$15/share	35 shares, + $5
fund A	$530	$15/share	35.333 shares

Don't confuse the mutual fund with the *company* that runs the fund. If you want to invest in the mutual funds run by those companies, you usually have to deal directly with the company or through your broker. You can invest in the shares of most mutual fund companies themselves through an exchange or over the counter.

What is different between stocks and funds?

	Stocks	**Mutual funds**
What you buy	You buy shares of a single company, usually in round lots of a hundred. You have voting rights in the corporation.	You buy shares in the fund, which is a collection of stocks. You have no voting rights. ***Diversification***. Owning a wide variety of securities is one of the biggest advantages of mutual funds. A diversified portfolio of securities can shield you from large losses because, even if some securities falter, others may perform well.
What you pay	Stock price dictates the amount you need to invest.	You can invest any amount, provided it's above the minimum requirement. ***Flexible investing***. The usual minimum initial investment is $1,000, with subsequent investments normally either $250 or $500. A few groups have no minimum.
Who decides what	You (and your broker) determine what and when to buy and sell.	Fund managers decide what assets should be in a portfolio and when to trade the holdings. You determine when to buy or sell your shares in the fund. ***Professional management***. You can share the expense of hiring an expert and even avoid paying commissions on every trade.
Who gets the dividends	Dividends are paid to you directly or to your brokerage firm for you. You have to decide how to reinvest dividends and interest payments.	Dividends can be reinvested to purchase more shares, or paid directly to you as cash. ***Automatic reinvestment or payment***. Every mutual fund has an optional automatic reinvestment program or, on request, will forward dividends to you in cash.
How *liquid* is your investment	When you sell, you must wait five business days before the trade settles and your money can be released to you.	You can transfer money back and forth very quickly. ***Easy access to your money***. To receive your money, you can simply call the fund and place an order to sell your shares. The sale occurs at the end of the day (in some funds, sooner), and money is available to you the next morning. Many funds even let you write checks against the money in the fund, although there is usually at least a $250 minimum per check.

Kinds of Mutual Funds

While you can trade some mutual funds through the stock exchanges, most of the time you'll deal directly with the mutual fund company – or ask your broker to do it for you.

What are closed-end funds?

Closed-end funds comprise only a small fraction of the mutual funds in existence. Like stocks, closed-end funds have only a limited number of shares available for trading. And, like stocks, these funds trade on an exchange or over the counter.

Closed-end funds are not listed in the mutual funds tables. You'll find them listed alphabetically in the stock tables, according to the exchange on which they trade.

You will also find them listed in a special, weekly table in ***The Wall Street Journal***.

Publicly traded means these closed-end fund shares are traded in the open market.

What are open-end funds?

The typical mutual fund is an ***open-end fund***. Open-end means that the fund will sell as many shares as investors want.

You can't trade shares of open-end funds in the stock market. You can only buy or sell them through the mutual fund company itself. Finding a buyer for your shares, however, is not a problem; every fund is required to buy back your shares immediately upon your request.

All mutual funds listed in ***The Wall Street Journal's Mutual Funds*** quotation table are open-end funds.

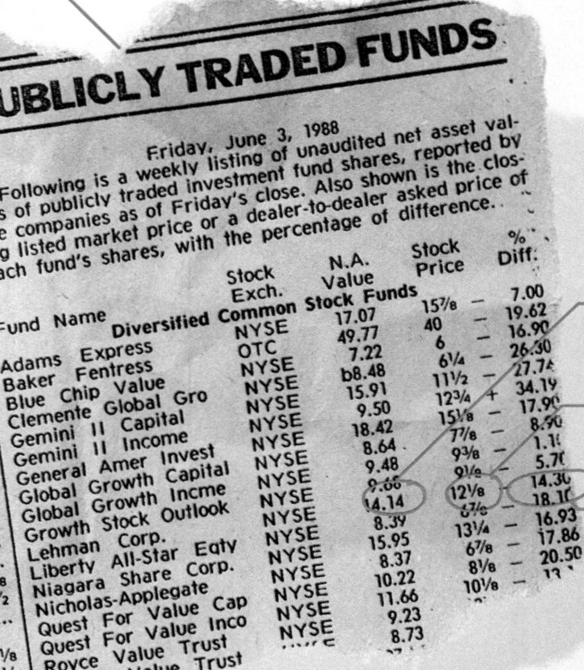

UBLICLY TRADED FUNDS

Friday, June 3, 1988

Following is a weekly listing of unaudited net asset val-
es of publicly traded investment fund shares, reported by
ne companies as of Friday's close. Also shown is the clos-
ng listed market price or a dealer-to-dealer asked price of
each fund's shares, with the percentage of difference.

Fund Name	Stock Exch.	N.A. Value	Stock Price		% Diff.
Diversified Common Stock Funds					
Adams Express	NYSE	17.07	15 7/8	–	7.00
Baker Fentress	OTC	49.77	40	–	19.62
Blue Chip Value	NYSE	7.22	6	–	16.90
Clemente Global Gro	NYSE	b8.48	6 1/4	–	26.30
Gemini II Capital	NYSE	15.91	11 1/2	–	27.74
Gemini II Income	NYSE	9.50	12 3/4	+	34.19
General Amer Invest	NYSE	18.42	15 1/8	–	17.90
Global Growth Capital	NYSE	8.64	7 7/8	–	8.90
Global Growth Incme	NYSE	9.48	9 3/8	–	1.1[illegible]
Growth Stock Outlook	NYSE	9.66	[illegible]	–	5.70
Lehman Corp.	NYSE	14.14	12 1/8	–	14.30
Liberty All-Star Eqty	NYSE	8.39	[illegible]	–	18.10
Niagara Share Corp.	NYSE	15.95	13 1/4	–	16.93
Nicholas-Applegate	NYSE	8.37	6 7/8	–	17.86
Quest For Value Cap	NYSE	10.22	8 1/8	–	20.50
Quest For Value Inco	NYSE	11.66	10 1/8	–	13[illegible]
Royce Value Trust	NYSE	9.23			
Schafer Value Trust	NYSE	8.73			
Source Capital					
-Contine					

If you sold all the shares in the Lehman Corp. fund on the date shown here, each share would be worth this ***net asset value*** figure, $14.14 – the total value of the fund's holdings divided by the number of shares of stock.

The ***stock price***, $12.125, is today's price for one share in the Lehman fund bought through a stock exchange.

% Diff is the % difference between the actual value per share of the fund and the price at which it's actually trading in the market. This difference indicates, therefore, how speculators think the fund will perform in the future.

What are load funds?

Load funds charge commissions when you invest and withdraw money. Loads can run as high as 8.5%.

Load funds are often sold through brokerage firms.

Load funds are also sometimes called ***front-end load funds***. There are also ***back-end load funds*** which charge fees if you sell your shares within a specified period of time.

What are no-load funds?

No-load funds charge no sales fee and don't use brokers to deal with the public. All of your money is invested in the fund.

All funds, however, have a management fee, whether or not they have a sales charge. Usually, this fee is about one-half to one percent.

There's no correlation between the amount of sales commission you pay and a fund's performance.

Keeping Tabs on Mutual Funds

The daily performance of mutual funds is measured differently from the performances of the stocks and bonds held in the funds.

MUTUAL FUND

		Offer NAV	
	NAV	Price	Chg.
Specl r	34.51	34.51−	.10
CommonSense Trust:			
Govt	11.04	11.84+	.03
Growth	10.65	11.64−	.08
Gro Inc	10.25	11.20−	.08
Commonwealth Trust:			
A & B	1.42	1.54	...
C	1.98	2.14	...
Composite Group:			
Bond Stk	p10.00	10.42−	.03
Growth	p10.67	11.11−	.02
Income	p8.94	9.31−	.01
NW Pt	p14.47	15.07−	.03
Tax Ex	p7.15	7.45−	.01
US Gov	p.99	1.03−	.01
Value	10.83	11.28+	.01
Conn Mutual:			
Govt	10.29	10.98−	.01
Growth	10.70	11.41−	.07
Totl Ret	11.63	12.41−	.03
Concord In	6.86	7.15−	.02
Concrd TE	6.90	7.19	...
...ental Equities:			
		9.55−	.02
		−	.02

Monday, June
Price ranges for investment c...
National Association of Securitie...
net asset value per share; the
value plus maximum sales cha...

		Offer NAV	
	NAV	Price	Chg.
SelEng r	12.90	13.16−	.03
SelEn r	8.28	8.45+	.03
SelEUt r	8.96	9.14−	.02
SelFd r	16.37	16.70−	.08
SelFnS r	27.84	28.41−	.03
SelHlth r	34.10	34.80−	.29
Sel Hs r	11.60	11.84−	.03
SelInd r	13.64	13.92−	.07
SelLesr r	22.77	23.23−	.11
SelMD r	7.29	7.44−	.02
SelMetl r	13.61	13.89−	.02
SelPap r	12.32	12.57+	.03
SelPrp r	10.45	10.66−	.06
SelReg r	9.50	9.69−	.05
SelRetl r	11.77	12.01−	.06
SelSL r	8.82	9.00−	.05
SelSoft r	14.36	14.65−	.1
SelTec r	18.40	18.78−	.1
SelTele r	17.16	17.51−	.0
Util r	25.78	26.31−	

The ***sponsoring company's name*** is listed first. Its funds appear below in alphabetical order.

Investors in the Composite Group, for example, have a choice between putting money in the Bond & Stock Fund, the Growth Fund, the Tax-Exempt Fund, etc. No matter which they choose, they may want to follow other funds offered by this company. Many companies allow transfers between certain funds within a family at no charge.

r after the fund name means the fund charges a fee to redeem shares for cash. This is also known as ***back-end load***.

p after the fund name means the fund charges a fee for marketing and distribution costs.

NAV stands for ***net asset value***. It refers to the dollar value of one share of the fund's stock – i.e., the amount the fund would pay you for the share if you wanted to sell it back. Since every share in a mutual fund represents tiny portions of hundreds of different securities, the NAV figure is calculated by adding up the value of all the fund's holdings and dividing by the number of shares. The NAV of the IDS Bond Fund, for example, is $4.62 – that's what a share sells for.

oday, there are over 2600 funds – more than he entire number of stocks listed on the New ork Stock Exchange.

...TATIONS

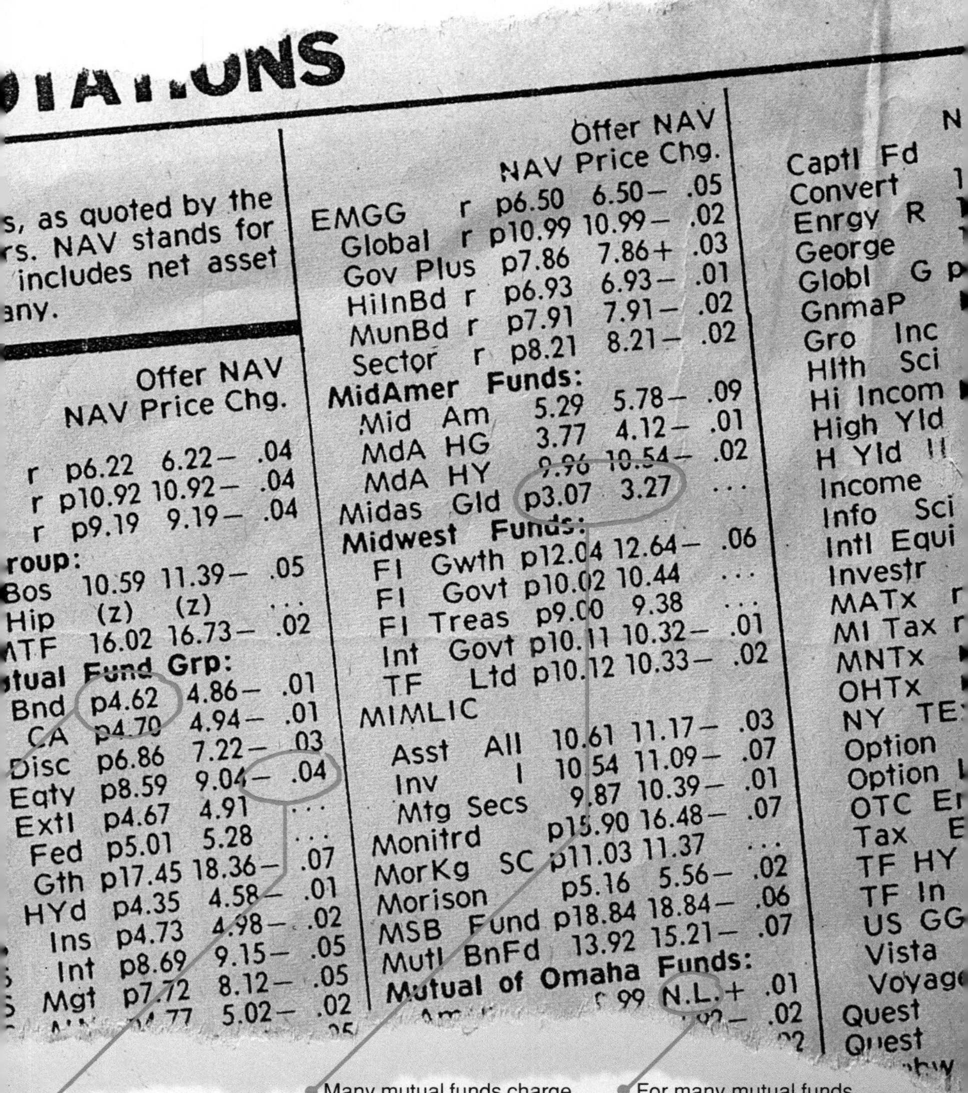

s, as quoted by the rs. NAV stands for includes net asset any.

		Offer	NAV
	NAV	Price	Chg.
	r p6.22	6.22–	.04
	r p10.92	10.92–	.04
	r p9.19	9.19–	.04
roup:			
Bos	10.59	11.39–	.05
Hip	(z)	(z)	...
ATF	16.02	16.73–	.02
tual Fund Grp:			
Bnd	p4.62	4.86–	.01
CA	p4.70	4.94–	.01
Disc	p6.86	7.22–	.03
Eqty	p8.59	9.04–	.04
Extl	p4.67	4.91	...
Fed	p5.01	5.28	...
Gth	p17.45	18.36–	.07
HYd	p4.35	4.58–	.01
Ins	p4.73	4.98–	.02
Int	p8.69	9.15–	.05
Mgt	p7.72	8.12–	.05
[illegible]	[illegible]	5.02–	.02

		Offer	NAV
	NAV	Price	Chg.
EMGG	r p6.50	6.50–	.05
Global	r p10.99	10.99–	.02
Gov Plus	p7.86	7.86+	.03
HiInBd	r p6.93	6.93–	.01
MunBd	r p7.91	7.91–	.02
Sector	r p8.21	8.21–	.02
MidAmer Funds:			
Mid Am	5.29	5.78–	.09
MdA HG	3.77	4.12–	.01
MdA HY	9.96	10.54–	.02
Midas Gld	p3.07	3.27	...
Midwest Funds:			
FI Gwth	p12.04	12.64–	.06
FI Govt	p10.02	10.44	...
FI Treas	p9.00	9.38	...
Int Govt	p10.11	10.32–	.01
TF Ltd	p10.12	10.33–	.02
MIMLIC			
Asst All	10.61	11.17–	.03
Inv I	10.54	11.09–	.07
Mtg Secs	9.87	10.39–	.01
Monitrd	p15.90	16.48–	.07
MorKg SC	p11.03	11.37	...
Morison	p5.16	5.56–	.02
MSB Fund	p18.84	18.84–	.06
Mutl BnFd	13.92	15.21–	.07
Mutual of Omaha Funds:			
[illegible]	[illegible] 99	N.L.	+ .01

Captl Fd
Convert
Enrgy R
George
Globl G
GnmaP
Gro Inc
Hlth Sci
Hi Incom
High Yld
H Yld
Income
Info Sci
Intl Equi
Investr
MATx
MI Tax
MNTx
OHTx
NY TE
Option
Option
OTC E
Tax E
TF HY
TF In
US GG
Vista
Voyag
Quest
Quest

NAV Change indicates he difference between today's et asset value quote and that f the previous day. The IDS quity Fund, for example, fell ¢. That means that today's AV figure of $8.59 is 4¢ wer than yesterday's NAV gure, which must have been 8.63.

Many mutual funds charge a commission, or ***load***, to buyers. This fee is reflected in a higher price quoted in the ***offering price*** column. Most funds carry loads. For example, you would pay $3.27 for a share in the Midas Gold Fund, but receive only $3.07 when you sell it back. The fund makes 20¢ from every share customers buy and sell back.

Some funds quote the same price in the NAV and the offer. This means they assess no up-front fee, but instead charge a fee when you sell.

For many mutual funds, however, there's only one price, whether you're buying or selling. No commissions – loads – are involved. That's why for some funds, the offer price column contains an ***N.L.*** entry, standing for ***No-Load*** – no commission charged.

Funds for Different Objectives

Not long ago, mutual funds were simply broad-based investments. Today, they can be highly specialized, and they serve very specific investment objectives.

What are the goals of the different funds?

There are mutual funds to meet almost any investment objective.

goal	kind of fund	potential price rise	potential current income	safety
maximum price rise	***aggressive growth funds*** invest in common stock of fledgling companies and industries, out-of-favor companies and industries	very high	very low	low to very low
high capital gains	***growth funds*** invest in common stock of settled companies and industries	high to very high	very low	low
price rise and current income	***growth and income funds*** invest in companies with solid track records of consistent dividend payments	moderate	moderate	low to moderate
high current income	***fixed income and equity income funds*** both invest in high-yielding stocks and bonds	very low	high to very high	low to moderate
high current income	***option income funds*** invest in dividend paying common stock on which call options are traded	moderate	high to very high	low to moderate
current income and maximum safety	***general money market funds*** invest in short-term debt securities ***US Gov't money market funds*** invest in treasury and agency issues	none	moderate to high	very high
current income, long-term growth and safety	***balanced funds*** invest in a mixture of bonds, preferred stock and common stock	low	moderate to high	high
tax-free income and safety	***tax-free money market funds*** invest in short-term municipal notes and bonds	none	moderate to high	very high
tax-free income	***municipal bond funds*** invest in bonds exempt from state, local and federal taxes	low to moderate	moderate to high	moderate

Why investors choose mutual funds over other financial investments

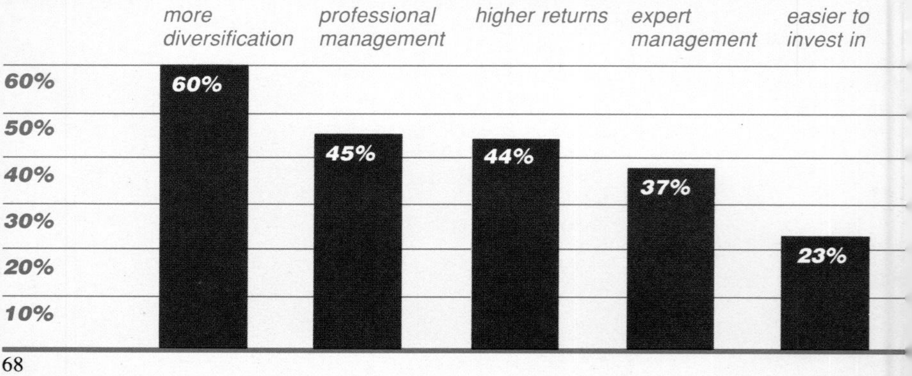

more diversification	professional management	higher returns	expert management	easier to invest in
60%	45%	44%	37%	23%

Money Market Funds

A money market account is simply a mutual fund which invests only in the money market.

What is the money market?

Money market can be a confusing term, since all investment markets involve money. Markets hat trade only in very ***short-term debt securities***, however, are usually referred to as the money market because they're most quickly turned into spendable cash. In other words, the money you invest in a money market account is being used for short-term loans to various companies and governmental bodies.

In contrast, longer-term securities, like stocks and bonds, are known as the ***capital market***.

What do money market funds invest in?

Money market funds invest in a number of different kinds of short-term debt securities. Some of the most common are:

Commercial paper, corporate bonds, representing short-term loans to corporations.
Certificates of Deposit, issued by large banks, with maturities ranging from one month to several years.
Bankers' acceptances, short-term loans to importers and exporters.
Short-term loans to municipalities and government agencies.
Treasury bills, issued by the US government, maturing in 30 to 90 days.

MONEY MARKET MUTUAL FUNDS

Fund	Avg. Mat.	7Day Yld.	e7Day Yld.	Assets
FFB Cash	46	6.79	7.02	389.2
FFB USGovt	32	6.78	7.01	224.9
FFB TxFrMM	50	4.46	4.56	129.8
FFB USTreas	32	6.72	6.95	121.0
FidelCal TaxFr	38	4.51	4.61	559.7
FidelCash Resv	52	6.65	6.88	9547.1
FidelDlyIncm b	31	6.55	6.77	2891.7
FidDly MM Prt	28	6.72	6.95	534.6
FidDly Tax Ex	32	4.24	4.33	203.8

Fund	Avg. Mat.	7Day Yld.	e7Day Yld.	Assets
LexGvtScMM a	20	6.31	6.52	16.6
LexMoneyMkt a	29	6.46	6.67	199.9
LexTaxFrDly c	58	4.38	4.48	86.1
LFRoth EarnLq	(z)	(z)		
LF Roth Exmpt	(z)	(z)		
LibertyUS Govt	31	6.37	6.57	1320.7
LiquidCapitl Tr	28	6.64	6.86	
LiquidCAshTR f	1	7.55		746.0
Liquid[illegible]		[illegible]	4.71	45.1

Fund
ScuddCashI
ScuddCaTF
ScuddNYTF
ScuddrGvt
ScuddrTaxF
Seagate
Seagate Tax
Seagate
Secur Cash
Select Mny

The ***fund name*** and the name of the company running the fund, the Fidelity Tax-Free Fund. Most companies, like Fidelity, offer stock and bond funds as well as money market funds.

Average maturity indicates the length of the average loan. In this fund, loans will be outstanding, on average, for 38 days.

7Day Yld shows the average interest rate, 4.51%, on the outstanding loans in the portfolio. ***e7Day Yld***, the effective 7-day yield, is based on the price the fund paid for the bond. The effective yield is a more meaningful figure; investors in this fund receive a 4.61% return.

Assets show how much money, in millions, is invested in the fund. Investors have put $559,700,000 of their savings into this fund.

How does the money market work?

Shares in your money market mutual fund are always worth $1. You earn income by receiving interest on the money the fund lends to governments and corporations. The rate of interest fluctuates every day because the loans are so short-term that every day at least one loan is completed and a new one begins at a new rate.

Although you can't predict how much interest you'll earn (it depends on the trends in interest rates), money market funds offer tremendous investment safety. Virtually the only downside is the possibility of earning more money through another investment.

Since 1980, only $1 of every $4 has been invested in stock funds. The other $3 have gone into bond funds and money market funds.

The money market as economic indicator

In today's economy, the amount of money flowing in and out of money market accounts provides economists with valuable information about the country's savings trends. In fact, ***The Wall Street Journal*** often publishes a chart highlighting the rise and fall of assets stored in money market accounts.

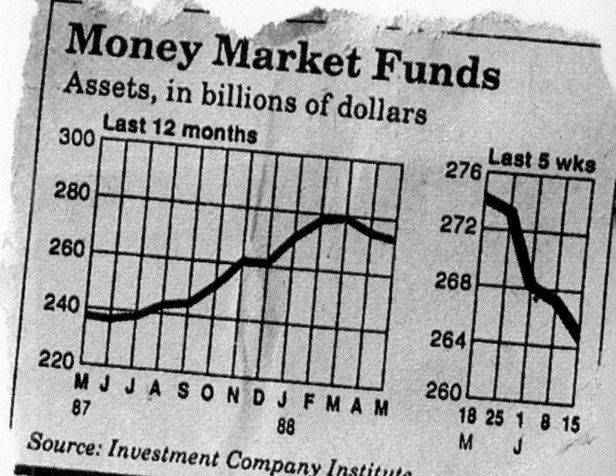

Anatomy of a Fund

Typically, a mutual fund's portfolio will include between 50 and 100 different stocks, bonds or options. Some mutual funds limit their scope to specific – sometimes very specific – aspects of the world economy.

The first funds were ***Equity Funds***, which invest in stocks, and ***Bond Funds***, which invest in bonds.

The Value Line Fund, Inc.:

Medical supplies	5.4%
Computer service & software	4.8
Financial services	2.9
Insurance	2.6
Telecommunications	2.4
Grocery	2.1
Common stocks in 42 other industries	74.6
Other assets & debt	5.2

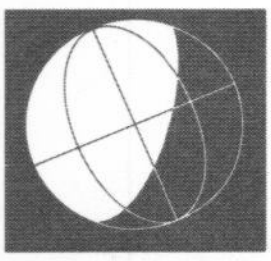

International Funds, also known as ***Overseas Funds***, invest in foreign stock or bond markets. Some invest only in one market; others diversify among many foreign markets.

The Van Eck World Trends Fund:

Australia	4.7%
Canada	4.8
EEC	3.2
France	6.4
Germany	10.0
Hong Kong	1.3
Japan	30.0
Netherlands	1.6
Singapore	.8
Switzerland	2.4
United Kingdom	3.9
United States	30.9

Megafunds, or the funds of funds, invest in mutual funds themselves, diversifying among funds rather than particular stocks or bonds.

Unit Investment Trusts or ***UIT*** are highly predictable funds. They invest in corporate bonds with fixed yields and do not alter the investments during the life of the trust. Fees are very low, since there is little management activity.

Tax-Free Funds invest in government bonds which provide tax-free income. Investors usually receive less interest than from corporate bonds, but the after-tax considerations may make them a better investment.

Van Kampen Merritt Insured Tax Free Income Fund:

Alabama	3.12%
Alaska	.54
Arkansas	1.32
California	4.07
Investments in 39 other states	88.70
Short-term investments	6.07
Other assets & debt	(3.82)

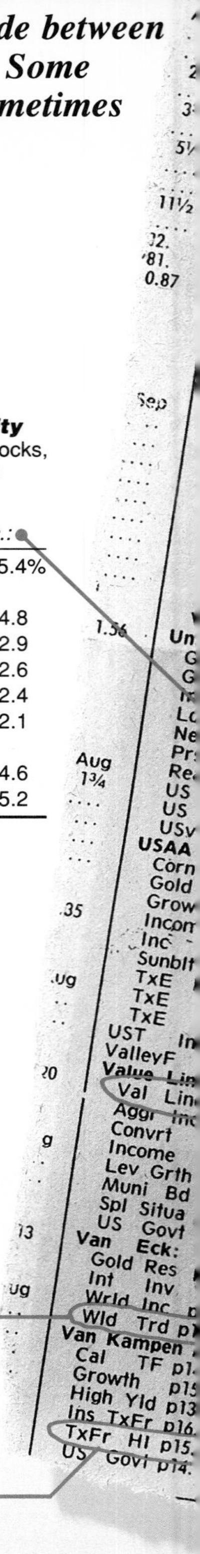

...ued From Preceding Page

	NAV	Offer Price	NAV Chg.
Vance Exch Funds:			
Capt Ex	98.26	N.L.	– .41
Dep Bos	55.71	N.L.	– .28
Dvrs Fd	104.49	N.L.	– .43
Ex Fd	146.97	146.97	– .50
Ex Bost	130.77	N.L.	– .71
Fid Exch	83.01	N.L.	– .37
2nd Fid	81.87	N.L.	– .42
Vanguard Group:			
Bd Mkt	9.14	N.L.	...
Convrt	8.82	N.L.	+ .03
Explor	28.60	N.L.	+ .01
Explr II	19.85	N.L.	+ .02
Morgan	10.99	N.L.	– .02
Naess T	35.58	N.L.	– .01
Prmcp	46.03	N.L.	+ .09
VHY Sk	14.01	N.L.	– .04
V Prefrd	7.95	N.L.	...
V ARP	21.03	N.L.	...
Quant	10.68	N.L.	– .07
Star Fnd	10.83	N.L.	– .03
TCF Int	31.34	N.L.	+ .01
TCF usa	26.60	N.L.	– .05
GNMA	9.40	N.L.	+ .02
HiY Bnd	8.49	N.L.	– .01
IG Bond	7.77	N.L.	– .01
ST Portf	10.33	N.L.	...
ST Govt	9.91	N.L.	– .01
US Treas	9.01	N.L.	– .05
Indx Ex	11.53	N.L.	+ .01
Index 500	26.46	N.L.	– .18
Mun HiY	9.63	N.L.	...
Mun Insr	11.08	N.L.	+ .01
Mun Intr	11.68	N.L.	– .01
MunLtd	10.16	N.L.	...
Mun Lng	9.96	N.L.	...
Mun Shrt	15.28	N.L.	...
Cal Ins	9.47	N.L.	– .01
NJ Ins	(z)	(z)	...
NY Ins	9.05	N.L.	...
Penn Ins	9.51	N.L.	+ .01
VSPE r	11.50	N.L.	– .02
VSPGl r	11.05	N.L.	– .04
VSP Hl r	17.87	N.L.	– .09
VSP Sv r	14.02	N.L.	.10
VSP Tc r	11.46	N.L.	+ .04
Welsley	15.04	N.L.	– .04
Wellgtn	16.24	N.L.	– .07
Windsr	12.74	N.L.	– .07
Wndsr II	11.93	N.L.	– .08
WF US	7.36	N.L.	– .03
WF Intl	11.27	N.L.	+ .05
Venture Advisers Group:			
Incm Pl	8.45	9.23	...
MuniPl r	p9.29	9.29	+ .01
NY Vent	7.69	8.40	– .02
RPFBd r	p7.03	7.03	+ .01
RPFEq r	p18.72	18.72	+ .03
Vik Eqlnd	13.95	N.L.	– .10
Wall Street	6.41	6.78	+ .03
Wealth M	p7.03	N.L.	+ .01
Weiss Peck Greer:			
Tudor	20.97	N.L.	+ .09
WPG	20.05	N.L.	– .09
WPG Gv	9.79	N.L.	– .01
WPG Gr	93.40	N.L.	+ .51
Wells F IRA:			
AssetA f	11.46	N.L.	– .01
Bond f	10.64	N.L.	...
Cp Stk f	17.94	N.L.	+ .04
Small f	13.87	N.L.	+ .05
W Hum Gr	p13.76	N.L.	– .03
Westrgrd	(z)	(z)	...
Wstwd	11.94	12.44	– .03
Wood Struthers Winthrop:			
Neuwth	14.01	N.L.	+ .01
Pine StF	11.37	N.L.	– .06
WinG r	p10.00	10.00	– .03

The first fund in the US was The Massachusetts Investors Trust, organized in Boston in 1924.

Index Funds hold only the stocks of a particular index, like the Dow Jones Industrial Average. Their function is to perform exactly as the index performs.

Vanguard S&P 500:

Capital goods	5.0%
Consumer durables	4.0
Consumer non-durables	31.0
Energy	12.0
Finance	6.0
Materials & services	13.0
Technology	13.0
Transportation	3.0
Utilities	13.0

Precious Metals Funds may invest in some bullion but chiefly trade mining stocks. Some avoid South African companies.

Vanguard Specialized Portfolios, Gold and Precious Metals:

Common stock	
Australia	17.8%
North America	27.3
South Africa	31.0
United Kingdom	3.3
Bullion	17.5
Other assets & debt	3.1

Sector Funds are the newest breed of funds; each fund focuses only on a particular industry, like automotive, defense or electronics.

Vanguard Specialized Portfolios, Technology:

Computer equipment	40.0%
Computer service & software	11.0
Communications	3.2
Aerospace/Defense	9.3
Electrical equipment	5.0
CAD/CAM/CAE	3.5
Semiconductors	16.1
Medical technology	9.8
Temporary cash invest.	.3
Other assets & debt	1.8

Buying Mutual Funds

Advertisements for mutual funds often appear in* The Wall Street Journal *and other financial publications. While these ads often include toll-free numbers to call for more information, they are never offerings. A fund company must always send you a prospectus before accepting any of your money.

How do you find a mutual fund?

For guidance in choosing a fund, you can consult any of the following: a broker, a financial planner, prominent business magazines that periodically carry feature articles describing and evaluating mutual funds, or specialized investment newsletters.

Some mutual funds allow you to conduct your business with them through Automatic Transaction Machines (bank machines) 24 hours a day, every day. Some funds allow you to use a home computer to trade and check your account balance or the fund's current holdings. You can even have money deposited directly from your paycheck into a fund.

How do you choose a mutual fund?

The first thing you should always do is determine your objectives. Once you've zeroed in on a few funds, you can write or call them to request detailed information.

A prospectus gives the fund's investment objectives and offers clues to management's ability to meet them.

An annual report and/or quarterly report provide analyses of the fund's present and past performance. These are useful tools in evaluating a fund's long-term success.

What is a prospectus?

A fund must provide a copy of ***the prospectus*** to investors before accepting their initial nvestment. Its purpose is to provide complete lisclosure of information about the fund. By ısing the table of contents on the cover, you ;an pinpoint the important information.

The date. A prospectus must be updated at east every 16 months, so make sure you have he latest copy.

The minimum. Initial investments are ısually between $250–$1,000. There are also ninimums for further investments.

The objective. This allows you to find a und that matches your investing objective.

Performance. This describes how the fund ıas performed in the past. Since funds may hange managers or limit choices to particular ectors of the economy, past performance loes not guarantee future success.

Risk. Each fund must list the level of risk ıvolved in achieving its objectives.

Features. Can you trade over the phone, or do you have to put everything in writing? Write checks against your money? Transfer your investments among the company's different funds (called ***exchange privilege***)? Can your dividends be reinvested automatically? This section will tell you.

Fees. How much is the sales charge and management fee? Do you pay a fee for withdrawing money? For exchanging between funds? Are there any other fees?

SAI. If you want more information than you can find in the prospectus, the fund must supply you with its ***Statement of Additional Information*** free of charge. This includes the compensation for officers of the fund, the fund's audited financial statement and other information.

How do you measure a fund's performance?

Since mutual funds are now categorized by investment objective and by industry, it seems only natural that mutual fund indexes have been created to keep tabs on the performance of groups of funds. Once a week, ***The Wall Street Journal*** publishes a table called ***Lipper Indexes*** (named after Lipper Analytical Services, which provides the information for the table). In it, you can see the aggregate performances of a variety of groups of mutual funds over the past week.

When choosing among specific funds, it's also a good idea to ask for their 1, 5 and 10-year performance records.

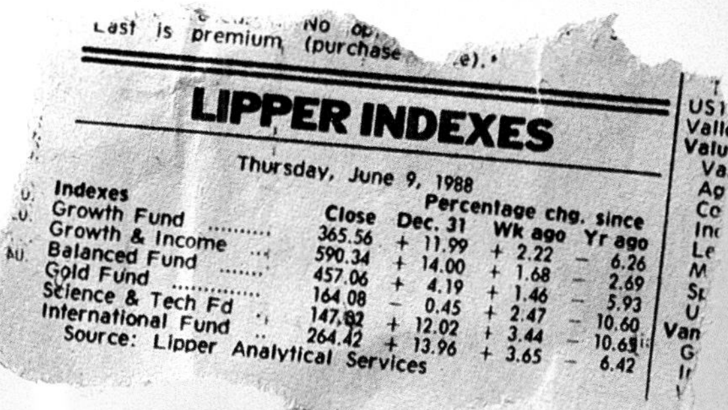

LIPPER INDEXES

Thursday, June 9, 1988

Indexes	Close	Percentage chg. since Dec. 31	Wk ago	Yr ago
Growth Fund	365.56	+ 11.99	+ 2.22	– 6.26
Growth & Income	590.34	+ 14.00	+ 1.68	– 2.69
Balanced Fund	457.06	+ 4.19	+ 1.46	– 5.93
Gold Fund	164.08	– 0.45	+ 2.47	– 10.60
Science & Tech Fd	147.82	+ 12.02	+ 3.44	– 10.65
International Fund	264.42	+ 13.96	+ 3.65	– 6.42

Source: Lipper Analytical Services

Does past performance guarantee future success?

No. Many funds are geared toward particular industries, securities and countries, and there are many different investment objectives. Consequently, some funds perform very well in certain economic climates and poorly in others. And some funds perform consistently in virtually any economic climate. But don't forget: the fund managers may leave and be replaced by others who are less (or more) adept at managing assets.

That's why mutual funds are usually rated according to their previous 1-year, 5-year and even 10-year performances. ***The Wall Street Journal*** publishes its mutual funds ratings four times a year.

Futures

A futures contract is a deal made now to take place in the future. The order ticket, used by traders on the exchange floor to record a trade, is the only written agreement between the parties.

Each customer has an ***account number*** at the brokerage house that handles the trade.

Exec. Brkr # is the broker executing the trade.

CTI # identifies the type of trader. In this case ***4*** means a broker for a brokerage firm.

H/C tells whether the trade was made for a brokerage house or a customer.

Opposite broker identifies the other trader in the deal. The broker jots down the opposite broker's initials and badge number.

B/S signifies whether this broker is a buyer or a seller.

Quantity represents the number of contracts traded.

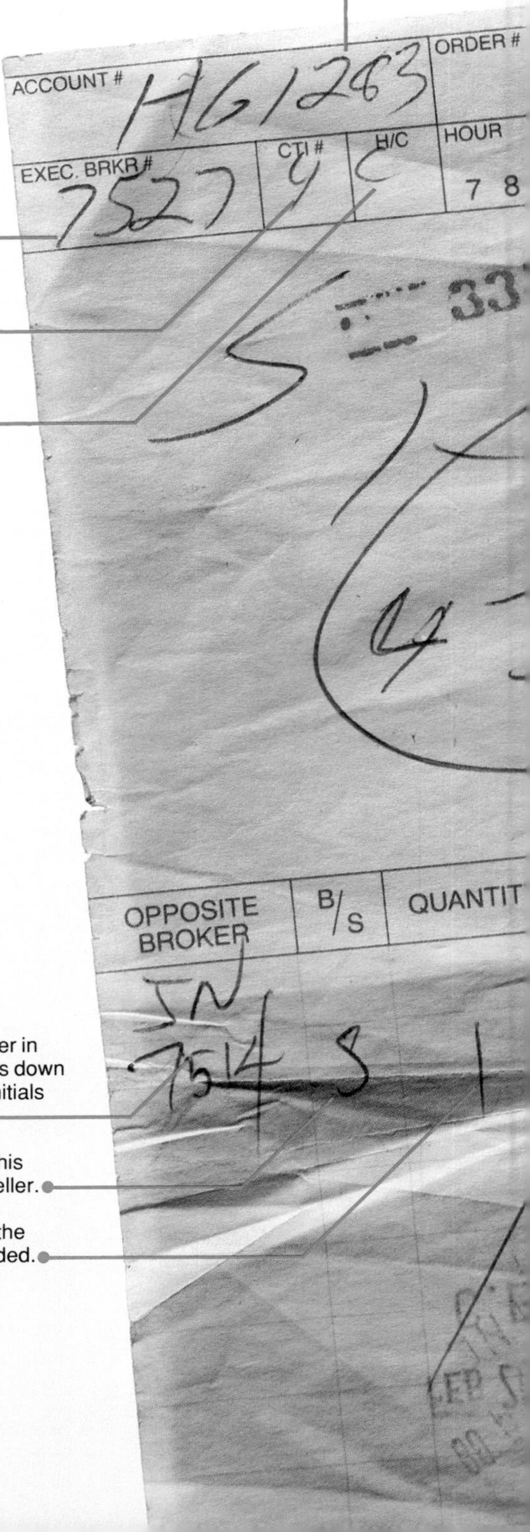

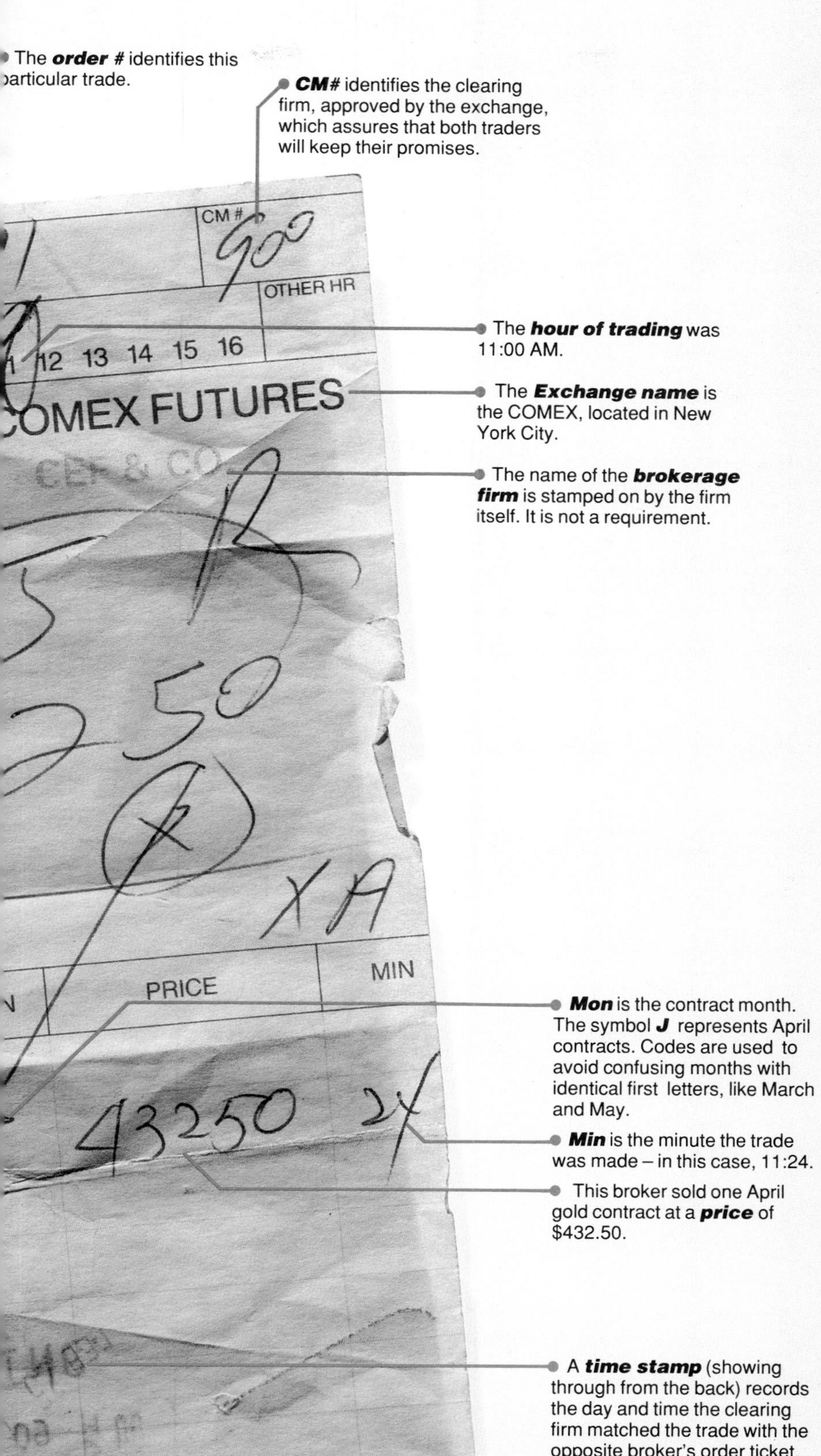

The ***order #*** identifies this particular trade.

CM# identifies the clearing firm, approved by the exchange, which assures that both traders will keep their promises.

The ***hour of trading*** was 11:00 AM.

The ***Exchange name*** is the COMEX, located in New York City.

The name of the ***brokerage firm*** is stamped on by the firm itself. It is not a requirement.

Mon is the contract month. The symbol ***J*** represents April contracts. Codes are used to avoid confusing months with identical first letters, like March and May.

Min is the minute the trade was made – in this case, 11:24.

This broker sold one April gold contract at a ***price*** of $432.50.

A ***time stamp*** (showing through from the back) records the day and time the clearing firm matched the trade with the opposite broker's order ticket, confirming the trade.

The Cash Market

The cash market is the loading platform, the dock — anywhere commodities are picked up or delivered.

What are commodities?

They're the raw materials which go into making the products we use every day of our lives: wheat for bread, rubber for tires, oil for thousands of petroleum-based products like gasoline and plastic cups.

Most businesses buy and sell commodities in the ***cash market***, also commonly called the ***spot market***, since the full cash price is paid "on the spot." Businesses keep a close watch on the cash market. They want to gauge current events, and use current prices as a basis for projecting where prices may be in the future.

Even if you're not in a commodity business, you can learn from watching prices in this market. You may be able to spot price trends on products you frequently buy at the supermarket.

How are cash prices determined?

Commodity prices are based on ***supply and demand***. If a commodity is plentiful, its price will be low. If a commodity is difficult to come by, its price will be high.

Supply and demand for many commodities ebb and flow in fairly predictable seasonal cycles. For example, wheat prices should be lowest at harvest when supplies are plentiful. As supplies are used up, prices should rise. The high season for gold and silver prices usually is around September, when jewelers gear up for the holiday season.

Large white eggs sold in Chicago at wholesale prices of 50¢–56¢ a dozen on Wednesday; sold for between 48¢-54¢ on Tuesday; but were more expensive a year ago at 60¢. Changes in cash prices may be reflected in prices you pay at your local grocery.

CASH PRICES

Wednesday June 22, 1988.
(Quotations as of 4 p.m. Eastern time)

GRAINS AND FEEDS	Wed	Tues	
Barley, top-quality Mpls., bu	3.75-4.40	3.90-4.40	
Bran, wheat middlings, KC ton	101.00	97.00	
Corn, No. 2 yel. Cent-Ill. bu	bp3.21	3.14	
Corn Gluten Feed, Midwest, ton ..	95.-130.	95.-130.	
Cottnsd Meal, Clksdle,Miss. ton ..	255.00	245.00	
Hominy Feed, Cent-Ill. ton	93.00	90.00	
Meat-Bonemeal, 50% pro. Ill. ton .	380.00	380.00	
Oats, No. 2 milling, Mpls., bu	b3.90	3.90	
Sorghum, (Milo) No. 2 Gulf cwt ...	6.30	6.07	
Soybean Meal, Decatur, Illinois ton............	321.-324.	318½-321½	
Soybeans, No. 1 yel Cent.-Ill. bu ...	bp9.95	10.04	
Sunflwr Sd No. 1 Duluth/Supr cwt	12.45	12.45	
Wheat, Spring 14%-pro Mpls. bu ..	4.62	4.66	3
Wheat, No. 2 sft red, St.Lou. bu	3.46	3.51½	
Wheat, No. 2 hard KC, bu	3.91¾	4.01½	2.
FOODS			
Beef, 700-900 lbs. Mid-U.S.,lb.fob .			
Broilers, Dressed "A" NY lb	z	1.05	
Butter, AA, Chgo., lb.	x.6428	.6340	
Cocoa, Ivory Coast, $metric ton ...	1.36	1.36	
Coffee, Brazilian, NY lb.	g1,873	1,862	2
Eggs, Lge white, Chgo doz..........	n1.23	1.23	
Flour, hard winter KC cwt	.50-.56	.48-.54	
Hams, 17-20 lbs, Mid-US lb fob	9.80	10.20	8
Hogs, Iowa-S.Minn. avg. cwt	.65	.67	
Hogs, Omaha avg cwt	47.25	48.75	62
Pork Bellies, 12-14 lbs Mid-US lb ..	46.25	47.75	62
Pork Loins, 14-17 lbs. Mid-US lb ...	.40	.43	
Steers, Tex.-Okla. ch avg cwt	1.09	1.10	1.
Steers, Feeder, Okl Cty, av cwt ...	68.25	68.25	69.
Sugar, cane, raw, world, lb. fob ...	78.90	78.90	80.
FATS AND OILS	.1097	1092	.06
Coconut Oil, crd, N. Orlears lb. ...	xxn.30½		
Corn Oil, crd wet mill, Chgo. lb. ...		.31	.23
Corn Oil, crd dry mill, Chgo. lb. ...	.29	.28½	.2
Cottonseed Oil, crd Miss Vy lb. ...	n.25	.25	.2
Grease, choice white, Chgo lb.	n.30	.30	.19½
Lard, Chgo lb.	.15¼	.15	
Linseed Oil, raw Mpls lb.	.18	.17½	.16
Palm Oil, ref. bl. deod. N.Orl. lb. .	n.a.	n.a.	.25
Peanut Oil, crd, Southeast lb.	n.25½	.25½	.17
Soybean Oil, crd, Decatur, lb.	n.35	.34½	.25½
Tallow, bleachable, Chgo lb.	.3062	.2966	.1592
Tallow, edible, Chgo lb.	n.17¼	.17¼	.12½
FIBERS AND TEXTILES	n.19½	.19½	.16½
Burlap, 10 oz. 40-in. NY yd			
Cotton 1 1/16 in str lw-md Mphs lb	n.2820	.2820	.2405
Print Cloth, poly/cot. 48-in. NY yd	.6580	.6625	.6808
Wool, 64s, Staple, Terr. dd. lb.	5.49	.49	.65
METALS	4.50	4.50	2.70
Aluminum ingot lb. del. Midwest .	q1.28-.34	1.28-.34	.73¾
Copper cathodes lb	p1.16-.17	1.16-.17	.74¼
Copper Scrap, No 2 wire NY lb	k.86	.85	.54
Lead, lb.	p.36-.38	.36-.38	.37
Mercury 76 lb. flask NY	q365-380	365.-380.	310.00
Steel Scrap 1 hvy mlt Chgo ton	108.-113.	108.-113.	83.50
Tin composite lb.	q4.4011	4.3975	4.1086
Zinc High grade lb	p.63-.66	.63-.66	.46½
MISCELLANEOUS			
Rubber, smoked sheets, NY lb.	n.70	.71⅛	.50½
PRECIOUS METALS			
Gold, troy oz			
Engelhard indust bullion	449.91	453.07	443.37
Engelhard fabric prods	472.41	475.72	465.37
Handy & Harman base price	448.50	451.65	441.75
London fixing AM 449.80 PM ...	448.50	451.65	441.75
Krugerrand, whol	a449.50	452.25	445.00
Maple Leaf, troy oz.	a464.00	467.75	459.50
American Eagle, troy oz.	a464.00	467.75	459.50
Platinum, (Free Mkt.)	564.00	579.50	554.50
Platinum, indust (Engelhard)	571.25	586.25	552.00
Platinum, fabric prd (Engelhard)	671.25	686.25	602.00
Palladium, indust (Engelhard) ...	129.50	131.75	135.00
Palladium, fabrc prd (Englhard)	144.50	146.75	150.00
Silver, troy ounce			
Engelhard indust bullion			
Engelhard fabric prods ...			
& Harma			

Gold is very rare. All the gold ever mined could fit on one oil tanker. Platinum is even harder to find, ten times rarer than gold.

Pork bellies are just that, the bellies of hogs. They're used to make bacon. What happens to the rest of the pig? You'll also find hams and pork loins traded in the cash market.

The Futures Contract

The futures market was created to help businesses minimize risks. It's a misconception that futures is primarily a game for high-risk speculators.

Why are there futures contracts?

Commodity prices are unpredictable. From the time farmers plant their crops to the time they ship the crops to market, all kinds of uncontrollable forces can intervene to affect the supply or demand.

Weather

Insects/Disease

Price Supports

Labor Negotiations

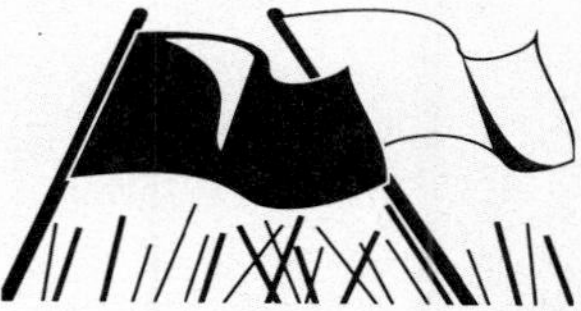

Political Turmoil

Changing Tastes

For years, commodity producers and users worked at the mercy of these disruptive forces. Farmers estimated how large a crop they could sell at harvest and planted accordingly. At harvest time, though, few buyers or an abundance of supply could force them to sell at a loss. Likewise, manufacturers took customers' advance orders only to find, when they needed the raw material to make their product, that it was scarce and prices were sky high.

What are futures contracts?

The antidote to unpredictable prices became the futures contract, ***a deal made now to take place in the future***. In a futures contract, the buyer and seller agree on:

- a future date for delivery;
- the price to be paid on that future date; and
- the quantity and quality of the commodity.

In fact, in some ways, a futures contract is like a house sale. The buyer and seller agree on:

- a future date for delivery (the closing date);
- the price to be paid the seller on that date; and
- the quantity (1 house) and quality (the same condition but with a fixed roof, for instance).

In the house sale, the buyer puts down a 10% good faith deposit to assure the seller that he won't renege. But in a futures contract, both parties put down deposits to ensure that neither will renege.

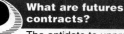

What is in a contract?

It's not profitable or efficient for businesses to trade one bushel or pound at a time. That's why each futures contract represents a ***large quantity*** of a commodity.

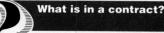

1 contract of wheat = 5,000 bushels

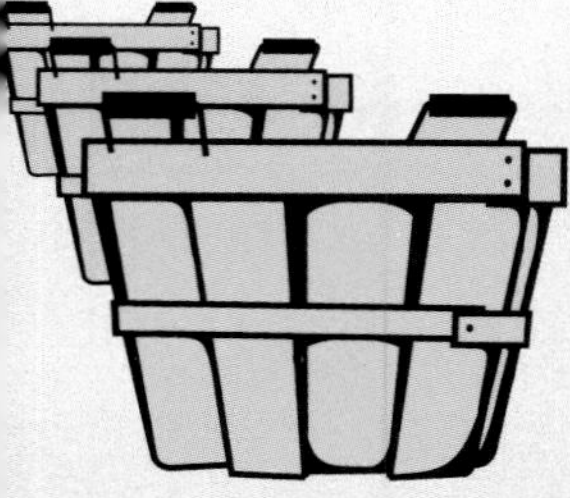

If wheat is $2.50/bu, one contract is worth $12,500.

1 contract of gasoline= 42,000 gallons

If gasoline is worth 55¢/gal, one contract is worth $23,100.

1 contract of sugar = 112,000 pounds

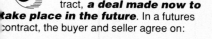

If sugar is 9¢/lb, one contract is worth $10,080.

The Futures Market

Even before the cotton seed grows into a cotton boll, farmers can know in advance what they will be paid, and shirtmakers can know their costs for the material – if they enter into a futures contract.

The ***futures market*** was created for those who use commodities in their businesses. Businesses which produce or use commodities, however, routinely buy and sell in the ***cash market***. They enter the futures market only to protect themselves against risks from volatile prices.

The futures contract is like an insurance policy against changes in price. Contracts are rarely used to trade actual commodities. In fact, nearly 98% of them are cancelled before the delivery period.

There are two distinct classes of traders in the futures market:

Hedgers are businesses who use commodities. They're producers, like farmers, mining companies, foresters, oil drillers. And they're users, like bakers, jewelers, paper mills, oil distributors.

Speculators, on the other hand, trade futures strictly for the money, and they're the ones who can make fortunes or lose their shirts. If you trade futures but never use the commodity itself, you're a speculator.

Hedger: *"All I want is today's contract price. I would rather give up making more money to avoid suffering a loss."*

Speculator: *"I'm willing to risk losing money. I just want the chance to profit from commodity prices without being in the commodity business."*

How hedgers use the market...

Hedgers are mainly interested in using the market to lock in a price. Once they hedge, they are protected against changes in the cash price.

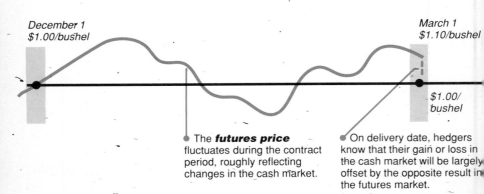

December 1
$1.00/bushel

March 1
$1.10/bushel

$1.00/
bushel

The ***futures price*** fluctuates during the contract period, roughly reflecting changes in the cash market.

On delivery date, hedgers know that their gain or loss in the cash market will be largely offset by the opposite result in the futures market.

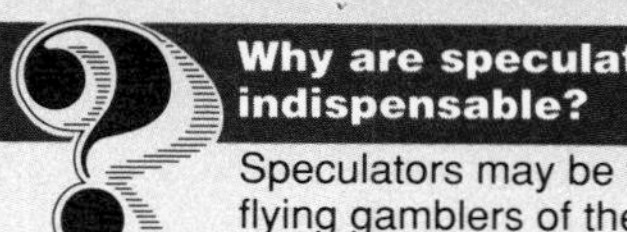

Why are speculators indispensable?

Speculators may be the highest flying gamblers of the financial world. Still, they're crucial to the success of the futures market because they complete a symbiotic relationship between those wishing to avoid risk and those willing to assume it.

Wanting to plan ahead, businesses need to transfer the risk to others. Speculators accept that risk because they want the opportunity to profit.

Speculators also keep the market active. If only businesses traded futures contracts, there simply wouldn't be enough traders in the market. Even worse, all the traders would be commercial traders: no one would be willing to take the risks.

What changes when they enter the futures market?

Hedgers and speculators then enter the futures market – where they become either buyers or sellers...

...It doesn't matter whether the buyer and seller are two hedgers, two speculators or a speculator and a hedger. The buyer always makes one promise and the seller always makes the opposite promise:

Seller: *"I promise that if the price of this commodity becomes more expensive than today's price, I'll subsidize the difference for you."*

Buyer: *"I promise that if the price of your commodity drops below today's price, I'll pay you the difference to cover your loss."*

How speculators use the market...

Speculators hoping to make a profit are only concerned with price fluctuations. They must watch the market carefully every day.

December 1
$1.00/bushel

March 1
$1.10/bushel

The ***futures price*** fluctuates during the contract period, roughly reflecting changes in the cash market.

Since they don't trade in the cash market, their gain or loss in the futures market is the final outcome.

Trading Futures Contracts

When you trade futures, you enter into contracts to buy or sell commodities.

To trade futures, you give your broker an order to enter you into a contract as either a buyer or a seller, depending on which way you think the market is headed. The "cost of the contract" is really what the commodity will cost if delivered. The contract itself costs virtually nothing.

When your order is filled, you go into a pool at the Exchange with all the other traders. An agent for the Exchange then pairs buyers and sellers anonymously.

At the start, the Exchange will require your broker to collect from you a good faith deposit. This deposit, called the ***initial margin***, required by the Exchange is usually 2-5% of the contract's full value. Brokers often charge speculators more.

The Exchange is responsible for seeing that you keep your promise. Consequently, at the end of every day, based on the amount the contract price moves, you will either have money added to or taken from your account. In other words, every day, you either subsidize someone else or someone else subsidizes you. This daily crediting or debiting of your account is called ***marking to the market***.

Entering and leaving the market

to enter the market	***which means***	***to leave the market***	***which means***
you can ***go long***	you take a position as a buyer	you ***go short***	offsetting contracts cancel each other; you have no more obligations – you are out of the market
or you can ***go short***	you take a position as a seller	you ***go long***	

How is a commodity's future price set?

If you agree to buy a commodity for immediate delivery, your price will be ***today's cash price***. But if someone agrees to hold the commodity until you're ready for it, you'll also be charged for storage, insurance and other ***carrying costs*** to cover the daily expenses until delivery.

Speculation also determines a commodity's price. It can drive the price way up or down. Price volatility creates more speculation in the market because even though there's a greater risk of losing money, there's also a greater chance to make a big profit.

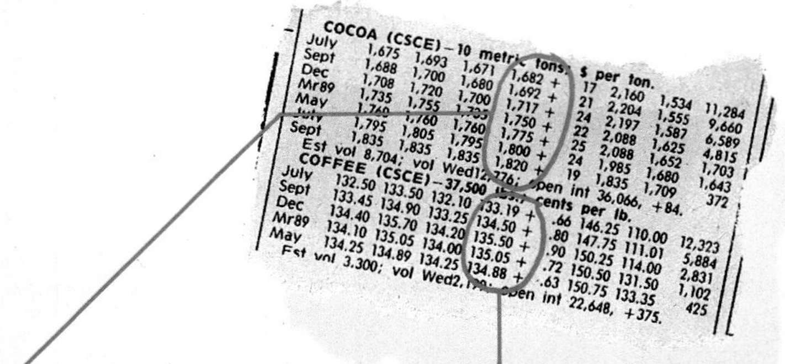

COCOA (CSCE)–10 metric tons; $ per ton.

July	1,675	1,693	1,671	1,682	+ 17	2,160	1,534	11,284
Sept	1,688	1,700	1,680	1,692	+ 21	2,204	1,555	9,660
Dec	1,708	1,720	1,700	1,717	+ 24	2,197	1,587	6,589
Mr89	1,735	1,755	[illegible]	1,750	+ 22	2,088	1,625	4,815
May	1,760	1,760	1,760	1,775	+ 25	2,088	1,652	1,703
July	1,795	1,805	1,795	1,800	+ 24	1,985	1,680	1,643
Sept	1,835	1,835	1,835	1,820	+ 19	1,835	1,709	372

Est vol 8,704; vol Wed12,776; open int 36,066, +84.

COFFEE (CSCE)–37,500 lbs.; cents per lb.

July	132.50	133.50	132.10	133.19	+ .66	146.25	110.00	12,323
Sept	133.45	134.90	133.25	134.50	+ .80	147.75	111.01	5,884
Dec	134.40	135.70	134.20	135.50	+ .90	150.25	114.00	2,831
Mr89	134.10	135.05	134.00	135.05	+ .72	150.50	131.50	1,102
May	134.25	134.89	134.25	134.88	+ .63	150.75	133.35	425

Est vol 3,300; vol Wed2,[illegible]; open int 22,648, +375.

• You're looking at the prices parties have promised to pay for cocoa when delivered in various months. The farther away the delivery day, the more carrying costs involved. Even so, prices rarely rise progressively in consecutive months. When they do, the relationship is called a ***contango***.

• More often than not, seasonal cycles and the supply and demand projections of speculators cause prices to be higher in some months, dip in later months, then rise again later. Notice that coffee would cost you less if you were willing to wait until March 1989 than if you would want it in December 1988.

The first futures contracts were made in Japan

The first recorded cases of futures trading occurred in Japan in the 1600s. Landlords, collecting a share of each rice harvest as rent, found weather and other conditions made payments too unpredictable.

In need of ready cash at all times, the landlords shipped rice to major cities for storage in warehouses. They then began selling warehouse receipts, which gave the holder the right to receive a certain amount of rice, of a certain quality, at a date in the future. As the holders periodically cashed in these receipts for rice, ***rice tickets*** *became an accepted form of currency.*

Rice tickets gave landlords steady income. And merchants had a steady supply of rice – plus an opportunity to profit by selling the tickets to others at a higher price.

What's the risk in speculating?

You can lose a lot more money than you invested because of ***leverage***. In financial terms, leverage means using a little bit of money to control something of much greater value. For example, it's possible to put down only $5,000 of your own money to control one gold contract worth $50,000. With that kind of leverage, every time the price of gold goes up 10¢ you earn or lose $10. That means a mere 50¢ move could make you – or cost you – $50. And, with just a $50 move, you could double your money – or lose it all.

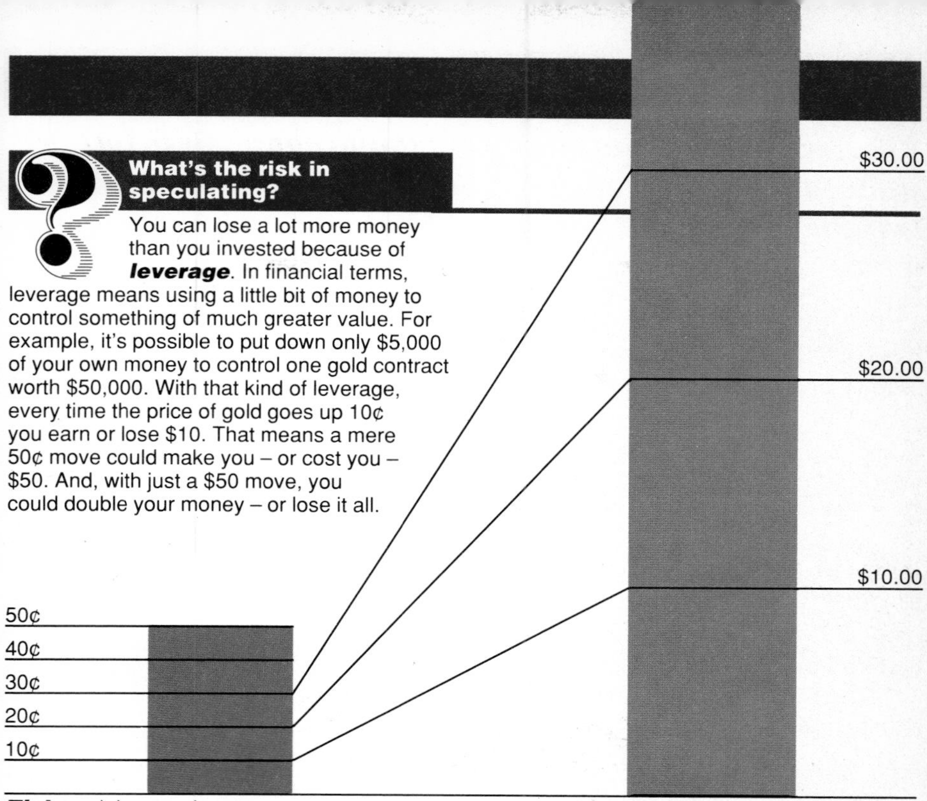

$30.00
$20.00
$10.00

50¢
40¢
30¢
20¢
10¢

Ticks: minimum price moves of a gold contract

Contract: corresponding changes in the value of a gold contract (100 oz. of gold)

What other risks are there?

The minimum amount a price can move up or down is called a ***tick***. The minimum amount varies, however, from commodity to commodity. A trade at a higher price is called an ***uptick***; at a lower price, a ***downtick***.

To protect traders from truly disastrous losses, many exchanges impose daily ***price limits*** on each contract trading. These are the maximum price movements (up or down) permissible in a trading day. Once a price reaches this ceiling or floor, the only trades executed will be ones at the limit price or within the limit.

How can traders reduce risks?

Frequent futures traders may try to coordinate trading between two different markets or two different commodities through a strategy called ***spread trading***.

Spread trading means buying one contract and simultaneously selling another, related contract. You will always make money on one contract and lose money on the other; but the object is to make more money on the one contract than you lose on the other.

The key to this strategy is the **spread** – the difference between the two contracts' prices. For example, a ***time spread***, shown below, involves buying and selling contracts for the same commodity but with different delivery months. Your hope is that the same events will affect these two contracts differently, narrowing or widening the spread over time.

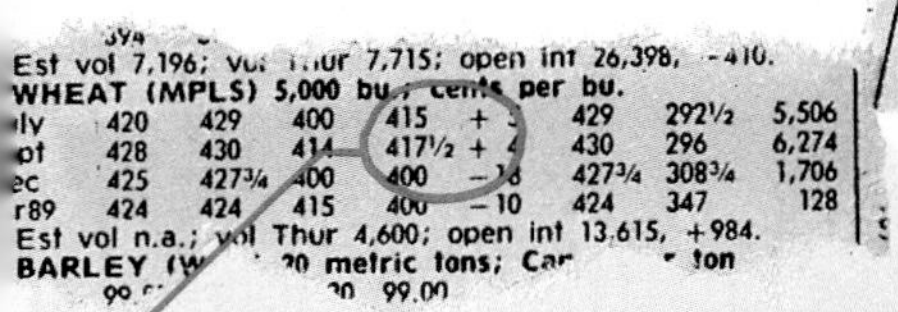

Est vol 7,196; vol Thur 7,715; open int 26,398, -410.
WHEAT (MPLS) 5,000 bu.; cents per bu.
July 420 429 400 415 + 429 292½ 5,506
Sept 428 430 414 417½ + 430 296 6,274
Dec 425 427¾ 400 400 – 427¾ 308¾ 1,706
Mr89 424 424 415 400 – 10 424 347 128
Est vol n.a.; vol Thur 4,600; open int 13,615, +984.
BARLEY (W... 20 metric tons; Can... ton

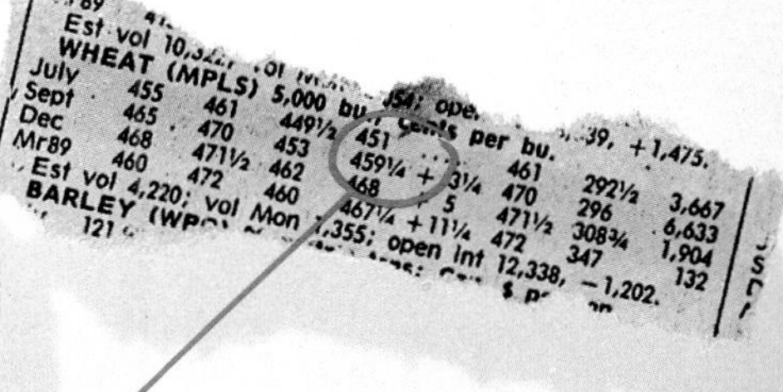

You agree to sell wheat in July at $4.15 a bushel and, simultaneously, agree to buy wheat in September at $4.17½ a bushel. The 2½¢ difference is the spread.

30 days later, prices have risen substantially. You've lost 36¢ a bushel on the July contract, but you've made 41¾¢ on the September contract.

The spread has now widened to 8¼¢, and this 5¾¢ increase is your profit. (Had you *bought* the July contract and *sold* the September contract instead, you would have made 36¢ and lost 41¾¢. In that case, the 5¾¢ change would have been the amount of your loss.)

Keeping Tabs on Futures Prices

Futures tables are easier to read than stock tables. And since futures prices relate directly to world conditions, learning to read the futures pages can help bring the world a little closer.

Open refers to the price at which cotton first sold when the exchange opened in the morning. Depending on overnight events in the world, the opening price may not be the same as the closing price from the day before. Since prices are expressed in terms of cents per pound, the 69.40 means cotton opened for sale at 69.4¢ a pound. Multiply 69.4¢ times 50,000 pounds and you've calculated the full value of one contract at the open of trading for the day.

High, low and ***settle*** tell you the contract's highest, lowest and closing prices for the day. These figures, viewed together, provide a good indication of how volatile the market for that commodity was during the trading day. After opening at 69.4¢ a pound, cotton for July delivery never sold for more than 69.5¢ a pound and never for less than 68¢. Trading finally ended, or settled, at 68.7¢.

Change compares the closing price given here with the previous closing price (listed in the previous day's paper). A plus (+) sign indicates prices ended higher; a minus (-) means prices ended lower. In this case, orange juice for July delivery settled 1/2 cent lower than it did the previous day. Orange juice for November delivery edged up 1/4 of a cent.

FUTURES PRICES

Tuesday June 21, 1988

Open Interest Reflects Previous Trading

	Open	High	Low	Settle	Change	Lifetime High
COTTON (CTN) – 50,000 lbs.; cents per lb.						
July	69.40	69.50	68.02	68.70	– .75	81.40
Oct	68.65	68.85	67.70	68.25	– .45	73.0[illegible]
Dec	67.50	68.20	66.85	67.58	– .25	70.2[illegible]
Mr89	68.25	68.90	67.80	68.20	– .30	68.[illegible]
May	68.60	68.70	67.90	68.65	– .05	68.[illegible]
July	....	....	....	68.65	– .05	65.[illegible]
Est vol 7,500; vol Mon 6,239; open int 3[illegible]						
ORANGE JUICE (CTN) – 15,000 lbs.; cents per lb.						
July	176.00	176.10	175.25	175.50	– .50	178
Sept	173.70	174.00	172.75	173.25	– .30	17[illegible]
Nov	167.10	167.30	166.80	167.10	+ .25	17[illegible]
Ja89	161.10	162.60	161.10	162.50	+ 1.40	17[illegible]
				161.85	+ 1.55	16[illegible]

The product is listed alphabetically within its particular grouping. Orange juice is listed under the heading ***Foods & Fibers***.

This shows a commodity's ***expiration cycle.*** Every contract expires during a certain month. *Ja89* indicates January of 1989. When the delivery date is reached, the expired contract is dropped from the table. The cycles usually coincide with activity in the commodity. For example, trading in grains follows a cycle in keeping with planting, harvesting and exporting. Rarely will you see a contract month that is more than 24 months away. Usually, the more distant contract months see the least trading activity anyway.

This is the ***exchange*** on which the futures contracts are traded. A list of what each abbreviation means is printed at the bottom of the page each day. Here CTN is the New York Cotton Exchange.

Some commodities trade on more than one exchange. The table on the futures page lists activity on the exchange watched most closely by those dealing in that commodity.

The size of each contract reflects the bulk trading units used during the normal course of commercial business. One contract of lumber covers the rights to 150,000 board-feet of lumber. ***The price per unit*** is expressed in either dollars or cents. The lumber prices in the table are expressed in dollars per 1,000 board-feet. To find the full value of the contract, multiply the day's settlement price by 150 since the contract is 150 times the unit.

Lifetime highs and lows indicate how much volatility there has been in the trading of this particular contract – an indication of risk and reward. You can see that lumber's July price of $192.70 is approximately halfway between the lifetime high and low for this particular contract.

Open Interest allows you to see how much interest there is in trading a particular contract. The closest months usually attract the most activity, as you can see from the difference in July lumber versus November lumber. The term *open interest* refers to the total number of outstanding contracts; that is, those that have not been cancelled by offsetting trades.

—WOOD—

LUMBER (CME)–150,000 bd. ft.; $ per 1,000 bd. ft.

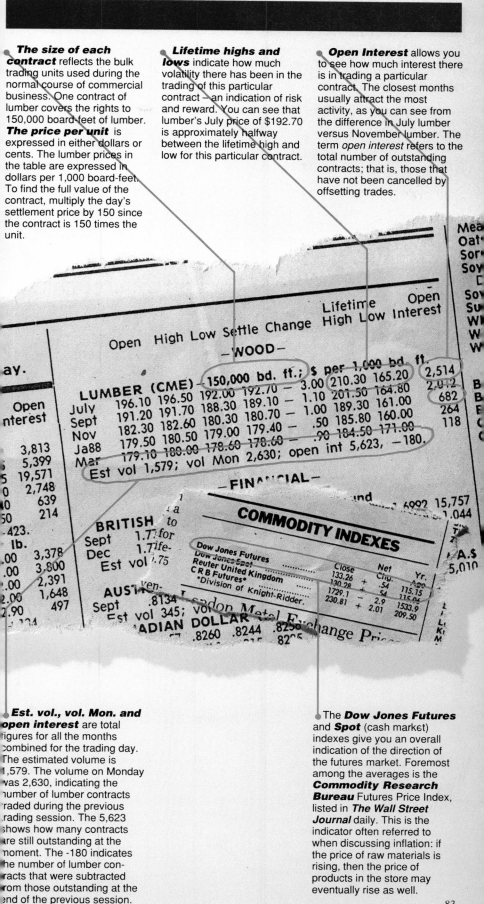

	Open	High	Low	Settle	Change	Lifetime High	Lifetime Low	Open Interest
July	196.10	196.50	192.00	192.70	– 3.00	210.30	165.20	2,514
Sept	191.20	191.70	188.30	189.10	– 1.10	201.50	164.80	2,012
Nov	182.30	182.60	180.30	180.70	– 1.00	189.30	161.00	682
Ja88	179.50	180.50	179.00	179.40	– .50	185.80	160.00	264
Mar	179.10	180.00	178.60	178.60	– .90	184.50	171.00	118

Est vol 1,579; vol Mon 2,630; open int 5,623, –180.

COMMODITY INDEXES

	Close	Net Chg.	Yr. Ago
Dow Jones Futures	133.26	+ .54	115.15
Dow Jones Spot	130.28	+ .54	115.06
Reuter United Kingdom	1729.1	– 2.9	1533.9
C R B Futures*	230.81	+ 2.01	209.50

*Division of Knight-Ridder.

Est. vol., vol. Mon. and open interest are total figures for all the months combined for the trading day. The estimated volume is 1,579. The volume on Monday was 2,630, indicating the number of lumber contracts traded during the previous trading session. The 5,623 shows how many contracts are still outstanding at the moment. The -180 indicates the number of lumber contracts that were subtracted from those outstanding at the end of the previous session.

The ***Dow Jones Futures*** and ***Spot*** (cash market) indexes give you an overall indication of the direction of the futures market. Foremost among the averages is the ***Commodity Research Bureau*** Futures Price Index, listed in ***The Wall Street Journal*** daily. This is the indicator often referred to when discussing inflation: if the price of raw materials is rising, then the price of products in the store may eventually rise as well.

The Futures Market in Action

The cash price table tells you what it cost to take delivery of a commodity yesterday. The futures table tells you how much it will cost to take delivery of a commodity in future months.

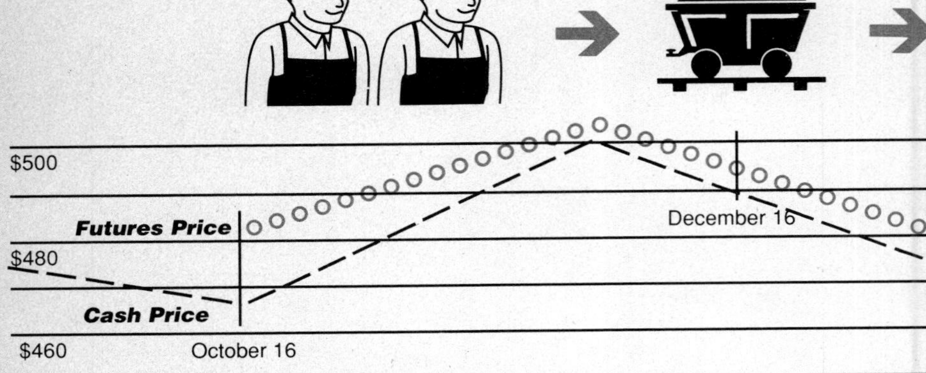

On October 16, 1987, a jeweler received an order for gold bracelets which the customer wanted delivered in May. Knowing she would need the gold to make the bracelets in April, the jeweler bought 5 April gold contracts (500 ounces). A mining company expected to have 800 ounces of gold to sell in April, so the company sold 8 April contracts (800 ounces). A speculator bet that prices would rise and bought 3 April contracts (300 ounces).

PRECIOUS METALS

Gold, troy oz			
Engelhard indust bullion	468.04	462.23	425.90
Engelhard fabric prods	[illegible]	485.34	447.20
Handy & Harman base price	466.60	460.80	425.50
London fixing AM 461.75 PM ...	[illegible]	460.80	425.50
Krugerrand, whol	a462.75	460.75	423.50

In the cash market, on October 16, 1987, at the New York firm of Handy & Harman, you would have paid $466.60 for immediate delivery of an ounce of gold.

Est vol 12,500; vol

GOLD (CMX)—100 troy oz.; $ per troy oz.

Oct	462.20	468.50	462.20	462.90	+ 2.10	494.00	361.00	[illegible]
Dec	466.80	472.50	466.50	467.80	+ 2.00	501.00	365.00	[illegible]
Fb88	474.50	480.00	473.80	[illegible]	+ 2.20	510.00	371.00	[illegible]
Apr	482.00	487.00	482.00	482.60	+ 2.40	514.00	378.00	[illegible]
June	489.00	494.50	489.00	[illegible]	+ 2.60	523.00	399.00	[illegible]
Aug	496.00	502.00	496.00	[illegible].60	+ 2.70	526.00	425.00	
Oct	504.50	510.50	504.50	[illegible].40	+ 2.80	531.00	429.00	
Dec	512.00	519.00	511.00	[illegible].10	+ 2.80	544.00	430.00	
Fb89	520.50	525.00	520.50	[illegible]1.00	+ 2.80	540.00	480.00	[illegible]

In the futures market, on the same day, futures traders agreed to buy and sell gold for April delivery at prices ranging from $482.00 to $487.00. Trading ended the day at $482.60. In other words, on October 16, buyers were willing to pay significantly more than the cash price ($466.60) in order to guarantee a price for gold to be delivered 6½ months later.

For simplicity's sake, assume the jeweler, miner and speculator all agreed to a price of $482.60.

On December 16, 1987, the Soviet Union (the world's second largest gold producer) sold a large amount of gold. Rumors of a massive gold sell-off began to circulate. After having reached $500 an ounce, the price of gold began to drop.

PRECIOUS METALS

Gold, troy oz			
Engelhard indust bullion	493.99	501.25	394.61
Engelhard fabric prods	[illegible]	526.31	414.34
Handy & Harman base price	492.50	499.75	393.10
London fixing AM 493.70 PM ...	[illegible]	499.75	393.10
Krugerrand, whol	a485.00	497.00	394.00
Maple Leaf, troy oz.	a499.00	511.50	[illegible]
American Eagle, troy oz.	[illegible]	511.50	[illegible]

In the cash market, on December 16, you could have bought an ounce of gold for $492.50.

Est vol 10,000;

GOLD (CMX)—100 troy oz.; $ per troy oz.

Dec	493.50	494.20	480.00	482.70	−12.80	502.30	365.00	1,738
Fb88	498.80	499.20	484.50	487.20	−13.20	510.00	371.00	65,519
Apr	505.00	506.00	490.50	493.60	−13.50	514.00	378.00	38,322
June	512.00	512.00	495.00	499.80	−13.80	523.00	399.00	14,696
Aug	510.00	510.00	505.50	506.20	−14.10	527.00	425.00	8,995
Oct	526.00	526.00	520.50	512.90	−14.40	533.50	429.00	8,719
Dec	531.80	532.50	519.50	519.60	−14.70	546.00	430.00	10,682
Fb89	535.50	535.50	532.00	526.60	−14.90	549.50	480.00	4,995
Apr				533.80	−15.10	550.00	501.00	2,864

In the futures market, that same day, the cost of gold for delivery in April ended the trading day at $493.60.

Buyers were now willing to pay only a small premium over the cash price ($492.50). This may have meant that the market didn't expect prices to rise very much during the next four months.

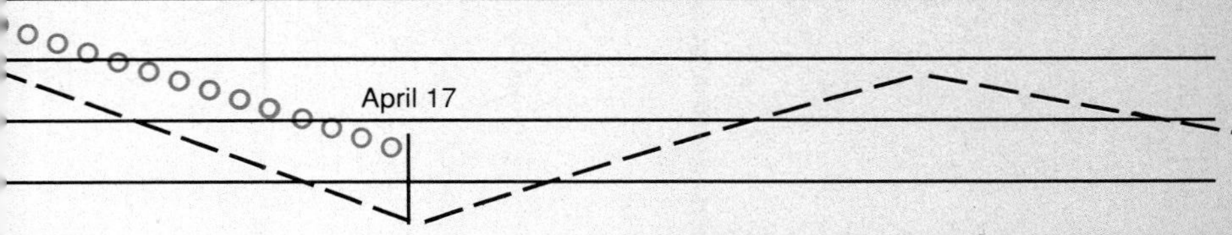

On April 17, 1988, everyone knew that all April contracts would expire at the end of the next trading day. Traders either had to take delivery or cancel their obligations by offsetting their contracts. (Those who had agreed to buy now had to agree to sell. Those who had agreed to sell now had to agree to buy. The opposite obligations cancel out each other.)

troy oz	PRECIOUS METALS		
gelhard indust bullion	451.72	448.41	450.64
gelhard fabric prods	[illegible]	470.83	473.14
ndy & Harman base price	450.30	447.00	449.00
don fixing AM 449.10 PM ...	450.30	447.00	449.00
gerrand, whol	a451.00	448.00	455.75
ple Leaf, troy oz.	a467.00	464.25	466.25
	a467.00	[illegible]	[illegible]

In the cash market, on April 17, you could have bought gold for $450.30 an ounce. (Back in October, gold for April delivery sold for $482.60.)

ol 5,500; vol Tues 8,042; open ...

(CMX)–100 troy oz.: $ per troy oz.

450.50	453.20	449.50	452.30	+	2.50	514.00	378.00	730
451.00	455.00	450.80	454.30	+	3.00	523.00	399.00	67,513
455.60	459.20	455.60	458.70	+	3.00	527.00	425.00	16,303
461.60	464.00	461.60	463.40	+	3.00	533.50	429.00	11,945
465.00	468.50	465.00	468.20	+	3.00	546.00	430.00	17,375
....	....	....	473.00	+	3.00	549.50	446.00	9,033
		....	478.00	+	3.00	550.00	[illegible]	[illegible]

In the futures market, the April contract settled at $452.30 The cash price is virtually the same as the contract price on the last day it trades, because futures traders and cash traders agree to the same thing: delivery of gold at the end of the day. Fees charged by the Exchange for processing, delivery and other costs account for the actual difference in the price you see. (Also, you don't see the last day of trading in the newspaper. When a contract expires, newspapers drop it from the table.)

How the hedgers fared:

At the April delivery date, the mining company made $30.30 profit and the jeweler lost $30.30 on their contracts. However, since the cash market price in April was $450.30 – much less than the $482.60 contract price – the end result was what they both expected, for the following reasons:

The mining company:
The mining company profited on the futures contracts, but was forced to sell the gold at a lower than anticipated price.

Futures contract price	+ sold at	$482.60
Delivery price in April	- bought at	$452.30
Outcome of futures trade	= profit	$ 30.30
Cash market price	+ sold at	$450.30
	+ futures profit	$ 30.30
Final outcome	= net sell price	$480.60

The jeweler:
The jeweler lost money on the futures contracts but was able to buy the gold at a lower than anticipated price.

Futures contract price	- bought at	$482.60
Delivery price in April	+ sold at	$452.30
Outcome of futures trade	= loss	-$ 30.30
Cash market price	- bought at	$450.30
	- futures loss	$ 30.30
Final outcome	= net buy price	$480.60

How the speculator fared:

Assume the speculator stayed in the futures market until December 16, then sold the three futures contracts. (In practice, however, many speculators hold their contracts for only a day or two.)

Futures contract price	- bought at	$482.60
December contract price	+ sold at	$493.60
Final outcome	= profit	$ 11.00

Financial Futures

Stocks, bonds and currencies are the commodities of the investment business. Futures contracts also protect those who use these commodities in their business.

What kind of financial futures are traded?

There are a wide variety of futures, and new kinds are constantly being added. Most futures contracts are pegged to widely used currencies or widely followed indexes, including:

- ***British pounds***
- ***Canadian dollars***
- ***Japanese yen***
- ***Eurodollars***
- ***Treasury bonds, notes, bills***
- ***Municipal Bond Index***
- ***S&P 500 Index***
- ***Major Market Index***

Treasury bond futures are the most heavily traded financial futures contracts. The most highly publicized, however, have been ***stock index futures*** – a group which includes the last two on this list.

What are stock indexes?

Stock indexes are ***mathematical indicators*** used to measure the collective performance of specific groups of stocks. For example, the Major Market Index comprises 30 major industrial stocks listed on the New York Stock Exchange (even though it's produced by the American Stock Exchange).

The S&P 500 Index is composed of 500 stocks listed on the NYSE, AMEX and OTC. The S&P 500 Index futures contract is the most widely traded financial futures contract.

Who uses stock index futures?

They were created for hedgers, such as mutual fund investment managers, pension fund managers, securities firms – ***anyone who owns and trades large portfolios of stock***.

Mutual fund managers, owning many of the stocks included in the S&P 500 Index, take sell positions in an S&P 500 Index futures contract. This protects them from declining stock prices, just as the wheat futures contract protects the farmer from falling wheat prices.

Investors planning to buy the stock in the future can lock in a price by taking a buy position in a futures contract. And those who want to speculate will be either sellers or buyers, depending whether they think the stocks in the index will rise or fall in value.

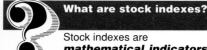

–FINANCIAL–

RITISH POUND (IMM) – $ per pound
t 1.7788 1.7860 1.7782 1.7832 + .0072 1.9012 1.699
c 1.7720 1.7784 1.7720 1.7760 + .0072 1.9000 1.698
Est vol 4,122; vol Mon3,746; open int 16,844, –25

USTRALIAN DOLLAR (IMM)–100,000 dlrs.; $
pt .8134 .8146 .8129 .8140 +.0051 .8146 .700
Est vol 345; vol Mon 501; open int 5,035, –224.
CANADIAN DOLLAR (IMM)–100,000 dlrs.; $ pe
pt .8257 .8260 .8244 .8256 +.0007 .8260 .73
ec .8223 .8230 .8215 .8225 +.0007 .8230 .73
r89 .8195 .8200 .8188 .8194 +.0007 .8200 .75
Est vol 7,302; vol Mon 4,627; open int 36,682, +
JAPANESE YEN (IMM) 12.5 million yen; $ per
pt .7978 .7991 .7972 .7979 –.0007 .8485 .7
ec .8050 .8055 .8036 .8045 –.0006 .8530 .7
r89 .... .8113 –.0007 .8590 .7
Est vol 15,297; vol Mon 16,785; open int 39,97
SWISS FRANC (IMM)–125,000 francs-$ per fr
ept .6913 .6946 .6908 .6939 +.0034 .8120
ec .6995 .7024 .6980 .7019 +.0036 .8210
Est vol 18,309; vol Mon 17,448; open int 28,63
W. GERMAN MARK (IMM) 125,000 marks; $
ept .5744 .5757 .5738 .5750 .0018 .6555
ec .5792 .5807 .5787 .5801 +.0018 .6610
Est vol 13,614; vol Mon 18,380; open int 49,4
EURODOLLAR (LIFFE)–$1 million; pts of
Sept 91.91 91.97 91.85 91.96 + .10 93.19
Dec 91.53 91.57 91.47 91.57 + .10 92.93
Mr89 91.32 91.37 91.29 91.37 + .11 92.33
June 91.16 91.16 91.16 91.21 + .11 92.10
Est vol 10,046; vol Mon 8,090; open int 28,15
STERLING (LIFFE)–£500,000; pts of 100%
Sept 90.11 90.30 90.11 90.29 + .18 91.47
Dec 90.04 90.16 90.00 90.15 + .15 91.45
Mr89 89.98 90.12 89.98 90.09 + .12 90.94
June 89.92 89.97 89.92 89.99 + .11 90.66
Sept 89.95 89.95 89.95 89.97 + .11 90.47
Dec 89.89 89.89 89.87 89.87 + .10 90.22
Mr90 89.81 89.81 89.77 89.81 + .09 89.98
Est vol 13,587; vol Mon 20,166; open int 2
T–BONDS (LIFFE) $1 mil.; pts of 100%
June .... 88-02 + 0-23 90-1
Sept 86-21 87-07 86-17 87-06 + 0-24 89-2
Est vol 10,039; vol Mon 5,793; open int 7,3
LONG GILT (LIFFE)–£50,000; 32nds of
June 120-00 120-01 119-21 119-19 – 0-03 123-2
Sept 95-23 95-29 95-16 95-19 98-2
Est vol 18,361; vol Mon 18,801; open int 3
EURODOLLAR (IMM)–$1 million; pts o

	Open	High	Low	Settle	Chg	Sett
Sept	91.90	91.97	91.86	91.89	– .05	8.1
Dec	91.50	91.58	91.47	91.51	– .04	8.4
Mr89	91.28	91.39	91.27	91.30	– .04	8.7
June	91.13	91.22	91.12	91.14	– .04	8.
Sept	90.99	91.08	90.99	91.00	– .04	9.
Dec	90.93	90.98	90.88	90.89	– .04	9.
Mr90	90.82	90.89	90.80	90.80	– .04	9.
June	90.74	90.80	90.72	90.72	– .04	9.
Sept	90.73	90.73	90.64	90.65	– .03	9.
Dec	90.63	90.65	90.56	90.58	– .02	9
Mr91	90.56	90.57	90.48	90.51	– .01	9.
June	90.44	90.49	90.41	90.43	– .01	9

Est vol 135,712; vol Mon 111,183; o
+2,315.
U.S. DOLLAR INDEX (FINEX) 500 ti
Sept 92.30 92.33 92.09 92.21 – .16
Dec 92.48 92.50 92.40 92.51 – .16
Est vol 3,000; vol Mon 473; open int 6
The index: High 92.33; Low 92.10; Clo
CRB INDEX (NYFE) 500 times Index
July 269.25 269.70 265.30 267.95 + 1.20
Sept 269.70 270.90 265.80 268.60 + .90
Dec 267.00 267.00 265.50 266.90 + .20
Mr89 265.50 266.50 265.50 265.20 + .55
Est vol 3,106; vol Mon 1,964; open in
The index: High 269.55; Low 265.90;

TREASURY BONDS (CBT)–$100,000;
June 87-18 88-03 87-06 87-07 – 16
Sept 86-25 87-08 86-12 86-21 – 5
Dec 85-30 86-12 85-17 85-25 – 5
Mr89 85-06 85-15 84-24 84-30 – 5
June 84-11 84-21 83-30 84-04 –
Sept 83-29 83-29 83-07 83-12 –
Dec 82-29 82-29 82-18 82-22 –
Mr90 82-10 82-10 81-30 82-01 –
Est vol 315,000; vol Mon 272,861; o
TREASURY NOTES (CBT)–$100,00
June 93-08 93-16 92-31 93-00 –
92-11 92-17 –

What is program trading?

It's ***using computer programs to signal when to buy and sell***.

The computer program is designed to alert traders whenever the stock index futures contract price moves either higher or lower than the index itself. Comparing the actual index to the futures contract, the trader will quickly sell the more expensive of the two and buy the less expensive. The difference is the profit. This is an example of ***arbitrage.***

Often, this price difference is only $^{1}/_{32}$ or $^{1}/_{16}$ of a dollar. To reap huge profits, therefore, traders will trade a huge number of contracts at a time.

• On a currency contract's delivery day you can take delivery of the amount of currency in the contract. The price is shown in terms of the number of dollars per deutschemarks – one deutschemark will get you .5750 of a dollar.

–INDEXES–

MUNI BOND INDEX(CBT)$1,000; times Bond Buyer MBI

	Open	High	Low	Settle	Chg	High	Low	Open Interest
June	87-26	88-09	87-26	88-09	+ 11	89-26	70-03	2,835
Sept	85-08	85-27	85-03	85-19	+ 11	88-08	81-02	9,053
Dec	83-15	83-27	83-06	83-19	+ 10	86-29	80-16	532
Mr89	82-02	82-02	81-13	81-26	+ 10	85-05	78-25	502
June	80-12	80-12	79-23	80-03	+ 9	82-20	77-06	570

Est vol 7,000; vol Mon 4,760; open int 13,492, –336.
The index: Close 88-09; Yield 8.33.

S&P 500 INDEX (CME) 500 times index

Sept	273.30	275.50	268.60	275.40	+ 3.90	343.50	193.00	95,970
Dec	274.35	277.40	270.80	277.40	+ 3.90	282.10	252.20	1,587
Mr89	275.70	279.00	272.00	279.00	+ 4.00	283.50	253.90	101

Est vol 49,672; vol Mon 35,690; open int 97,659, –30,779.
Indx prelim High 271.67; Low 267.52; Close 271.67 +2.73

NYSE COMPOSITE INDEX (NYFE) 500 times index

Sept	154.00	155.70	151.80	155.65	+ 2.15	158.10	128.50	4,434
Dec	155.35	156.40	152.85	156.70	+ 2.15	159.20	137.95	851
Mr89	157.05	157.05	157.05	157.75	+ 2.15	157.05	144.25	230

Est vol 8,221; vol Mon 4,127; open int 5,516, –2.
The index: High 153.29; Low 151.30; Close 153.29 + 1.33

KC VALUE LINE INDEX (KC) 500 times index

Sept	245.50	247.45	241.40	247.45	+ 3.15	249.50	225.00	1,291
Dec	247.75	250.05	244.60	250.05	+ 3.00	250.05	237.25	10

Est vol 250; vol Mon 123; open int 1,301, –74.
New index: High 241.95; Low 240.07; Close 241

• ***The value of an index contract is calculated differently than for other futures contracts.*** Although there's a value to the contract, you can only take delivery of the contract's value, not the contract itself. In this example, the value of the September S&P 500 contract is 500 times the closing index of 275.40, or $137,700. On delivery day, all accounts are settled, and the contracts are cancelled. Those who want delivery receive the full cash value.

• These ***Treasury bond futures*** trade on the CBT, the Chicago Board of Trade. Each contract is worth $100,000 of Treasury bonds. (Notice that on the LIFFE, the London International Financial Futures Exchange, listed on this page, each Treasury bond futures contract equals $1 million of bonds.) The minimum tick, or price movement, is $^{1}/_{32}$ of a point. For instance, bonds for June delivery settled at $87^{7}/_{32}$ points ($870.21875) each. The bonds' yield settled at 9.432%, up .062% from the previous day.

*Some index futures are pegged to obscure indexes, even ones created by private companies. You'll find advertisements listing these indexes on the futures page of **The Wall Street Journal:***

- ***Financial News Network Index***
- ***Russell 2000/3000 Stock Indexes***
- ***CBOT Corporate Bond Index***

The Futures Exchanges

Exchanges are the only places where futures contracts are traded. No regulated over-the-counter futures market exists.

Customers' orders from all around the world are funneled here. When Saudi oil ministers, Texas oil barons, major oil companies and local independents want to buy or sell oil, they call their brokers who call their floorbrokers who step into the trading pit and make deals.

The Chicago Board of Trade is pictured here. Among many other commodities, financial futures are traded at the ***CBOT***.

Exchange floors are divided into ***pits*** and ***rings***.

The ***trading pit*** is usually tiered into three or four levels. During heavy activity, traders stand on the steps to see over the heads of the traders in front of them.

The ring is a smaller area, usually reserved for commodities with lighter trading. Traders stand around a circular table and, after completing a deal, drop their trading cards into an area in the middle where the pit recorder stands.

Usually, one commodity trades in each area, unless volume is too small to justify the use of space. Pits for soybeans, gold even stock index futures may stand side by side.

Options on the futures contracts always trade in an area adjacent to their corresponding futures trading area.

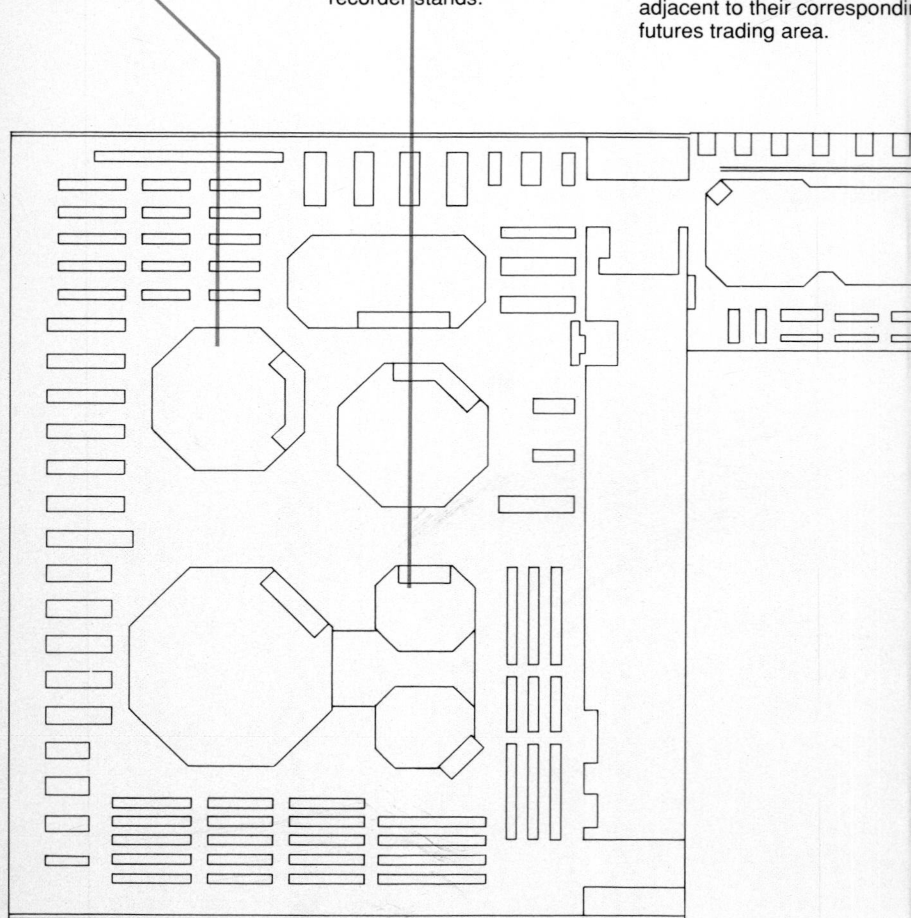

It's every man for himself. On a particularly hectic trading day in Chicago, in 1987, activity in one of the pits grew so rough that a trader was inadvertently shoved from the pit and suffered a broken arm.

Floor traders may try to trade in and out of contracts throughout the day, hoping to make numerous small profits. The practice is called ***scalping***.

Futures brokers only charge one commission, called ***round-turn commissions***, to open and close a position. This practice differs from stock trades, which involve one commission to buy a stock and another to sell it.

To trade on the floor of any exchange, one must hold a ***seat***, which can be purchased. The price can vary, as shown in this table. Brokers trade for their clients. ***Locals*** are individuals who hold seats and trade for their own accounts.

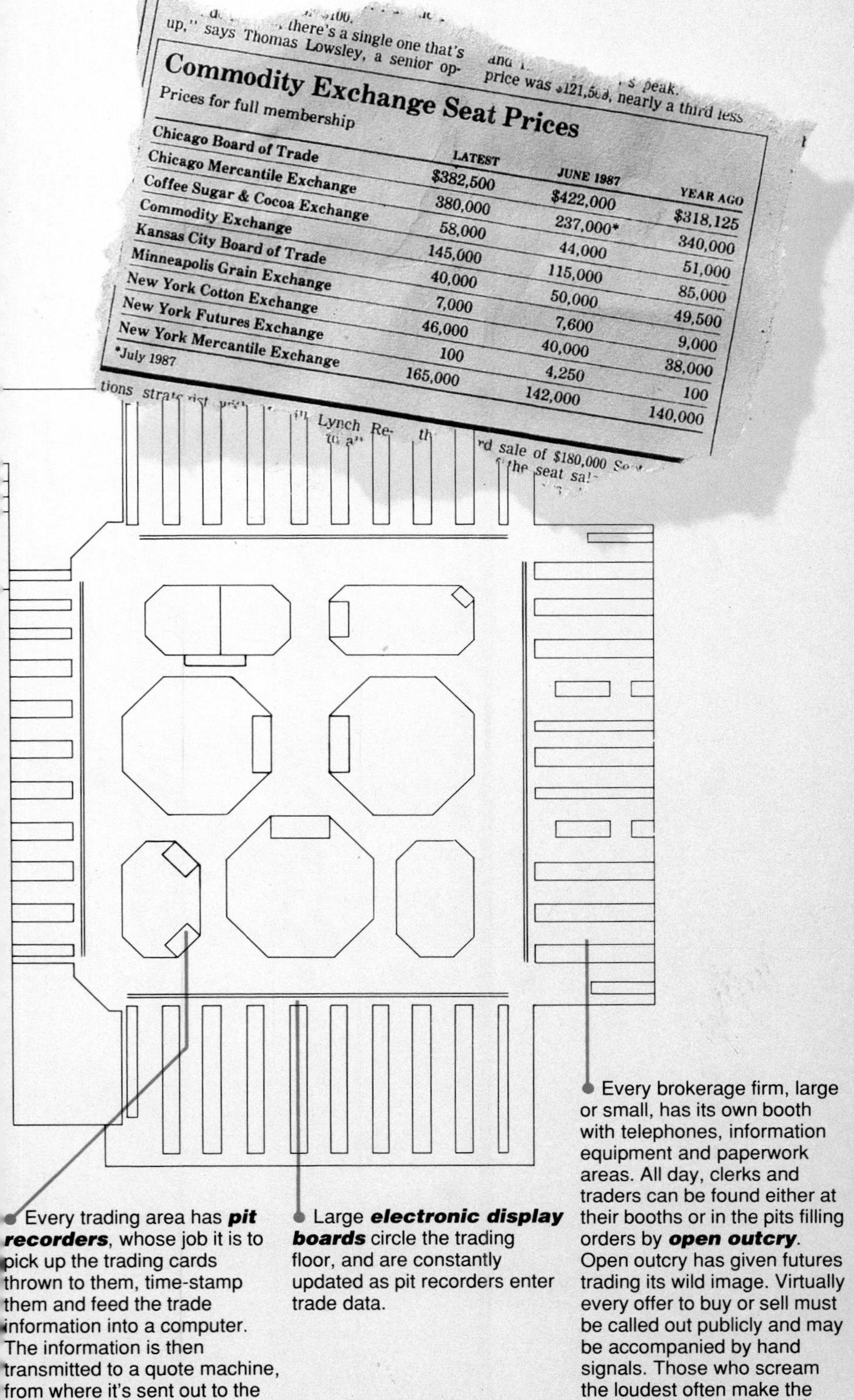

... there's a single one that's up," says Thomas Lowsley, a senior op- ...

... price was $121,500, nearly a third less ...

Commodity Exchange Seat Prices

Prices for full membership

	LATEST	JUNE 1987	YEAR AGO
Chicago Board of Trade	$382,500	$422,000	$318,125
Chicago Mercantile Exchange	380,000	237,000*	340,000
Coffee Sugar & Cocoa Exchange	58,000	44,000	51,000
Commodity Exchange	145,000	115,000	85,000
Kansas City Board of Trade	40,000	50,000	49,500
Minneapolis Grain Exchange	7,000	7,600	9,000
New York Cotton Exchange	46,000	40,000	38,000
New York Futures Exchange	100	4,250	100
New York Mercantile Exchange	165,000	142,000	140,000

*July 1987

... tions strategist ... Lynch Re- ... rd sale of $180,000 ... the seat sa- ...

Every trading area has ***pit recorders***, whose job it is to pick up the trading cards thrown to them, time-stamp them and feed the trade information into a computer. The information is then transmitted to a quote machine, from where it's sent out to the rest of the world.

Large ***electronic display boards*** circle the trading floor, and are constantly updated as pit recorders enter trade data.

Every brokerage firm, large or small, has its own booth with telephones, information equipment and paperwork areas. All day, clerks and traders can be found either at their booths or in the pits filling orders by ***open outcry***. Open outcry has given futures trading its wild image. Virtually every offer to buy or sell must be called out publicly and may be accompanied by hand signals. Those who scream the loudest often make the most deals.

The Futures Exchanges

Most of the world's futures exchanges are located in the United States.

What do exchanges do?

The exchanges ensure fairness in the markets by providing information to the Commodity Futures Trading Commission, ***CFTC***, which is to futures trading what the SEC is to stock trading. The exchanges also scrutinize trading activities and strictly enforce regulations. The National Futures Association, ***NFA***, also exercises self-regulation.

Exchanges also provide for standardized rules and orderly and timely trading with their clearing houses (subsidiaries of the exchanges which enable traders to cancel contracts whenever they want to). The exchanges never set prices or trade for themselves.

Since most of the world's exchanges are in the US, the greatest number of contracts are traded here. The most important exchanges are located in Chicago, Kansas City, Minneapolis and New York.

Exchanges around the world include those in London, Paris, Singapore, Tokyo, Sydney, Zurich and Winnipeg, among others.

Chicago:
– Chicago Board of Trade: corn, oats and other grains
– Chicago Mercantile Exchange: meat and livestock
– International Monetary Market: treasury bonds and notes, currencies, precious metals, financial indexes
– Chicago Rice and Cotton Exchange
– Mid America Commodity Exchange: financial futures

Minneapolis:
– Minneapolis Grain Exchange

Kansas City:
– Kansas City Board of Trade: grains, livestock and meats, food and fiber, stock indexes

Philadelphia:
– Philadelphia Board of Trade: foreign currencies

New York:
– COMEX: precious metals, copper
– New York Cotton Exchange
– Coffee, Sugar and Cocoa Exchange
– NYFE: commodity and stock indexes
– New York Mercantile Exchange: petroleum, precious metals

The Commodities Exchange (COMEX) was formed from the merger of the Rubber Exchange, Hide Exchange, Raw Silk Exchange and Metals Exchange.

What are these hand signals?

They look like shadow figures you'd make on the wall, but these are the hand signals traders use to save their vocal cords while buying and selling on the floor of the exchange.

These particular signals are used by grain traders on the Chicago Board of Trade. Other exchanges may use other signals.

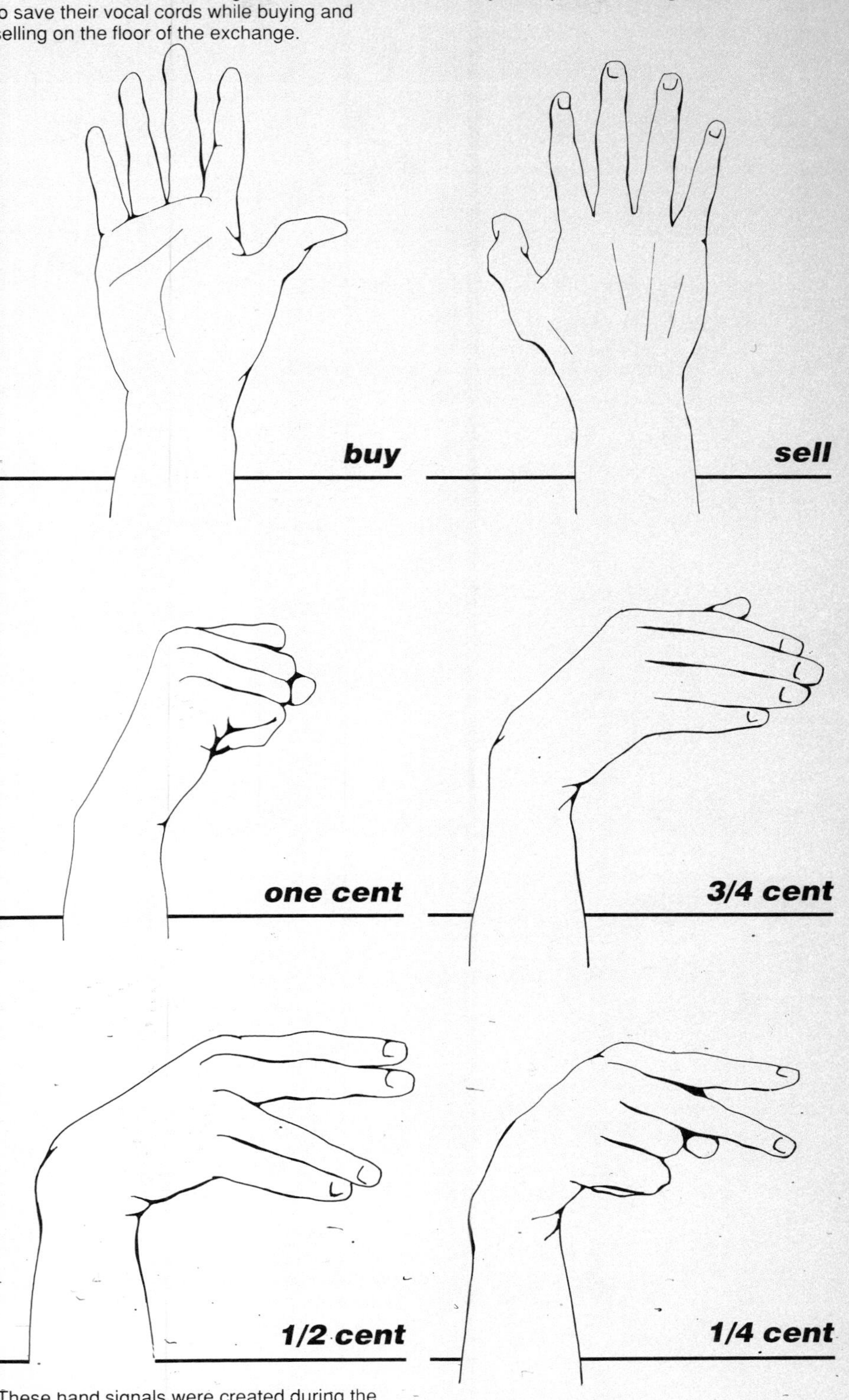

These hand signals were created during the days when the minimum amount a price could move was 1/8¢, not 1/4¢, as it is today. That's why four fingers represents 1/2; it meant 4/8.

Options

An option gives you the right – but not an obligation – to buy or sell something. Buyers pay a non-refundable amount in return for time to decide whether or not to conclude the deal.

What are the terms of an option?

The ***strike price*** is the agreed selling price of the stock or futures contract involved in the option.

Buyers and sellers can decide whether or not to go through with the deal any time up until the ***expiration date***. Only certain expiration dates are available. They're chosen by the exchange which lists the option.

In the meantime, the seller must always be ready to sell the stock or futures contract as soon as the buyer decides to buy. For this commitment, the seller receives money from the buyer, called an ***option premium***.

Nearly all stock options are for 100 shares of a stock. Every futures option is for one futures contract (which represents a large quantity of a commodity).

Why use options?

With options, you can delay buying or selling a stock or futures contract. Also, you can make large profits without having to tie up a lot of your own investment money.

FOREIGN CURRENCY OPTIONS

Philadelphia Exchange

Friday, June 10, 1988

Option & Underlying | Strike Price | Calls–Last: Jun, Jul, Sep | Puts–Last: Jun, Jul

Australian Dollars-cents per unit.

50,000 ADollr 80.75 / 80.75 / 80.75 — ...79, ...80, ...81, ...82 — 1.78, 0.81, r, r — r, 1.36, 0.82, 0.50 — r, r, 1.22, r — r, r, r, r

50,000 Australian Dollars-European Style.

FUTURES OPTIONS

Tuesday, June 21, 1988.

–AGRICULTURAL–

CORN (CBT) 5,000 bu.; cents per bu.

Strike Price	Calls–Settle Sep-c	Dec-c	Mar-c	Puts–Settle Sep-p	Dec-p	Mar-p
320	57	55	58	21	26	40
330	50	51	60	25	32	....
340	45	49	35	34	38	....
350	39	44	60	....	41	....
360	37	39	....	....	50	....
		35	....	....	....	....

... 2,522 puts

–OIL–

CRUDE OIL (NYM) 1,000 bbls.; $ per bbl.

Strike Price	Calls–Settle Aug-c	Sep-c	Ot-c	Puts–Settle Aug-p	Sep-p	Oct-p
14	....	....	....	0.01	0.04	0.08
15	1.38	1.60	....	0.02	0.10	0.60
16	4.70	0.81	1.01	0.11	0.31	0.39
17	0.05	0.31	0.48	0.68	0.80	0.86
18	0.02	0.09	0.20	1.66	1.59	1.58
19	0.01	0.04	0.10	2.65	2.54	2.48

Est. vol. 24,521; Mon vol. 9,512 calls; 9,664 puts
Open interest Mon; 81,671 calls; 96,131 puts

How much does an option cost?

The cost of an option depends a lot on what's happening with the stock or futures contract involved.

The more time there is until expiration, the larger the premium you must pay the seller.

Also, the greater the difference between the current stock price and the strike price, the greater the buyer's price. For example:

- XYZ stock is selling on the NYSE at $22 a share today.
- Option 1 gives you the right to buy XYZ stock at $15 a share.
- Option 2 gives you the right to buy XYZ stock at $25 a share.

Since you would rather have an option to pay $15 for a $22 stock instead of $25 for a $22 stock, Option 1 is more valuable. As a result, it costs more to buy Option 1 than to buy Option 2.

What are the risks of options?

If you have the right to buy a stock at $20 and it's selling in the market at $22, you could exercise your call option, pay $20 a share, then turn right around and sell the shares at $22. Obviously, the higher the stock's price goes, the more you can profit.

Sellers know this, so as the stock price rises and falls, the option price rises and falls with it. Consequently, you can profit just by trading the rights to your option for more money than you paid – without ever having to lay out the large sum needed to buy the 100 shares of stock or the futures contract.

Your risk in buying options is limited to the premium paid. If a stock price fell $10 a share and you owned the stock, you would have lost $10 a share. But if you only had an option to buy that stock, you could have lost only the cost of that option, no matter how far the stock price fell. As a result, when you buy an option, you know immediately the most you can lose. This is what the industry calls ***limited, predetermined risk***.

What kinds of options are there?

All options fall into two broad categories: ***puts*** and ***calls***.

	call	***put***
buy (long)	the right to buy the corresponding stock or futures contract at a fixed price until the expiration date	the right to sell the corresponding stock or futures contract at a fixed price until the expiration date
sell (short)	known as ***writing a call*** – selling the right to buy the stock or futures contract from you until the expiration date	known as ***writing a put*** – selling the right to sell the stock or futures contract to you until the expiration date

You can trade puts and calls on a huge assortment of investments. There are options on:

- ***Foreign currencies***
- ***Commodity and financial futures***
- ***Market indexes***
- ***Interest rate***

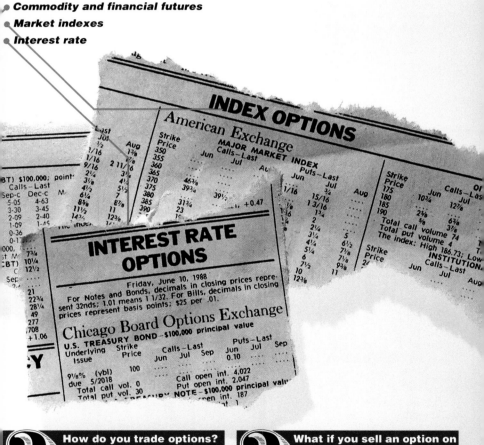

How do you trade options?

Any broker registered to trade stocks can also trade stock options. Only a commodity broker can trade options on futures.

Although some stock options are traded over-the-counter, the vast majority are ***listed on an exchange*** – not necessarily the same exchange that lists the corresponding stock.

What if you sell an option on something you don't own?

This is called ***naked writing***. It can be very risky because you must always be ready to buy the stock or futures contract and then immediately sell it to the option buyer on demand – no matter how much money you spend in the process. To eliminate this risk, cautious option writers only sell options on stocks and futures they already own, which is called ***covered writing***.

Keeping Tabs on Your Options

All option tables list the same types of information. But their formats vary slightly depending on the financial products being optioned.

Strike price is the price at which the option owner may buy or sell the corresponding futures contract by exercising the option.

Est. vol. and **Thurs. vol.** show an estimate of the amount of trading that occurred on this day (final figures will not be tabulated by press time) compared to the actual volume for the previous day, broken out into calls and puts.

Open interest shows the number of outstanding option contracts that have not been offset by an opposite transaction. This is as of the previous day, broken out by calls and puts.

The futures contract on which the option is based; **the exchange** on which the futures contract trades; **the number of units** in the contract; and the manner in which the price of the commodities contract is quoted.

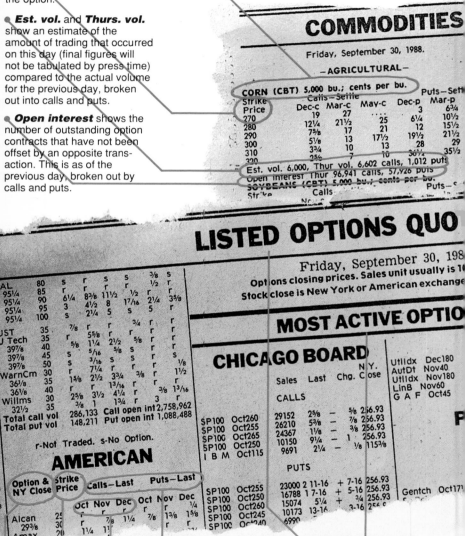

COMMODITIES

Friday, September 30, 1988.

–AGRICULTURAL–

CORN (CBT) 5,000 bu.; cents per bu.

Strike Price	Calls—Settle Dec-c	Mar-c	May-c	Puts—Settle Dec-p	Mar-p
270	19	27	....	3	6¾
280	12¼	21½	25	6¼	10½
290	7⅝	17	21	12	15½
300	5⅛	13	17½	19½	21½
310	3¾	10	13	28	29
320	2⅝	7	10	36½	35½

Est. vol. 6,000, Thur vol. 6,602 calls, 1,012 puts
Open interest Thur 96,941 calls, 57,926 puts
SOYBEANS (CBT) 5,000 bu.; cents per bu.
Strike Calls Puts—S

LISTED OPTIONS QUO

Friday, September 30, 198

Options closing prices. Sales unit usually is 1
Stock close is New York or American exchange

UAL	80	s	r	s	s	3/8	s
95¼	85	r	r	r	r	½	r
95¼	90	6¼	8⅜	11½	½	r	r
95¼	95	3	4½	8	1 7/16	2¼	3⅝
95¼	100	s	2¼	5	s	5	r
UST	35	7/8	r	r	¾	r	r
U Tech	35	r	5⅝	r	r	r	r
39⅞	40	5/8	1¼	2½	5/8	r	r
39⅞	45	s	5/16	5/8	s	r	r
39⅞	50	s	3/16	s	s	r	s
WarnCm	30	r	7¼	r	r	r	⅛
36⅞	35	1⅝	2½	3¾	3/8	r	1½
36⅛	40	r	r	1 3/16	r	r	r
Willms	30	2⅝	3½	4¼	r	3/8	1 3/16
32½	35	3/8	1	1¾	r	3	r

Total call vol 286,133 Call open int 2,758,962
Total put vol 148,211 Put open int 1,088,488

r-Not Traded. s-No Option.

AMERICAN

Option & NY Close	Strike Price	Calls—Last Oct	Nov	Dec	Puts—Last Oct	Nov	Dec
Alcan	25	r	r	r	r	r	¼
29⅜	30	r	7/8	1¼	7/8	1⅜	1⅝
Amax	20	1¼	[illegible]			r	r

MOST ACTIVE OPTIO

CHICAGO BOARD

		Sales	Last	Chg.	N.Y. Close
CALLS					
SP100	Oct260	29152	2⅝	– 5/8	256.93
SP100	Oct255	26210	5⅜	– 7/8	256.93
SP100	Oct265	24367	1⅛	– 3/8	256.93
SP100	Oct250	10150	9¼	– 1	256.93
I B M	Oct115	9691	2¼	– 1/8	115⅜
PUTS					
SP100	Oct255	23000	2 11-16	+ 7-16	256.93
SP100	Oct250	16788	1 7-16	+ 5-16	256.93
SP100	Oct260	15074	5¼	+ 3/4	256.93
SP100	Oct245	10173	13-16	3-16	256.9
SP100	Oct240	6990			

Utlldx Dec180
AutDt Nov40
Utlldx Nov180
LinB Nov60
G A F Oct45

Gentch Oct17½

Option & close lists the stock or the futures contract to which the group of options correspond. The prices listed underneath are the day's closing price of the stock or futures contract.

Strike price is the price at which the option owner may buy or sell the corresponding stock by exercising the option.

The prices for the two types of options, **calls** and **puts**, are grouped together. **Last** means the closing price on that option.

Stock options expire on the third Friday of their **expiration month**. The options available for trading, in this example, are October, November and December.

Listed options are stock options listed on major exchanges, though not necessarily on the exchange where the stock itself is listed.

Every day, the **Most Active Options** listing tells you which options were most heavily traded during the previous trading session on each of the exchanges. These could be index options, stock options or even futures options.

Futures options are categorized by ***industry group***, just as their related futures contracts are.

The various prices of ***call*** and ***put options*** on crude oil futures. The options expire in November, December and January; ***c*** and ***p*** simply indicate calls and puts. Settle indicates that the exchange has adjusted the price to reflect market values at the end of the trading. Because futures contracts and the options on those contracts may not trade at the same pace, the Exchange will adjust an option's price to coincide with its futures price at the end of the day.

URES OPTIONS

–OIL–

RUDE OIL (NYM) 1,000 bbls.; $ per bbl.

rike rice	Calls–Settle Nov-c	Dec-c	Jn-c	Puts–Settle Nov-p	Dec-p	Jan-p
	....	....	....	0.02	0.13	0.25
1	....	1.37	....	0.04	0.34	0.49
2	0.56	0.73	0.84	0.18	0.70	0.81
3	0.09	0.35	0.50	0.71	1.32	1.55
4	0.03	0.14	0.24	1.68	2.10	2.29
5	0.01	0.07	0.12	2.63	3.00	3.17
16						

Est. vol. 48,170; Thur vol. 10,154 calls; 12,729 puts
Open interest Thur; 107,233 calls; 111,134 puts

HEATING OIL No.2 (NYM) 42,000 gal.; $ per gal.

Strike Price	Calls–Settle Nov-c	Dec-c	Jn-c	Puts–Settle Nov-p	Dec-p	Jan-p
	....	....	....			
	.0150	....	...			

ONS

Option & NY Close	Strike Price	Calls–Last Oct	Nov	Dec	Puts–Last Oct	Nov	Dec
Time	90	r	r	23½	r	r	r
110	95	r	19¾	r	r	1	r
110	100	13¾	[illegible]	r	½	r	r
110	105	7	11	12¾	1⅛	r	3⅜
110	110	3⅞	6½	9½	2⅞	4¾	5¾
110	115	2	4	7	r	r	r
110	120	1⅝	3½	5	r	r	r
110	125	r	3	3⅞	r	r	r
110	130	r	1¾	2	r	r	r
TriCtl	22½	1/16	r	r	r	r	r
Worthg	22½	r	r	1¼	r	r	r

Option & NY Close	Strike Price	Oct	Nov	Jan	Oct	Nov	Jan
Ashl O	32½	r	s	r	½	s	r
33⅜	35	r	r	1⅝	r	r	2⅝
Bard	40	6¼	r	r	3/16	r	¾
46⅛	45	1¾	2¾	3⅝	r	r	r
46⅛	50	¼	1/16	1⅝	4	r	r
CdnPac	15	r	r	3⅛	r	r	r
17⅝	17½	r	r	1⅜	r	r	r
CharmS	12½	r	r	2	r	r	r
14	15	⅛	r	r	r	r	r
Clorox	30	2⅞	r	3¾	r	r	r
32½	35	3/16	½	⅞	r	r	
Comcst	15	r	1½	r	r	r	
CPsy	22½	½	r	1¾	r	½	
22¾		3/16		11/16			

Last	Chg.	N.Y. Close
–	1⅛	186.02
+	⅜	36⅞
6	–15-16	186.02
–	½	60
–	1-16	49
–	3-16	16½
		40⅜

FIC

Option & NY Close	Strike Price	Oct	Nov	Dec	Oct	Nov	Dec
56⅛	60	s	15/16	2⅞	s	r	r
56⅛	65	s	½	s	s	r	s

Total call vol 41,962 Call open int 1,035,197
Total put vol 25,539 Put open int 470,323

r-Not Traded. s-No Option.

PACIFIC

Option & NY Close	Strike Price	Calls–Last Oct	Nov	Dec	Puts–Last Oct	Nov	Dec
A M I	15	2 5/16	r	2½	r	r	r
17	17½	5/16	11/16	1	¾	r	r
Bevrly	5	1		r	1/16	r	r
6	7½	1/16		5/16	r	r	r
Bowatr	30	½	1¼	1⅜	1⅜	r	r
29	35	r	r	9/16	r	r	r
CasCke	25	r	r	r	⅛	r	r
CombEn	30	r	r	2⅛	r	r	1⅛
30¾	35	1/16	r	½	r	r	r
Cray	65	r	r	r	¾	1⅛	1⅝
69½	70	2¼	3⅝	4¾	2½	2¾	3⅞
69½	75	½	1½	2½	5⅝	r	6¾
69½	80	⅛	9/16	1⅛	r	r	10½
69½	85	1/16	s	⅝	r	s	r
	90	s	s	¼	s	s	r
		[illegible]	r	2⅞	r	⅜	r

21
21
21
21
21
21
Mic
52
52
5
5
5
Mi
NY
Ni
P
P

An option is said to be ***in the money*** when exercising the option would be profitable. ***Out of the money*** options are unprofitable. Time, Inc. October calls at a strike price of $100 are in the money – you could buy stock worth $110 for $100.

But those with a strike price of $115 are out of the money – you'd pay $115 for a stock worth $110. If the stock price and the strike price happen to be the same, the option is ***at the money***.

An option's price is called its ***premium***. In this case, the C.R. Bard Inc. $45 October calls closed at 1¾ for the day. Options contracts are for 100 shares of stock, so the premium for this option is $175. An ***s*** means there is no option in this particular month at this strike price; ***r*** means none of these particular options were traded on this day.

At the end of the listings is a summary of the trading on that exchange. ***Total call volume*** and ***total put volume*** show the number of options traded that day. ***Call open interest*** and ***put open interest*** show the number of options outstanding. These figures should be multiplied by 100 to determine the number of shares covered by options.

Different options trade on different ***exchanges***. This table shows stock options traded on the American and Pacific Exchanges.

Money

Lincoln's Secretary of the Treasury, Salmon P. Chase, decided that the first United States legal tender banknotes should be green. That's why they're called greenbacks.

The Federal Reserve Bank which issued the bill is identified by the letter symbol in the center of the ***seal***, the name inside the circle, and the branch number that appears four times on the face of the bill. Each Reserve Bank was originally required to maintain a gold reserve of at least 40% against money in circulation. The requirement was reduced to 25% in 1945, and eliminated entirely in 1968.

Each Federal Reserve branch issues notes according to the needs of its region. On this bill, the ***B*** and the ***2*** both signify the New York Federal Reserve.

Until 1929, our currency measured 7.42 inches by 3.125 inches. At that time, all paper money was redesigned, and today's Federal Reserve notes measure 6.14 inches by 2.61 inches.

The serial number appears in two places on the face of all United States currency – in the upper right and lower left portions. All serial numbers have eight digits. No two notes of the same kind, denomination and series have the same serial number. Counterfeiters are often caught when they make batches of a bill bearing the same serial number.

Special paper, obtained from a private company, has been used for US currency since 1879. The paper is a blend of rag-bond, cotton and linen.

The number one, as a numeral or word, can be found 16 times on a dollar bill (front and back).

The series identification is found at the right of the portrait near the signature of the Secretary of the Treasury and shows the year the design was first used on a note. (A design change may be as simple as updating the name of the new Secretary of the Treasury.)

*The Federal Reserve issues currency, but the **Bureau of Engraving and Printing** actually prints it. The Bureau takes all possible precautionary measures against counterfeiting. For example, it makes its own inks according to secret formulas. For security reasons, each feature, such as the portrait, vignette, ornaments, lettering and script, is the work of a separate engraver specially trained in that particular facet of the art.*

The note position letter appears in the upper left hand area and again in the lower right hand corner. This letter indicates the position of the note on the printing plate. ***The plate serial number*** appears to the right of the note position letter and identifies the plate from which the particular note was printed.

The Great Seal of the United States contains two 13-letter Latin mottoes. ***E Pluribus Unum*** means "From Many, One." ***Annuit Coeptis*** means "He Has Favored Our Undertaking." The unfinished pyramid symbolizes future growth, while the eye represents the benevolent gaze of God.

Symbols on the back of the seal represent the ***13 colonies*** include the 13-star constellation above the eagle's head, 13 arrows, and an olive branch with 13 leaves and 13 olives held in the eagle's claws.

Federal regulations state that any reproduction of US currency must be at least $1\frac{1}{2}$ times larger, as it is here, or no bigger than $\frac{3}{4}$ of actual size. It is forbidden to reproduce the bills in color at any size.

Familiar names...

gelt	*greenbacks*
jack	*long green*
loot	*smackers*
simoleons	*the ready*
rocks	*moolah*
scratch	*shekels*
spondulicks	*wad*
wampum	*bucks*
sugar	*clams*
bread	*dough*
lettuce	*gravy*
ten-spot	*sawbuck ($10)*

The Story of Money

The value of a dollar is social, as it is created by society.

Ralph Waldo Emerson, 1860

The story of money is the story of how humans have learned to trade for the things they can't – or don't want to – make themselves. If you want an apple, you'll have to find someone who is willing to part with an apple in exchange for something else. That something else at one time might have been beads, shells, fish hooks, grain or any item once used as money.

What is barter?

Our hunter-gatherer ancestors lived in small, isolated communities, and took what they needed from the surrounding land. Surplus was rarely a problem: people were lucky if there were enough skins, nuts or oranges to go around.

At some point, however, a tribe with a few extra oranges but short on skins must have run into a tribe with skins to spare but no oranges – and barter began. As people became more economically sophisticated – inventing agriculture, domesticating animals, making better tools – surpluses grew and barter flourished.

But barter has its problems. You can spend days running around looking for the perfect match: someone who has what you want and wants what you have.

And barter isn't always fair. Some items, like animals, simply aren't divisible, and deals must be struck at uneven rates of exchange.

Finally, barter restricts productive capacities. As societies grew more sophisticated and produced a greater range of things, the exchange process became too complicated for barter alone.

A famous barter

In 1626, Dutch settler Peter Minuit traded $24 worth of beads to the local Indians for Manhattan Island.

Manhattan (1987 assessed land value only) = $17,047,781,983

*For small change, colonists often used gunpowder and bullets. Later, they cut up coins on the spot to make change. A half coin was **four bits**. A quarter coin was **two bits**.*

*Where did the dollar get its name? It originates from a silver coin called the **Joachimsthaler** minted in 1518 in the valley (thal) of St. Joachim in Bohemia. Thalers flourished throughout Europe, and each country transformed the name slightly. In Holland, it became **daalder**; in Scandinavia, the **daler**; and in England, the **dollar**.*

What were early forms of money?

Money wasn't always paper and metal. As barter lost its appeal, live animals and sacks of grain became commonly accepted – money that was dragged (often kicking and bellowing) rather than pocketed. In Europe, as recently as 1393, a pound of saffron was worth one plowhorse; a pound of ginger would buy a sheep; two pounds of maize would buy a cow.

When did coins first appear?

Obviously, this kind of money, like barter, also had its drawbacks. Grain rotted; salt scattered; cows were tough to take to market. Someone had to devise something more durable, something easy to carry.

The Egyptians were among the first to provide a solution. Around 2500 BC they began to make metal coins. True, these pieces of metal weren't usable for anything except money. But they were durable and portable and could be subdivided into denominations useful for small purchases. The practice of making change flourished.

In 1792, Congress authorized the minting of US silver dollars, which means that any silver dollar George Washington may have thrown across the Potomac as a young man would actually have been a Spanish peso. Since then, our dollars have come in gold, silver, paper and even pewter.

*A **googol**– a 1 followed by a hundred zeroes – was created by the very young nephew of a*

10,000,000,000,000,000,000,000,000,000,000,000,000,000,000,000,000,0

Who made the first paper money?

The roots of paper money can also be traced back to 2500 BC, when the Babylonians wrote bills and receipts on ***clay tablets***. The first true paper money, however, may have been issued by Kubla Khan, who in AD 1273 issued ***mulberry bark*** paper notes bearing his seal and his treasurers' signatures.

The oldest existing specimen of paper money is the ***Kwan***, a Chinese note issued between 1368 and 1399 during the Ming Dynasty. It's about the size of a sheet of typewriter paper.

The first paper money in the British Empire was the result of a failed siege of Quebec by Massachusetts soldiers. Lacking any winnings to pay for the cost of the fight, the colony issued ***promissory notes*** to the soldiers for payment. Soon other colonies followed suit.

During the American Revolution, the Continental Congress issued paper money because it was short of gold and silver to mint coins. So many bills were printed that, before long, inflation set in. The price of corn rose 10,000-fold... and by the war's end, a dollar had dropped in value from $1 of gold to $2\frac{1}{2}$ cents in gold.

Congress didn't try issuing paper money again for 70 years, until the Civil War, when similarly disastrous inflation occurred. In the interim, private banks engaged in a free-for-all of currency issuing. Whenever the public lost faith in a bank's ability to make good on its paper notes, people would rush to demand payment in silver and gold. Bank failure and economic panic were the frequent results of these early runs on the banks.

Where does "money" come from?

The term ***money*** goes back to the French *monnaie* (coin), and even farther, to the Latin *moneta*, which also gave us ***mint***.

Salary is really salt money, harking back to the days when Romans paid soldiers in salt – a precious commodity needed to preserve perishable food. A ***fee***, however, originated in Germany and meant sheep and cattle, a link to the days before metal money when livestock was the medium of exchange.

Maybe Thomas Jefferson's face should grace the ***dime*** instead of the nickel. After all, the dime was his creation. The name comes from the Old French, *disme*, which comes from the Latin *decima*, which means tenth.

This 1917 dollar bill is legal tender: you could spend it if you found someone who would accept it. To a collector, it's worth about $4.

nathematician. The man had run out of -illions, and found his inspiration in the child's baby talk.

,000,000,000,000,000,000,000,000,000,000,000,000,000,000,000,000

The Life of Money

When the US Mint prints new dollars and stamps new coins, it's not making new money. It's simply replacing the dollars and coins that have worn out from overuse.

The Treasury ships new money and coins to the Federal Reserve Banks.

The number of coins and dollars in circulation ebbs and flows according to seasons. Right before the holidays, when travel and buying are up, the demand for coins and currency is the highest. In the 1960s, when vending machines first began to proliferate, coin circulation increased dramatically.

The Fed distributes money to banks.

Customers withdraw money from banks and spend it at stores.

The bank takes the cash from the stores, separates the worn out from the usable bills, adds new bills from the Fed, and hands them out to the customers.

Money circulates

The stores take the money from customers and deposit it at their banks.

Worn out and dirty money is shipped back to the Federal Reserve Banks

Paper money is shredded and burned into a mulch. Coins are sent back to the Mint for melting and recasting.

Money wears out

The average life of a $1 bill is 13 to 18 months. Larger bills last longer because they're not circulated as often. The U.S government spends $120 million a year just replacing worn out bills.

The introduction of the Susan B. Anthony dollar coin was an attempt to save money. While it costs more to mint coins than to print bills, the much longer life of the coins makes them more economical.

In 1792, Congress established the first mint in Philadelphia. The first cents and half-cents, struck in 1793, were about the size of present-day quarters and nickels and made of copper.

How are coins made?

Metal alloys are rolled from ***ingots*** into flat sheets of the proper thickness. Blanks, or ***planchettes***, are punched from the metal sheets, and the good blanks are sorted from the scrap.

After being ***annealed*** (softened) and washed, blanks are put in an ***upsetting*** machine which gives them a raised edge.

Blanks are then weighed and inspected before stamping. Front and back are stamped simultaneously at pressures exceeding 40 tons.

Finally, the coins are weighed, counted and shipped to the Federal Reserve Banks for distribution.

Today, new coins are struck at the Bureau of the Mint's Philadelphia, Denver and San Francisco branches. Look for the mint mark on each coin: **D** means Denver, **S** means San Francisco, **P** (or no mark at all) means Philadelphia.

The only current coin which does not honor a past US President is the $1 coin, which honors the famed woman's rights advocate Susan B. Anthony.

Why do coins have ridges?

When coins were made of gold and silver, subtle cheating was a common occurrence. People would shave the edges of their coins before spending them, eventually collecting enough shavings to use as money. Milled edges, the ridges, were devised to thwart these cheaters. Today, the precious metals may be gone, but the style still remains.

The original dimes and quarters were made almost entirely from silver. That changed in 1965, as silver prices began rising and the government began protecting its silver holdings. Gradually, the silver coins were removed from circulation. Today, dimes and quarters are made of a copper core between two thin alloy layers: 75% copper and 25% nickel – the same alloy used to make nickels.

How is paper money made?

United States currency is printed by the ***intaglio*** method. The design of the bill is engraved on a printing plate and ink is held in grooves created by the engraving. Excess ink is wiped from the surface of the plate before printing. This technique allows for intricate design work, creating a complex engraving which is difficult to counterfeit.

US currency is printed in sheets of 50 bills. The printing plates used can make up to three million impressions before they need to be replaced.

Money goes extinct

In 1969, $500, $1,000, $5,000 and $10,000 notes were eliminated as currency because of declining demand. Salmon P. Chase, Treasury Secretary from 1861–64, was the face on the $10,000 note. But the granddaddy of them all, the $100,000 note, redeemable on demand in gold bullion, bore the face of Woodrow Wilson.

Familiar Faces

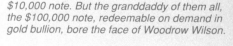

Jefferson
$2

Lincoln
$5

Hamilton
$10

Jackson
$20

Grant
$50

Franklin
$100

Larger bills, not currently in circulation, include: $500 – McKinley; $1,000 – Cleveland; $5,000 – Madison; $10,000 – Chase; and $100,000 – Wilson.

The Bank Account

Stop the presses: most of our money is now checkbook money.

In recent decades there has been still another change in our money agreement, away from the use of currency. Although we may still picture money as green paper and silver coins, those are now the petty cash of our economy. Most of what people use for spending is in the form of deposits – ***checking accounts*** – at banks.

Checkbook money doesn't exist as hard currency at all. Your checking account isn't a shoebox full of dollars in the bank basement. It exists only as computer entries – electronic records. These entries represent the bank's promise to make good on the checks you write, up to the limit of your deposit amount.

So instead of picturing bills and coins, think of money as immediate spending power: deposit a check in your account, and your spending power increases by the amount of the check.

New Yorker gives check to a Columbus, Ohio store owner for shoes...

Owner deposits check in bank...

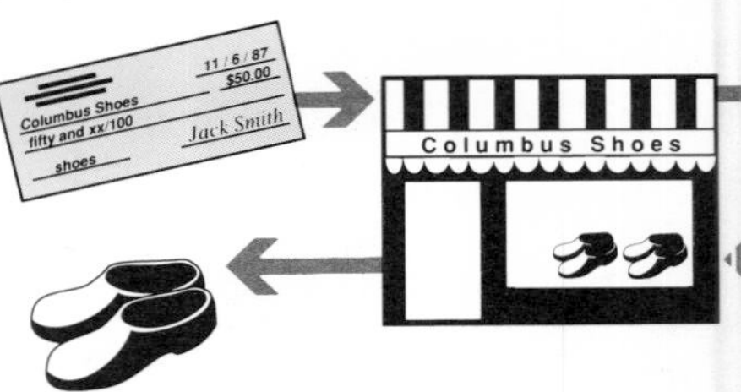

which then credits store owner for the amount of check.

How do banks read checks?

High-speed electronic equipment ***reads*** the sorting instructions printed in magnetic ink along the bottom of the check. Nearly 100,000 checks are processed every hour.

Check routing number. The first two digits show your bank's Federal Reserve district. The third digit identifies the main Federal Reserve branch. The fourth digit shows your bank's state. The last digit in this sequence, combined with the first eight, verifies the routing number's accuracy in computer processing.

Your bank account number.

The check number.

There's nothing here when you write your check, but it's filled in when your check is in your monthly statement. The number is the dollar amount, printed by the first bank to receive the check.

Bank sends check to Cleveland Federal Reserve Bank...

which sends it to NY Fed for collection...

which sends it to the buyer's NY bank...

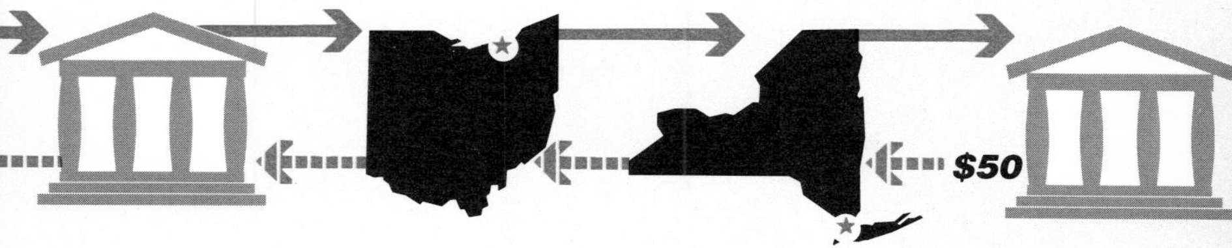

Cleveland Fed adds the amount to Columbus bank's account...

NY Fed pays Cleveland Fed from its own reserves...

which deducts the amount from the buyer's account and then tells NY Fed to deduct the amount from the bank's account.

The routing number is repeated here in a different format. This number is used in manual processing. The first number indicates the city code. The second indicates the bank. The numbers on the bottom are the Federal Reserve branch.

The bank where the check was deposited stamps it on the back.

The payment stamp indicates that your bank has certified that there are sufficient funds in your account to cover the check and that it has been paid.

The depositor's endorsement; businesses must use a stamp, while an individual may use a stamp or signature endorsement.

The process date and processing bank. The bottom line tells that this was the 112,615th check processed by machine 10 on that date.

Automatic Teller Machines (ATM)

*Today, in addition to our credit cards, many of us also carry **bank cards** which permit us to do our banking 24 hours a day. The first ATM was installed by the People's National Bank of Glouster, Virginia in December, 1962.*

Credit cards are not money

*The card signifies that you have permission to **buy now and pay later.** In other words, every time you use a credit card, you're taking out a loan – and the credit card company is extending you the credit.*

The Federal Reserve

Unlike the central banks of most countries, the Fed is not one, but twelve banks, with 25 regional branches spread across the nation.

Each Federal Reserve branch issues money according to the needs of its region. The following letters and numbers on our bills stand for the different banks:

A	**1**	Boston	**G**	**7**	Chicago
B	**2**	New York	**H**	**8**	St. Louis
C	**3**	Philadelphia	**I**	**9**	Minneapolis
D	**4**	Cleveland	**J**	**10**	Kansas City
E	**5**	Richmond	**K**	**11**	Dallas
F	**6**	Atlanta	**L**	**12**	San Francisco

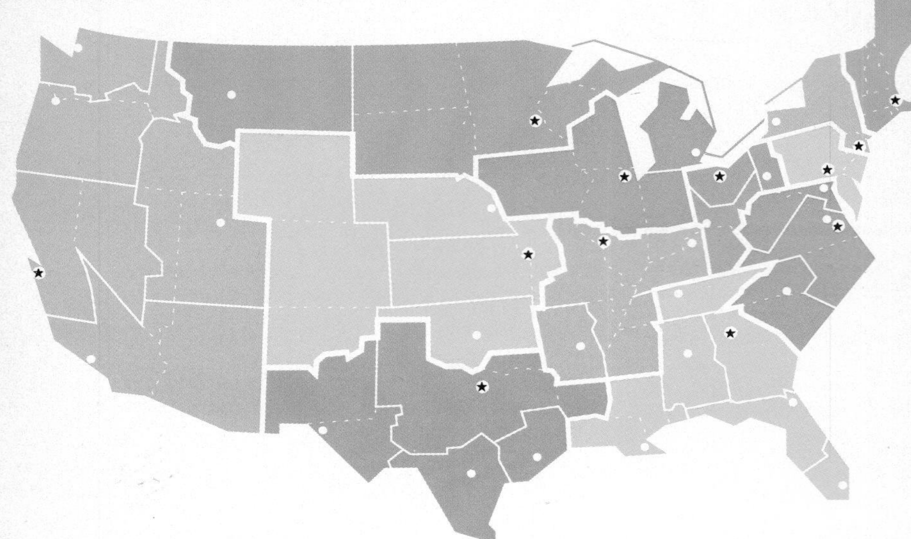

What is the Fed?

The Federal Reserve (The Fed) is our national bank. Its origins go back to 1907, when a sudden nationwide financial scare resulted in a disastrous run on the banks. J.P. Morgan saved the day by importing $100 million worth of gold from Europe. The government, however, decided it couldn't continue to rely on industry giants to save the economy.

In 1913, Congress created the Federal Reserve to stabilize and secure the nation's financial system. Since then, the trend has increased toward coordination. Today, all banks are part of the Federal Reserve system.

Who runs the Federal Reserve?

The Federal Reserve is run by a seven-member Board of Governors appointed by the President and confirmed by the Senate. No two members may come from the same Federal Reserve district. Terms of office last 14 years to insulate governors from political pressures. Terms are staggered, with one expiring every two years. There's one chairman and one vice-chairman, both of whom hold terms of four years.

Popular myths about the Federal Reserve

Myth: *The Federal Reserve is an agency of the US Government.*

Truth: *No. It's a corporation, accountable to the government but owned by banks which have purchased shares of stock.*

Myth: *The FDIC symbol displayed in a bank means that the bank is a member of the Federal Reserve.*

Truth: *No. FDIC stands for the Federal Deposit Insurance Corporation, which insures each deposit account for up to $100,000.*

Myth: *Fort Knox is part of the Federal Reserve.*

Truth: *No. Fort Knox is a US military installation where much of the nation's gold is stored. Most gold stored by the Fed is foreign-owned – probably because the US is considered the world's safest haven for money.*

What does the Fed do?

The bankers' banker

If your bank wants to lend more money to customers, it has to borrow money from its own bank – the Fed. The interest the Fed charges banks is called the ***discount rate***.

The watchdog

The Fed is also the bank's auditor. Fed officials regularly examine every bank's records to make sure loan decisions are based on sound judgments and that regulations are being followed.

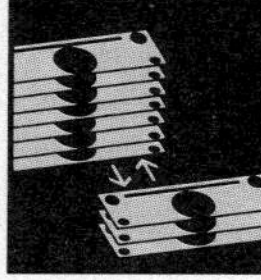

The regulator of the money supply

In our economy, if there's a lot of money around, we spend too much. If there's too little, we don't spend enough. The Fed tries to maintain just the right balance of money so the dollar will buy roughly the same amount of goods and services every year. If prices remain stable, so will the value of our money.

The controller of the currency

As coins and paper money become damaged, the Fed takes them out of circulation and orders the Treasury to replace them with fresh new coins and bills.

The US Government's bank

The Fed, through the Reserve Banks, is where the Treasury has its bank account – and where many governmental and quasi-governmental agencies also have their accounts – depositing and withdrawing funds like any other customer. In fact, the Fed processes over 80 million Treasury checks each year.

The Fed directs the Treasury to deposit federal unemployment taxes, withholding taxes, corporate income taxes and certain excise taxes. The Reserve Banks issue savings bonds and Treasury securities for the government, and release funds to pay the government's bills such as social security and interest payments on T-Bills.

The clearinghouse

The Fed performs the monumental task of serving as the nation's check-clearing system, processing over 15 billion checks a year. That's over 41 million checks a day.

The keeper of the gold

One of the most popular tourist attractions in the US is the gold vault at the New York Federal Reserve Bank. This massive underground vault, resting right on the bedrock of Manhattan, contains the largest known accumulation of gold in the world – about 13,000 tons. Actually, most of the gold doesn't belong to the US. In fact, it constitutes about one-third of the official gold reserves of the world's non-communist nations.

The Fed also performs related transactions such as implementing exchanges between nations (literally, moving gold bars to different shelves or rooms).

The Money Supply

The Federal Reserve Bank has a strong say in controlling just how much money, or buying power, is created. In fact, you could say it holds the nation's purse strings.

The Fed, like other institutions and individuals, buys and sells government securities in the open market. While others trade for investment reasons, the Fed trades to affect the country's buying power.

When the Fed buys securities, it pumps new money into the system because it allows the banks to add cash to their assets. When the Fed sells securities, it siphons off money from the system, causing banks to deduct cash from their assets.

How does the Fed increase the money supply?

Once banks have funds in their accounts, the real magic of money growth in the economy begins. It's based on something called the ***reserve requirement*** – the amount of money the Fed requires banks to keep in their own accounts. If the requirement is 10%, a bank must keep $100 on reserve in the Fed's vaults for every $1,000 of its customers' deposits. Once this requirement is satisfied, the bank may create $9 for every additional $1 on reserve by providing loans, etc.

This is one way the Fed stimulates the creation of new money. The cycle keeps going, and for every $1,000 of new money released by the Fed, at a 10% reserve level, almost $10,000 of new money will end up in circulation.

What is the discount rate?

When banks need more funds to conduct business, they ask to borrow funds from the Federal Reserve. The Fed creates new money and pumps it into the system by making the loan. The interest rate the Fed then charges on the loan is called the ***discount rate***. If the discount rate is too high, banks will be discouraged from borrowing. If it's low, banks may be tempted to borrow a lot. Thus, the discount rate also regulates the flow of money into the economy.

How the Fed uses the reserve requirement to expand the money supply

$1,000 The Fed buys bonds in the open market. Bond sellers deposit the money in bank accounts.

$100 reserve ***$900 to lend*** Bank A now has $1,000 in new money. Keeping 10%, or $100, on reserve, it lends $900 to John.

$90 reserve ***$810 to lend*** John gives a $900 check to Anne who deposits it in Bank B. Keeping 10%, or $90, on reserve, Bank B lends Ted $810. He deposits it in Bank C.

$81 reserve ***$729 to lend*** The bank keeps 10%, or $81, and lends $729.

$1,000+ ***$900+*** ***$810+*** ***$729+*** **=*$3,439*** has already been created.

There is no ideal money supply – other than what's needed at the moment to keep the economy running smoothly.

The money supply has a powerful effect on inflation, unemployment and production. Economists have found a close link between how fast the money supply is expanding or shrinking and how fast the economy as a whole is expanding or shrinking. By law, the Fed is responsible for targeting the growth rates for money supply.

How do we measure the money supply?

If you're like most people, you keep careful track of your personal money supply. And you probably have several different ways of counting it. You know, for instance, how much you have in immediately spendable form – the cash in your wallet and the money in your checking account. You also know which investments can be turned into cash quickly: savings accounts, CDs and so on.

Economists and policy-makers keep equally careful track of the nation's money supply. Every week the latest figures are published in ***The Wall Street Journal,*** listed in a table called ***Federal Reserve Data***, divided into the categories ***M1***, ***M2*** and ***M3***.

M1, M2 and M3 are simply three ways of measuring money supply – and they are very similar to the ways you count your own money.

The Ms are ***monetary aggregates***. They are an attempt to group assets which people use in roughly the same way. The lines between groups can seem pretty arbitrary. The object, however, is to separate savings money from money used in transactions.

- ***M1*** is the narrowest measure of money supply. It contains all money in ***immediately spendable*** forms: currency plus checkbook money.
- ***M2*** is a broader measure. It includes M1 but adds ***savings*** money and money in small ***time deposits*** (like CDs): money that can't be used directly for payments but can be converted easily into spendable forms.
- ***M3*** is the broadest measure of money supply. It includes all of M1 and M2 plus the ***financial instruments of large institutions***, which are not converted easily into spendable forms.

A run on the bank *used to occur when a bank didn't have enough money on reserve to satisfy all the customers who wanted to withdraw their deposits. It became a matter of first come, first served – causing people to run to the bank to be first. Today, however, the FDIC has virtually eliminated this phenomenon.*

FDIC, the ***Federal Deposit Insurance Corporation****, was established by Congress to insure depositors against losses up to $100,000 should their banks go bankrupt. An FDIC sticker in the bank window doesn't mean the bank is run by the government. It does mean your money is safe.*

Measuring the Health of the Economy

How do we measure the health of the economy?

Imagine a team of distinguished doctors monitoring a difficult patient around the clock – performing tests, watching vital signs, taking constant readings of dozens of physical functions.

Imagine, too, that the doctors have very few medicines at hand. When the patient goes downhill, often they can only cross their fingers and wait.

Finally, imagine that the vigil never stops. Even when the patient seems hale and hearty, the doctors keep right on testing, worrying about when his condition might worsen again.

Now you have an idea of how thousands of experts – and countless more interested amateurs – watch the economy. National economic health is measured in every way enterprising economists can think of, and the results are reported regularly in the media.

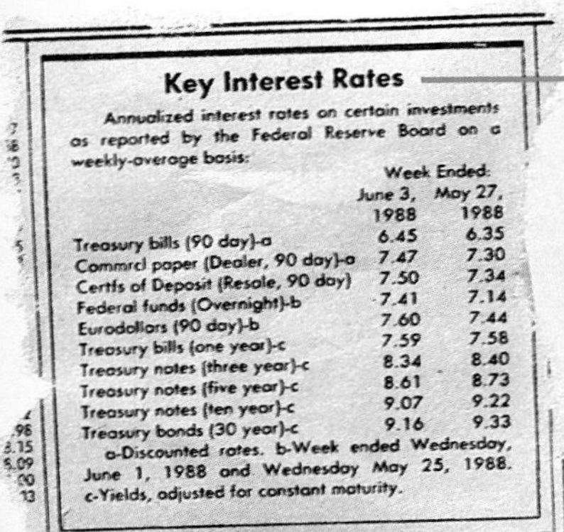

Key Interest Rates

Annualized interest rates on certain investments as reported by the Federal Reserve Board on a weekly-average basis:

	Week Ended: June 3, 1988	May 27, 1988
Treasury bills (90 day)-a	6.45	6.35
Commrcl paper (Dealer, 90 day)-a	7.47	7.30
Certfs of Deposit (Resale, 90 day)	7.50	7.34
Federal funds (Overnight)-b	7.41	7.14
Eurodollars (90 day)-b	7.60	7.44
Treasury bills (one year)-c	7.59	7.58
Treasury notes (three year)-c	8.34	8.40
Treasury notes (five year)-c	8.61	8.73
Treasury notes (ten year)-c	9.07	9.22
Treasury bonds (30 year)-c	9.16	9.33

a-Discounted rates. b-Week ended Wednesday, June 1, 1988 and Wednesday May 25, 1988. c-Yields, adjusted for constant maturity.

A change in the prevailing ***interest rates*** indicates a change in the agreement about what it will cost to borrow money. When money is plentiful, banks will offer low interest rates in order to induce people to borrow. (If a bank can't lend its money – the product it has to offer – it can't make any money.) When money is tight – the supply is low – the competition for the available money is greater, causing interest rates to rise.

Government economists have assembled ***twelve leading indicators*** into a barometer of future economic activity. This index includes a variety of factors, from stock prices to the average number of hours clocked by factory workers each week. The government calculates the index and releases the results each month.

The index is expressed in percentages, with 100% representing the calculation for 1967. For example, an index of 192% in July, 1987 means that the index is 92% higher than the 1967 base. The higher the index, the more the economy has grown since 1967.

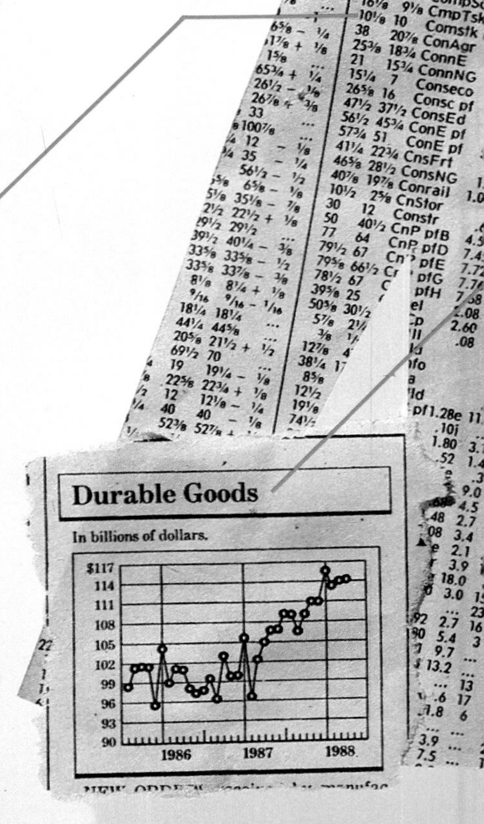

Durable goods orders are big ticket items purchased by corporations, like heavy machinery and large computers. Corporations will put off buying these items if money is tight. And they'll rush to fill as many orders as possible if they think prices will soon rise.

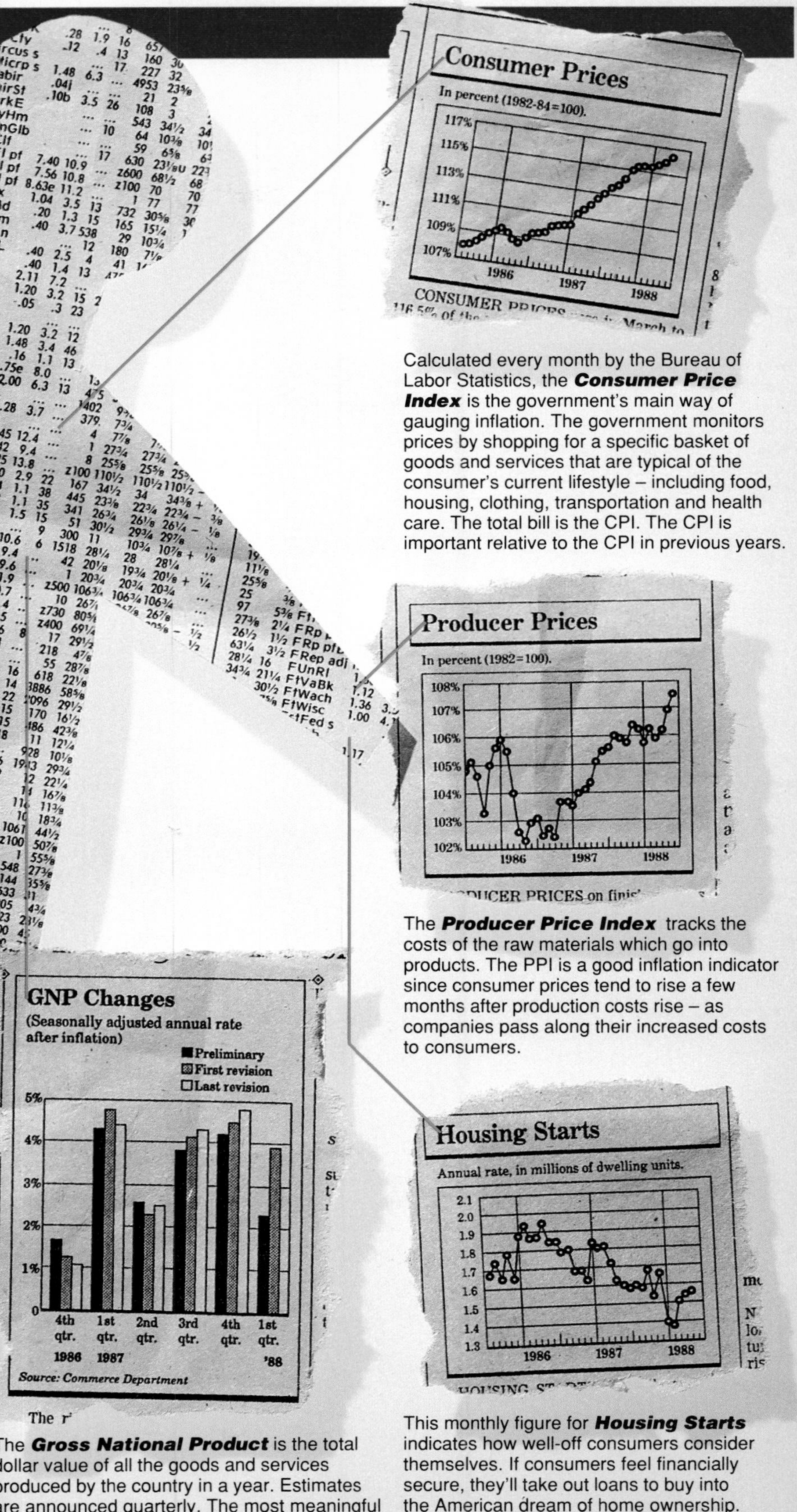

Calculated every month by the Bureau of Labor Statistics, the ***Consumer Price Index*** is the government's main way of gauging inflation. The government monitors prices by shopping for a specific basket of goods and services that are typical of the consumer's current lifestyle – including food, housing, clothing, transportation and health care. The total bill is the CPI. The CPI is important relative to the CPI in previous years.

The ***Producer Price Index*** tracks the costs of the raw materials which go into products. The PPI is a good inflation indicator since consumer prices tend to rise a few months after production costs rise – as companies pass along their increased costs to consumers.

The ***Gross National Product*** is the total dollar value of all the goods and services produced by the country in a year. Estimates are announced quarterly. The most meaningful analysis of GNP is in comparing it to other years. For instance, if the GNP is a lot higher than previous years, the economy is growing rapidly.

This monthly figure for ***Housing Starts*** indicates how well-off consumers consider themselves. If consumers feel financially secure, they'll take out loans to buy into the American dream of home ownership. Therefore, trends in housing starts can indicate overall consumer confidence.

Inflation and Recession

"A nickel ain't worth a dime anymore."

– Yogi Berra

"Invest in inflation. It's the only thing going up."

–Will Rogers

What is inflation?

Even economists can't agree on the hows and whys of inflation. The most common explanation is that inflation is caused by a money supply that expands too rapidly. This so-called ***easy money*** or ***loose money*** policy creates a situation, economists say, where there's too much spending money and not enough goods and services on which to spend it all. In other words, supply is lower than demand. The result? As consumers compete for limited goods, ***prices escalate***.

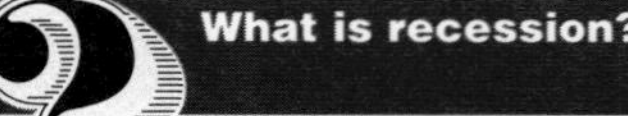

What is recession?

Recession is not as easy to spot as inflation. In inflationary times, you can actually see the prices of products rising. Recessions, however, are much more amorphous. In fact, the best definition of a recession is ***a downturn in economic activity***, indicated by two consecutive drops in the quarterly GNP figures. That is not the kind of occurrence which you're likely to observe very easily in your day-to-day life.

Is inflation bad for everyone?

In fact, it's good for debtors. In inflationary times, earning the $1,000 you borrowed five years ago becomes easier. What you actually repay in ***real*** terms is much less than $1,000, since the money you use to repay the lender won't buy nearly what it would have bought five years before.

Time is money

Looking only at increased costs can be misleading. Time savings can also be important.

In 1800, you traveled from New York to Philadelphia by stage coach. The trip cost about $4, but the coach left at 1:00 p.m. and arrived the next day at 7:00 a.m. Today, the Amtrak Metroliner costs about $34 each way, but it only takes 75 minutes.

While the trip's price has ***inflated*** *about 750%, the travel time has* ***deflated*** *about 1,420%. So, if time is money, then the cost of a trip from New York to Philly has dropped 650% since 1800.*

The decline of the German mark

1918 *Germany loses the war and the government doubles the money supply*
1919 *prices increase 6-fold*
1920 *prices increase another 14-fold*
1921 *prices increase another 37-fold*
1922 *prices increase another 2,000-fold*
1923 *(early) prices increase another 150,000-fold*
1923 *(late) prices increase another 726-fold*

In 1918, at the time of the Armistice, 1 mark bought the same amount as 726,000,000 marks in late 1923. Many Germans took to burning their paper money because it was a cheaper source of fuel than firewood.

The buying power of a dollar *declined dramatically during the inflation-ravaged years of the early 1980s. Inflation seemed to many a way of life that would never end. This chart shows the rise in the cost of living from 1967 (the base year used in calculating the CPI) to 1985. It also shows the projected cost of living in the year 2000, based on a 16% annual inflation rate which, at the time, many considered a realistic estimate.*

item	***1967***	***1985***	***2000***
monthly housing expense	$114.00	$678.00	$6,288.00
monthly auto expense	82.00	369.00	3,428.00
loaf of bread	.22	2.02	18.73
coffee (2 lbs)	.49	2.59	24.01
steak (lb)	.98	2.49	23.08
gasoline (gallon)	.23	1.21	11.22
resident college tuition	294.00	1,581.00	14,655.87

The Consumer Price Index

'he CPI is the prime indicator of inflation and recession. t not only reflects economic trends, but influences them s well.

What is in the Consumer Price Index?

CPI components are reconsidered every few years to reflect the changes in our lifestyles. In 1986, r example, the CPI market basket was altered reflect higher spending on housing and on od eaten away from home.

Employer-employee contracts often stipulate that pensions or wages will rise each year by a percentage equal to the rise in the CPI. These are called cost-of-living increases.

'he current components of the CPI and their relative importance

18.5% ***Food***

- At home, including cereals and bakery products; meats, poultry, fish and eggs; dairy products; fruits and vegetables; other foods
- Away from home
- Alcoholic beverages

38% ***Housing***

- Shelter, including renter's costs; rent
- Homeowner's costs, including owner's equivalent rent
- Fuel, including fuel oil, coal and bottled gas; gas (piped) and electricity
- Household furnishings and operation

5% ***Clothing***

- Men's and boys' clothes
- Women's and girls' clothes
- Footwear

21.5% ***Transportation***

- Private transportation
- Public transportation

6.5% ***Medical care***

- Hospital stays

5% ***Entertainment***

- Ticket prices

5.5% ***Other goods and personal care services***

- Shampoos, toothpaste, soap

'he CPI percentage annual change

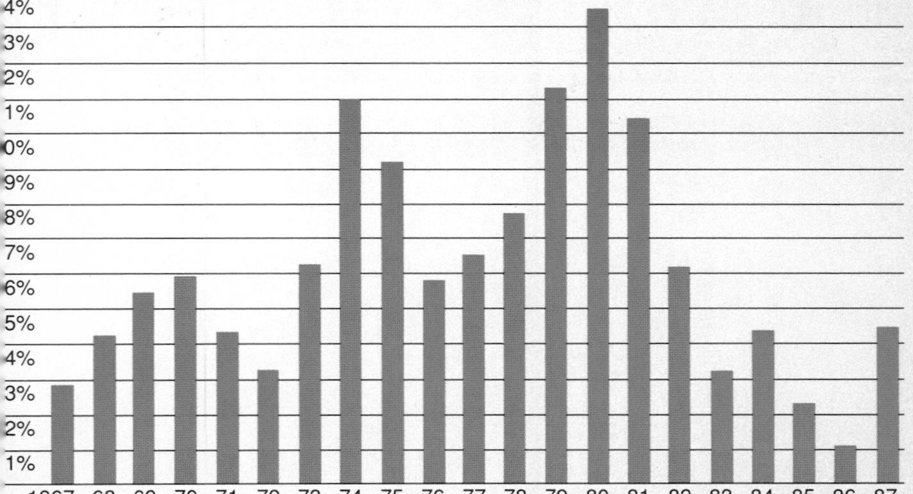

The World of Money

Exchange rates express the purchasing power of one country's money in another country's marketplace.

If you've ever tried to buy dinner in Paris, shoes in Rome or chocolate in Switzerland, you've had practice with exchange rates. It takes some figuring to realize that, in dollar terms, 20,000 lira for a pair of Italian shoes is a pretty good buy.

Tourists' calculations are small-scale example of the figuring that goes on constantly, all over the world, among bankers, financiers and business people dealing with flows of money across national borders. Exchange rates measure how much a country's currency is worth in relation to other currencies.

What is foreign exchange?

If everyone used US dollars, there would be no need for ***foreign exchange*** – the term for buying and selling things between countries using different currencies.

If a US store wants to sell a coat made in Milan, for example, the store will have to pay for it in Italian lira. After all, the Milanese coatmaker lives in a place where everyone uses lira.

So, the store owner must exchange her dollars for lira in order to buy the coat. But how many lira equal a dollar? The answer comes from the foreign exchange market, where currencies are traded just like stocks, bonds or any other financial product. The daily closing prices are available each day in ***The Wall Street Journal.***

If the going rate is 1204 lira for every dollar, and the cost of the coat is 250,000 lira, then the store owner will have to exchange $207.64 for lira to make the purchase.

How is currency exchanged?

There is no actual physical marke place where the world's currencie are traded. The foreign exchange market is a network of interconnected telephones and computers, and the going rate for every currency is continually revised as traders make their long distance deals.

Tourists exchanging their money use cash or travelers checks. Most businesses, however, exchange money simply by adding and subtracting from their bank balances.

When a New York rug dealer buys rugs from an Indian dealer, the New Yorker instructs the bank to pay the Indian. The bank then calculates the current exchange rate between dollar and rupees, deducts the dollars from the client account, then instructs the Indian's bank in Ne Delhi to credit the account with the appropriate number of rupees.

At the right is ***The Wall Street Journal's*** currency table showing what $1 is worth in many of the world's currencies. For example, in Burundi, $1 would have given you 117.8883 francs on 6/10.

What would products cost in another country?

If a product costs you more in France this year than last year, the maker of the product did not necessarily raise the price. The French price may be the same as last year. Your dollar, however, may simply buy fewer francs than it did last year. So you need to spend more dollars to buy the same number of francs, with which to buy the same product.

The chart to the right shows how many dollars it took to buy a pound of beef in four countries in 1985 and 1986. The amount of each currency that a dollar would buy is in parentheses.

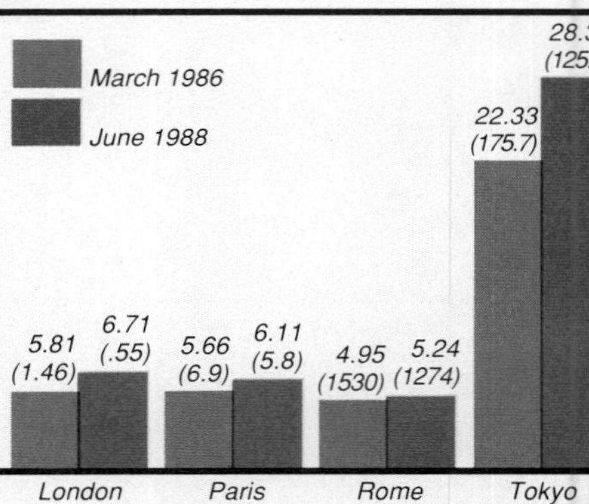

How the units of currency in other countries were named

Country	Currency	Named for
Brazil	cruzado	the Southern Cross
England	pound	a pound of silver (same as the lira)
France	franc	from Francorum Rex, a Latin inscription meaning King of the Franks, found on medieval French coins
Germany	mark	from old German meaning "to mark" – to keep a tally
India	rupee	comes from root meaning of silver
Italy	lira	from Latin libra (pound)
Japan	yen	means circle, because money should circulate
Peru	sol	the sun
Soviet Union	ruble	means "to cut"
Spain	peso	means weight (of a silver dollar)

World Value of the Dollar

The table below, compiled by Bank of America, gives the rates of exchange for the U.S. dollar against various currencies as of Friday, June 10, 1988. Unless otherwise noted, all rates listed are middle rates of interbank bid and asked quotes, and are expressed in foreign currency units per one U.S. dollar. The rates are indicative and aren't based on, nor intended to be used as a basis for, particular transactions.

BankAmerica International doesn't trade in all the listed foreign currencies.

Country (Currency)	Value 6/10	Value 6/3
Afghanistan		
(Afghani-o)	50.60	50.60
Albania(Lek)	5.5458	5.5946
Algeria(Dinar)	5.633	5.6131
Andorra(Fr Franc)	5.7938	5.827
(Sp. Peseta)	113.295	113.855
Angola(Kwanza)	29.918	29.918
Antigua		
(E. Caribbean $)	2.70	2.70
Argentina(Austral)	7.785	7.405
Aruba(Florin)	1.79	1.79
Australia(Dollar)	1.2398	1.2408
Austria(Schilling)	12.28	12.1025
Azores		
(Port. Escudo)	140.325	141.10
Bahamas(Dollar)	1.00	1.00
Bahrain(Dinar)	0.377	0.377
Balearic Islands		
(Sp. Peseta)	113.295	113.855
Bangladesh(Taka)	31.43	31.43
Barbados(Dollar)	2.0113	2.0113
Belgium(Franc-c)	35.86	35.485
(Franc-f)	36.02	36.68
Belize(Dollar)	2.00	2.00
Benin(CFA Franc)	289.6871	291.3583
Bermuda(Dollar)	1.00	1.00
Bhutan(Ngultrum)	13.6092	13.5704
Bolivia		
(Boliviano-o)	2.33	2.33
(Boliviano-f)	2.31	2.31
Botswana(Pula)	1.8005	1.806
Brazil(Cruzado-o)	172.62	166.085
Brunei(Dollar)	2.02	2.0206
Bulgaria(Lev)	0.827	0.827
Burkina Faso		
(CFA Franc)	289.6871	291.3583
Burma(Kyat)	6.2301	6.2558
Burundi(Franc)	117.8883	118.3737
Cameroun Rp		
(CFA Franc)	289.6871	291.3583
Canada(Dollar)	1.217	1.2303
Canary Islands		
(Sp Peseta)	113.295	113.855
Cape Verde Isl		
(Escudo)	70.675	70.675
Cayman Isl(Dollar)	0.83	0.83
Central Africa Rep'		
(CFA Franc)	289.6871	291.3583
Chad(CFA Franc)	289.6871	291.3583
Chile(Peso-o)	247.91	246.47
China		
(Renminbi Yuan)	3.722	3.722
Colombia(Peso-o)	295.10	293.79
Comoros		
(CFA Franc)	289.6871	291.3583
Congo, Ppls Rep of		
(CFA Franc)	289.6871	291.3583
Costa Rica(Colon)	75.60	75.25
Cote d'Ivoire		
(CFA Franc)	289.6871	291.3583
Cuba(Peso)	0.7616	0.7616
Cyprus(Pound*)	2.1805	2.1705
Czechoslovakia		
(Koruna-o)	5.20	5.20
Denmark(Krone)	6.5245	6.5585
Djibouti, Rp of		
(Franc)	170.00	170.00
Dominica		
(E Caribbean $)	2.70	2.70
Domin. Rp(Peso)	5.00	5.00
Ecuador(Sucre-d)	495.00	476.50
(Sucre-f)	249.50	249.50
Egypt		
(Pound-o)	0.70	0.70
(Pound-d)	2.2979	2.2878
El Salvador		
(Colon-o)	5.00	5.00
(Colon-d)	5.00	5.00
Eq'l Guinea		
(CFA Franc)	289.6871	291.3583
Ethiopia(Birr-o)	2.07	2.07
Faeroe Isl		
(Danish Krone)	6.5245	6.5585
Falkland Islands		
(Pound*)	1.8212	1.8053
Fiji(Dollar)	1.3928	1.3976
Finland(Markka)	4.07	4.107
France(Pranc)	5.7938	5.827
Fr. C'ty in Af		
(CFA Franc)	289.6871	291.3583
Fr. Guiana(Franc)	5.7938	5.827
Fr. Pacific Isl		
(CFP Franc)	105.3407	105.9484
Gabon(CFA Franc)	289.6871	291.3583
Gambia(Dalasi)	6.53	6.475
Germany, East		
(Ostmark-o)	1.7149	1.7216
Germany, West		
(Mark)	1.7149	1.7216
Ghana(Cedi)	184.00	184.00
Gibraltar(Pound*)	1.8212	1.8053
Greece(Drachma)	137.555	137.645
Greenland		
(Danish Krone)	6.5245	6.5585
Grenada		
(E Caribbean $)	2.70	2.70
Guadeloupe(Franc)	5.7938	5.827
Guam(US $)	1.00	1.00
Guatemala		
(Quetzal-o)	1.00	1.00
(Quetzal-h,i)	2.565	2.565
Guinea Bissau		
(Peso)	650.00	650.00
Guinea Rep(Franc)	440.00	440.00
(Franc-j)	300.00	300.00
Guyana(Dollar)	10.00	10.00
(Dollar-a)	20.00	20.00
Haiti(Gourde)	5.00	5.00
Honduras Rep		
(Lempira-o)	2.00	2.00
Hong Kong(Dollar)	7.809	7.8155
Hungary(Forint)	48.5074	48.6217
Iceland(Krona)	43.88	44.02
India(Rupee)	13.61	13.57
Indonesia(Rupiah)	1674.00	1675.00
Iran(Rial-o)	67.5844	67.8627
Iraq(Dinar)	0.3217	0.3108
Irish Rep(Punt*)	1.5604	1.5532
Israel(New Shekel)	1.584	1.585
Italy(Lira)	1275.05	1282.40
Jamaica(Dollar-o)	5.49	5.48
Japan(Yen)	124.785	125.65
Jordan(Dinar)	0.3675	0.3605
Kampuchea(Riel)	100.00	100.00
Kenya(Shilling)	16.5907	16.659
Kiribati		
(Aust Dollar)	1.2398	1.2408
Korea, North(Won)	0.94	0.94
Korea, South(Won)	728.60	733.20
Kuwait(Dinar)	0.2762	0.2756
Laos, Ppls D. Rep		
(Kip)	350.00	350.00
Lebanon(Pound)	359.50	363.00
Lesotho(Maloti)	2.2318	2.2363
Liberia(Dollar)	1.00	1.00
Libya(Dinar)	0.2811	0.2823
Liechtenst'n		
(Sw Franc)	1.4314	1.4339
Luxembourg		
(Lux Franc)	35.8552	35.4862
Macao(Pataca)	8.0431	8.05
Madagascar D.R.		
(Franc)	1295.6136	1303.0878
Maderia		
(Port. Escudo)	140.325	141.10
Malawi(Kwacha)	2.5193	2.5342
Malaysia(Ringgit)	2.58	2.5905
Maldive(Rufiyaa)	10.10	10.10
Mali Rep		
(CFA Franc)	289.6871	291.3583
Malta(Lira*)	3.0994	3.0994
Martinique(Franc)	5.7938	5.827
Mauritania		
(Ouguiya)	74.275	74.04
Mauritius(Rupee)	13.1965	13.2465
Mexico(Peso-d)	2300.00	2300.00
(Peso-e)	2284.50	2284.00
Miquelon		
(Fr Franc)	5.7938	5.827
Monaco(Fr Franc)	5.7938	5.827
Mongolia(Tugrik-o)	3.3555	3.3555
Montserrat		
(E Caribbean $)	2.70	2.70
Morocco(Dirham)	8.1396	8.065
Mozambique		
(Metical)	454.50	454.50
Namibia(S.A. Rand)	2.2318	2.2363
Nauru Isl.		
(Aust Dollar)	1.2398	1.2408
Nepal(Rupee)	22.30	22.30
Netherlands		
(Guilder)	1.9253	1.9328
Neth Ant'les		
(Guilder)	1.79	1.79
New Zealand		
(Dollar)	1.4286	1.4271
Nicaragua		
(New Cordoba)	11.20	11.20
Niger Rep		
(CFA Franc)	289.6871	291.3583
Nigeria(Naira-d)	4.1714	4.1714
Norway(Krone)	6.2615	6.3125
Oman, Sultanate of		
(Rial)	0.385	0.385
Pakistan		
(Rupee)	17.8445	17.7944
Panama(Balboa)	1.00	1.00
Papau N.G.(Kina)	0.8457	0.8486
Paraguay		
(Guarani-o)	320.00	320.00
(Guarani-p)	550.00	550.00
(Guarani-d)	887.00	883.00
Peru		
(Inti-o,n)	33.00	33.00
(Inti-f)	75.00	75.00
Philippines(peso)	21.015	21.015
Pitcairn Isl		
(N.Z. Dollar)	1.4286	1.4271
Poland(Zloty-o)	430.00	420.00
Portugal(Escudo)	140.325	141.10
Puerto Rico(US $)	1.00	1.00
Qatar(Riyal)	3.6408	3.6408
Reunion, Ile de la		
(Fr Franc)	5.7938	5.827
Romania(Leu-o)	8.55	8.55
Rwanda(Franc)	75.2069	75.5165
St. Christopher		
(E. Caribbean $)	2.70	2.70
St. Helena(Pound*)	1.8212	1.8053
St. Lucia		
(E. Caribbean $)	2.70	2.70
St. Pierre		
(Fr Franc)	5.7938	5.827
St. Vincent		
(E. Caribbean $)	2.70	2.70
Samoa, Western		
(Tala)	2.0242	2.0242
Samoa, Am(US $)	1.00	1.00
San Marino(It. Lira)	1275.05	1282.40
Sao Tome & Principe		
(Dobra)	73.2225	73.524
Saudi Arabia(Riyal)	3.7555	3.7555
Senegal		
(CFA Franc)	289.6871	291.3583
Seychelles(Rupee)	5.2973	5.3191
Sierra Leone		
(Leone)	30.00	28.00
Singapore(Dollar)	2.02	2.0206
Solomon Isl(Dollar)	2.0492	2.0538
Somali Rep		
(Shilling-d)	100.00	100.00
South Africa		
(Rand-f)	2.963	2.9542
(Rand-c)	2.2318	2.2363
Spain(Peseta)	113.295	113.855
Span Ports in N. Afr		
(Sp. Peseta)	113.295	113.855
Sri Lanka(Rupee)	31.0638	31.5037
Sudan Rep(Pound-o)	4.50	4.50
(Pound-k)	2.93	2.93
(Pound-f)	4.00	4.00
Surinam(Guilder)	1.785	1.785
Swaziland		
(Lilangeni)	2.2318	2.2363
Sweden(Krona)	5.9835	6.018
Switzerland		
(Franc)	1.4314	1.4339
Syria(Pound-h)	26.50	27.00
Taiwan(Dollar-o)	28.62	28.62
Tanzania(Shilling)	96.0254	96.2286
Thailand(Baht)	25.1535	25.20
Togo, Rep		
(CFA Franc)	289.6871	291.3583
Tonga Is(Pa'anga)	1.2398	1.2408
Trinidad & Tobago		
(Dollar)	3.60	3.60
Tunisia(Dinar)	0.8363	0.8401
Turkey(Lira)	1336.23	1329.81
Turks & Caicos		
(US $)	1.00	1.00
Tuvalu		
(Aust Dollar)	1.2398	1.2408
Uganda		
(Shilling-l)	60.0568	60.3858
Utd Arab Emir		
(Dirham)	3.671	3.671
Utd Kingdom		
(Pound Sterling*)	1.8212	1.8053
Uruguay(Peso-m)	342.50	340.00
USSR(Rouble)	0.601	0.59
Vanuatu(Vatu)	102.49	102.49
Vatican(Lira)	1275.05	1282.40
Venezuela		
(Bolivar-o)	14.50	14.50
(Bolivar-n)	7.50	7.50
(Bolivar-d)	32.60	31.425
Vietnam(Dong-o)	368.00	368.00
Virgin Is, Br(US $)	1.00	1.00
Virgin Is, US(US $)	1.00	1.00
Yemen(Rial)	9.755	9.755
Yemen PDR(Dinar)	0.343	0.343
Yugoslavia		
(Dinar)(1)	2031.69	1593.51
Zaire Rep		
(Zaire)	177.4057	172.50
Zambia(Kwacha)	8.0094	8.048
Zimbabwe(Dollar)	1.7753	1.786

*U.S. dollars per National Currency unit. (a) Freemarket central bank rate. (b) Floating rate. (c) Commercial rate. (d) Free market rate. (e) Controlled. (f) Financial rate. (g) Preferential rate. (h) Nonessential imports. (i) Floating tourist rate. (j) Public transaction rate. (k) Agricultural products. (l) Priority rate. (m) Market rate. (n) Essential imports. (o) Official rate. (p) Exports. (na) Not available.

(1) Yugoslavia, 27 May 1988: Dinar Devalued by Approx 24%

Further information available at BankAmerica International.

Source: Bank of America Global Trading, London

The World of Money

In today's global economy, currencies are valued by measuring (floating) them against each other.

Before the 1980s, investors around the world were quite content to invest their assets in the markets most familiar to them – their own domestic markets. Most parochial of them all, perhaps, were the Americans, who powered the American securities market – the most influential securities market in the world.

Buoyed by the euphoria of the '80s bull market – and, more importantly, by the advent of securities market deregulation – brokers and investors the world over began rushing to explore new financial arenas. They created entirely new investments and speculative products with seemingly endless permutations, and they began investing in nearly all the foreign markets.

Foreign investment has its risks. Each foreign market operates under its own set of rules, and the psychology of traders in each market often differs. Nevertheless, the profit opportunities have seemed too enticing to ignore.

In fact, investors began to understand that trading their American stocks for Japanese stocks was actually no different than selling the stocks of one industry to buy the stocks in another industry.

What is the gold standard?

For a long time, the relative value of currencies was measure against precious metals, most often gold and silver. For example, a French vintner and an American retailer would have known that a franc was worth X amount of go and the dollar was worth Y amount of gold. Using this ***gold standard*** made comparing francs to dollars relatively easy.

The gold standard became outdated in mode times, as national economies moved away from basing their own domestic money value on gold. In 1972, the nations of the world stopped using gold as a universal yardstick.

The factors affecting a currency's worth

It is important to remember that a currency is only strong or weak in relation to another currency For example, the dollar may be weak against the Swiss franc, but it might be strong against the Mexican peso.

	Strong currency	***Weak currency***
Exports/imports	Great demand for a nation's products means great demand for the currency needed to pay for those products.	Less demand for products means less currency is needed by foreigners to pay for the products.
Foreign investment	If a nation's securities, e.g., T-bills or CDs, are paying high interest, foreigners will want the currency needed to buy those securities.	Low interest rates mean lowe investment returns on securities, so foreigners are less attracted and need less currency to buy those securities.
Inflation	If inflation is low and stable, foreigners feel confident that money they invest in the country's assets, such as real estate and securities, will hold its value over time.	High inflation will cause foreigners to find other countries in which to invest. They'll avoid the loss of valu that comes simply from holding that country's inflatin currency.

People no longer simply use money to buy products. Now they use money to buy money, trading in and out of currencies as values change in relation to each other.

This table shows the relationship between the US dollar and other currencies. The first two columns show the number of dollars you could exchange for one yen. (The table shows figures for two days. On Monday, for one yen you could have received .007921 of a dollar.) The second two columns show how many yen you would receive in exchange for one dollar on the same day. (On Monday, for one dollar you would have received 126.25 yen.)

Some currencies, like the yen, are used very heavily in commercial transactions. Anticipating future needs for currency, many businesses often put down a deposit on the amount of currency they will need 30, 60 or 90 days before the need arises. These are called ***forward contracts***.

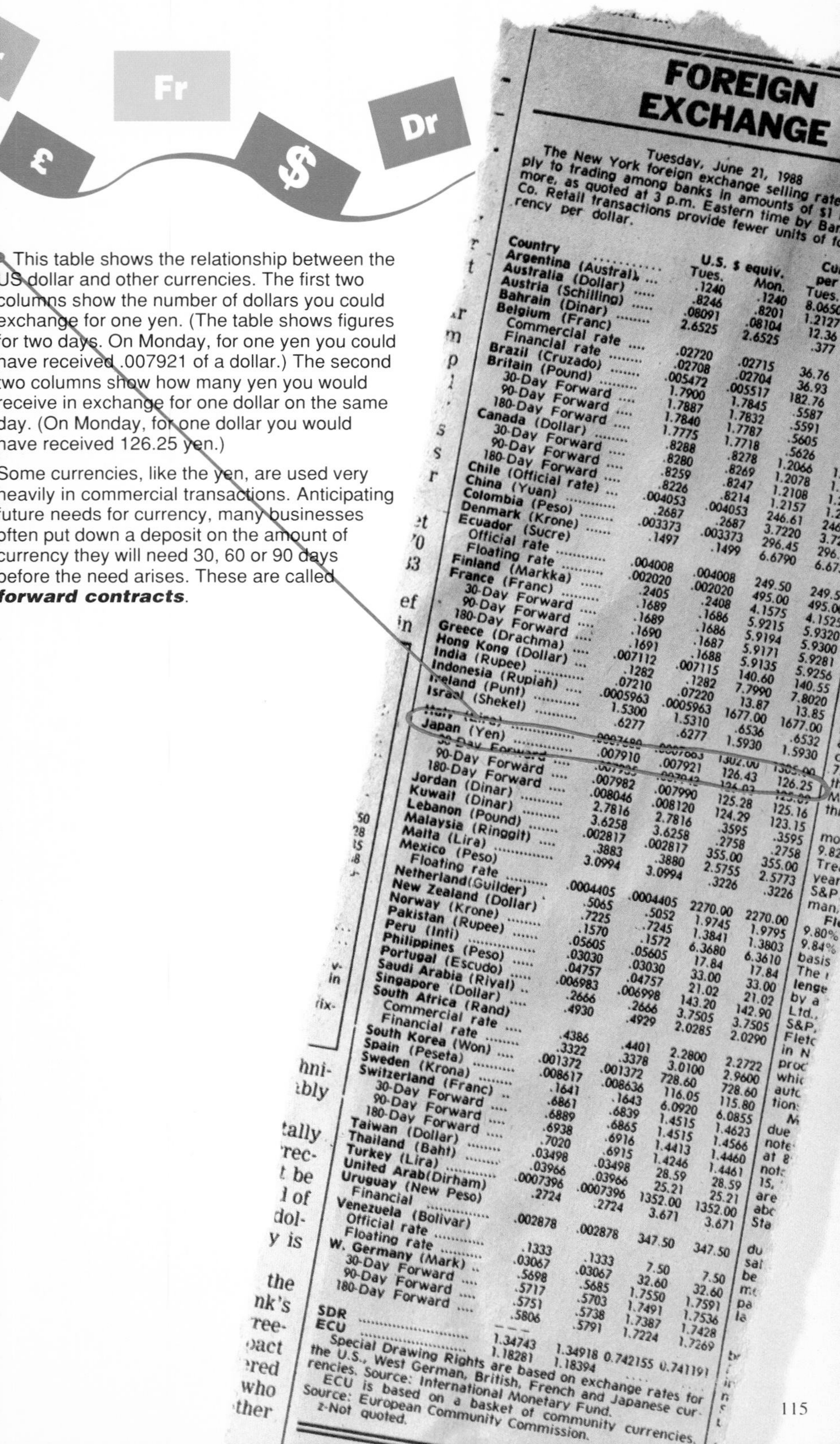

FOREIGN EXCHANGE

Tuesday, June 21, 1988

The New York foreign exchange selling rates apply to trading among banks in amounts of $1 m… more, as quoted at 3 p.m. Eastern time by Bank… Co. Retail transactions provide fewer units of for… rency per dollar.

Country	U.S. $ equiv. Tues.	U.S. $ equiv. Mon.	Curr per U… Tues.	
Argentina (Austral)	.1240	.1240	8.0650	
Australia (Dollar)	.8246	.8201	1.2127	
Austria (Schilling)	.08091	.08104	12.36	
Bahrain (Dinar)	2.6525	2.6525	.377	
Belgium (Franc)				
Commercial rate	.02720	.02715	36.76	
Financial rate	.02708	.02704	36.93	
Brazil (Cruzado)	.005472	.005517	182.76	1
Britain (Pound)	1.7900	1.7845	.5587	
30-Day Forward	1.7887	1.7832	.5591	.
90-Day Forward	1.7840	1.7787	.5605	.
180-Day Forward	1.7775	1.7718	.5626	.5
Canada (Dollar)	.8288	.8278	1.2066	1.2
30-Day Forward	.8280	.8269	1.2078	1.20
90-Day Forward	.8259	.8247	1.2108	1.21
180-Day Forward	.8226	.8214	1.2157	1.21
Chile (Official rate)	.004053	.004053	246.61	246.6
China (Yuan)	.2687	.2687	3.7220	3.722
Colombia (Peso)	.003373	.003373	296.45	296.4
Denmark (Krone)	.1497	.1499	6.6790	6.6730
Ecuador (Sucre)				
Official rate	.004008	.004008	249.50	249.50
Floating rate	.002020	.002020	495.00	495.00
Finland (Markka)	.2405	.2408	4.1575	4.1525
France (Franc)	.1689	.1686	5.9215	5.9320
30-Day Forward	.1689	.1686	5.9194	5.9300
90-Day Forward	.1690	.1687	5.9171	5.9281
180-Day Forward	.1691	.1688	5.9135	5.9256
Greece (Drachma)	.007112	.007115	140.60	140.55
Hong Kong (Dollar)	.1282	.1282	7.7990	7.8020
India (Rupee)	.07210	.07220	13.87	13.85
Indonesia (Rupiah)	.0005963	.0005963	1677.00	1677.00
Ireland (Punt)	1.5300	1.5310	.6536	.6532
Israel (Shekel)	.6277	.6277	1.5930	1.5930
Italy (Lira)	.0007680	.0007663	1302.00	1305.00
Japan (Yen)	.007910	.007921	126.43	126.25
30-Day Forward	[illegible]	[illegible]	[illegible]	[illegible]
90-Day Forward	.007982	.007990	125.28	125.16
180-Day Forward	.008046	.008120	124.29	123.15
Jordan (Dinar)	2.7816	2.7816	.3595	.3595
Kuwait (Dinar)	3.6258	3.6258	.2758	.2758
Lebanon (Pound)	.002817	.002817	355.00	355.00
Malaysia (Ringgit)	.3883	.3880	2.5755	2.5773
Malta (Lira)	3.0994	3.0994	.3226	.3226
Mexico (Peso)				
Floating rate	.0004405	.0004405	2270.00	2270.00
Netherland (Guilder)	.5065	.5052	1.9745	1.9795
New Zealand (Dollar)	.7225	.7245	1.3841	1.3803
Norway (Krone)	.1570	.1572	6.3680	6.3610
Pakistan (Rupee)	.05605	.05605	17.84	17.84
Peru (Inti)	.03030	.03030	33.00	33.00
Philippines (Peso)	.04757	.04757	21.02	21.02
Portugal (Escudo)	.006983	.006998	143.20	142.90
Saudi Arabia (Riyal)	.2666	.2666	3.7505	3.7505
Singapore (Dollar)	.4930	.4929	2.0285	2.0290
South Africa (Rand)				
Commercial rate	.4386	.4401	2.2800	2.2722
Financial rate	.3322	.3378	3.0100	2.9600
South Korea (Won)	.001372	.001372	728.60	728.60
Spain (Peseta)	.008617	.008636	116.05	115.80
Sweden (Krona)	.1641	.1643	6.0920	6.0855
Switzerland (Franc)	.6861	.6839	1.4515	1.4623
30-Day Forward	.6889	.6865	1.4515	1.4566
90-Day Forward	.6938	.6916	1.4413	1.4460
180-Day Forward	.7020	.6915	1.4246	1.4461
Taiwan (Dollar)	.03498	.03498	28.59	28.59
Thailand (Baht)	.03966	.03966	25.21	25.21
Turkey (Lira)	.0007396	.0007396	1352.00	1352.00
United Arab(Dirham)	.2724	.2724	3.671	3.671
Uruguay (New Peso)				
Financial	.002878	.002878	347.50	347.50
Venezuela (Bolivar)				
Official rate	.1333	.1333	7.50	7.50
Floating rate	.03067	.03067	32.60	32.60
W. Germany (Mark)	.5698	.5685	1.7550	1.7591
30-Day Forward	.5717	.5703	1.7491	1.7536
90-Day Forward	.5751	.5738	1.7387	1.7428
180-Day Forward	.5806	.5791	1.7224	1.7269
SDR	1.34743	1.34918	0.742155	0.741191
ECU	1.18281	1.18394	....	

Special Drawing Rights are based on exchange rates for the U.S., West German, British, French and Japanese currencies. Source: International Monetary Fund.

ECU is based on a basket of community currencies. Source: European Community Commission.

z-Not quoted.

The Changing Value of Money

How much is money worth?

When someone says you can receive 130 yen for every dollar you own, what does that mean? Is that a lot of yen or a little? Would you have been wiser to make the exchange years earlier when the currency was cheaper; or is it less expensive now. If you could have turned in your dollars for another currency in 1920, which one would have made you the biggest profit through 1988? The only way to answer these questions is to examine how currencies have changed in value over time.

The illustration on this page shows the history of exchanging dollars for rupees, francs, marks and yen since 1920. If you use the dollar as a benchmark, you can also see how these four currencies rose and fell in relation to each other since that time.

In 1960, the French franc was devalued. People recieved one new franc for every 100 old francs they held. So, if you used $100 to buy 1420 francs in 1920 (14.2 x 100), and exchanged the francs back to dollars in 1960, you would have lost a lot of money: your 1420 francs would have been converted into 14.2 francs, or $2.90 (at 4.9 francs to the dollar)

How much currency will your dollars buy?

As you look at this table, think of each currency in terms of how many of each your dollar would buy. For example, in 1920, $1 could buy 2.57 rupees. In 1955, rupees were cheaper; $1 could buy 4.79 of them.

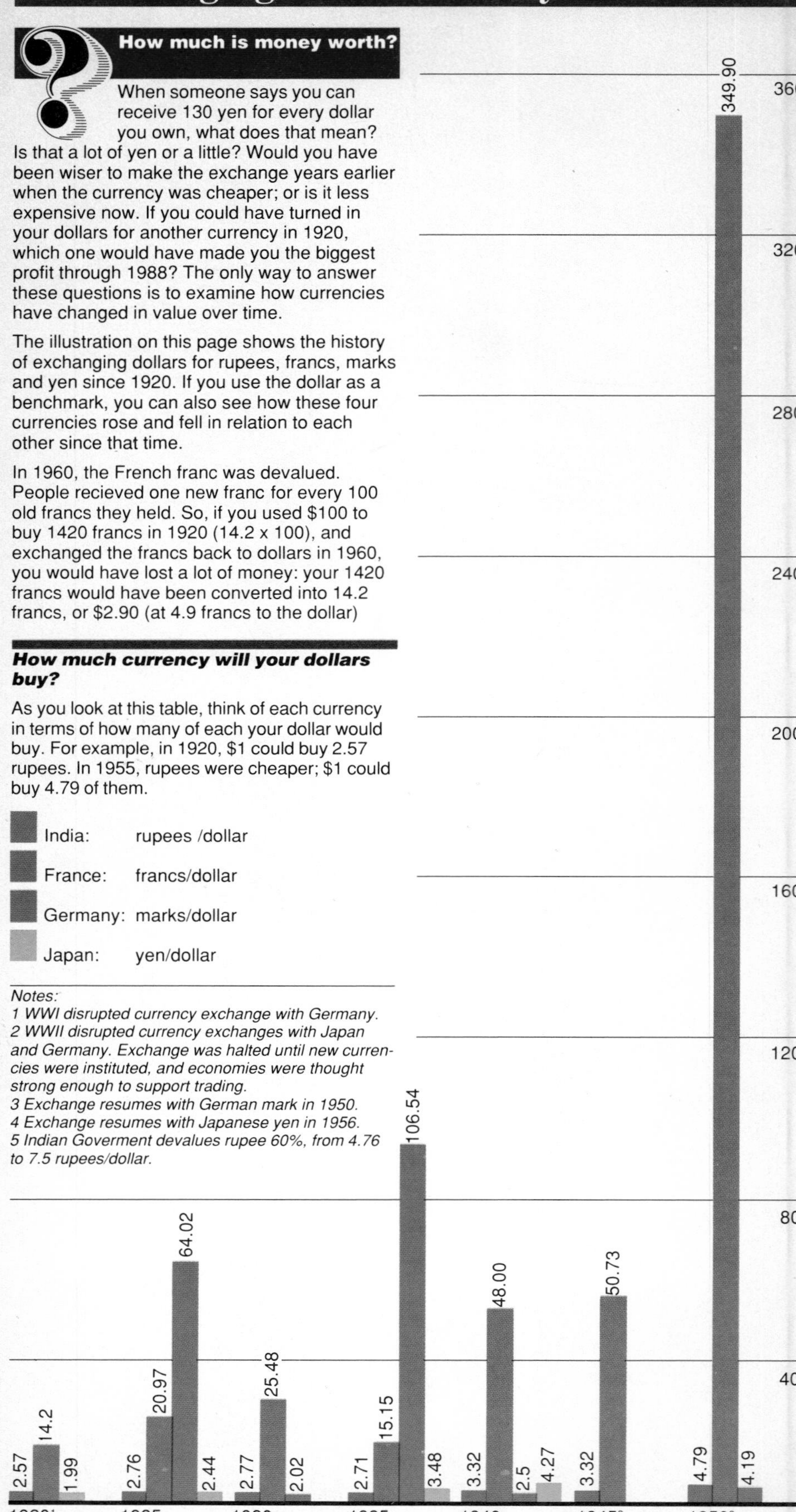

Notes:
1 WWI disrupted currency exchange with Germany.
2 WWII disrupted currency exchanges with Japan and Germany. Exchange was halted until new currencies were instituted, and economies were thought strong enough to support trading.
3 Exchange resumes with German mark in 1950.
4 Exchange resumes with Japanese yen in 1956.
5 Indian Goverment devalues rupee 60%, from 4.76 to 7.5 rupees/dollar.

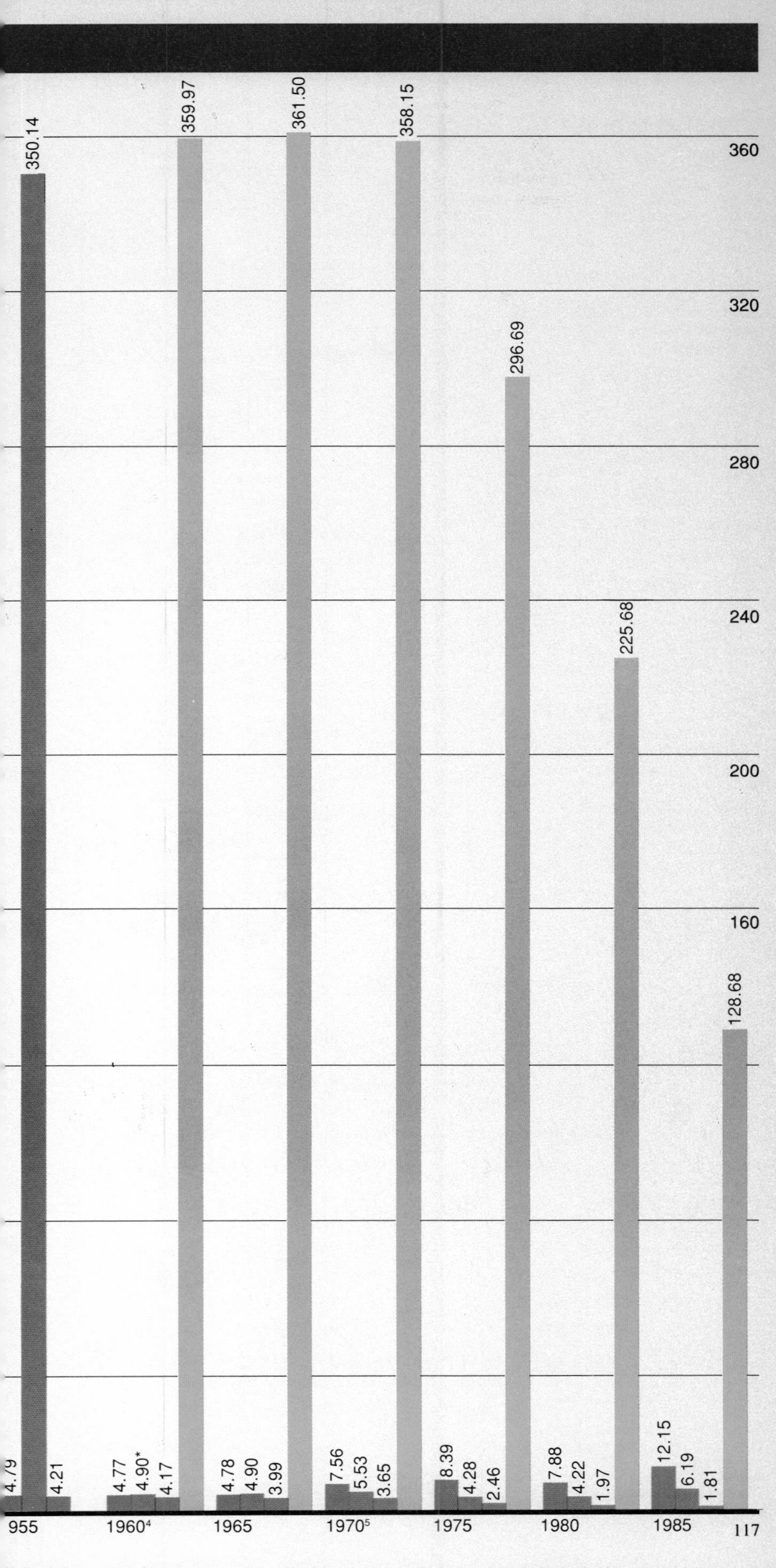
350.14
359.97
361.50
358.15
296.69
225.68
128.68
360
320
280
240
200
160
4.79
4.21
4.77
4.90*
4.17
4.78
4.90
3.99
7.56
5.53
3.65
8.39
4.28
2.46
7.88
4.22
1.97
12.15
6.19
1.81
955
1960[4]
1965
1970[5]
1975
1980
1985

Index

List of Charts, Graphs, and Tables

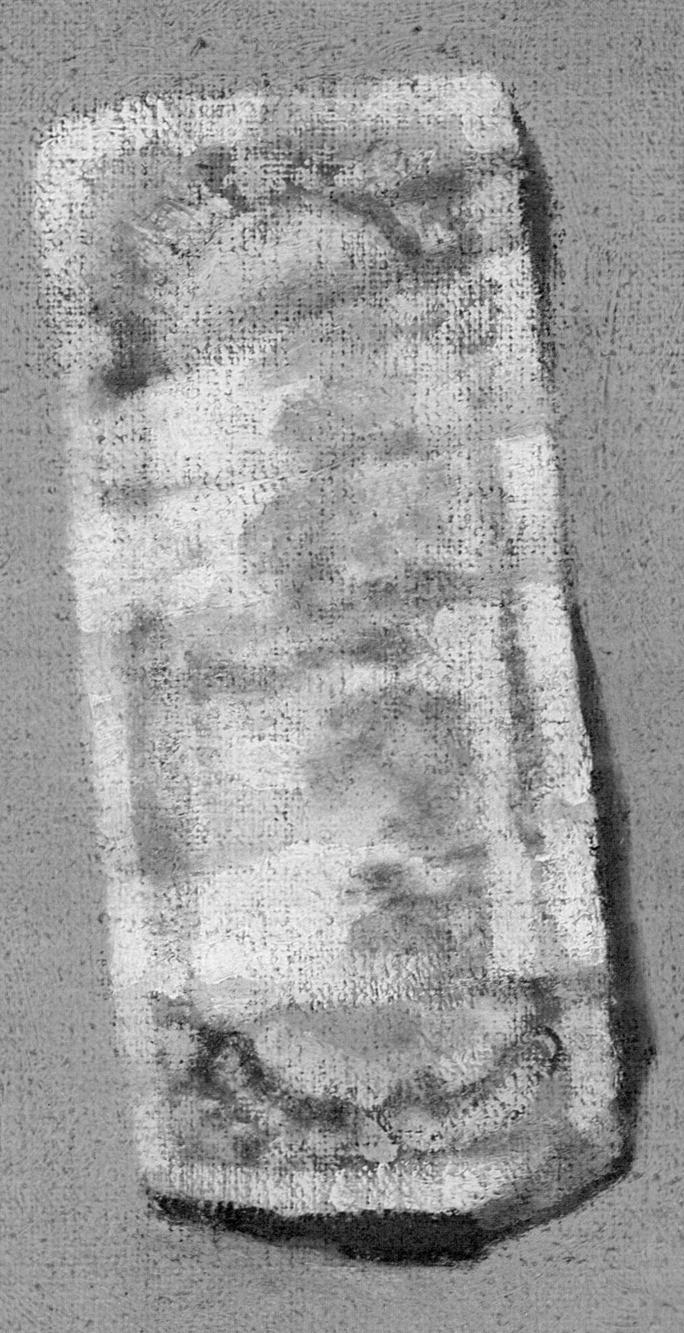